Expert internet searching

FOURTH EDITION

Phil Bradley

© Phil Bradley 1999, 2002, 2004, 2013

Published by Facet Publishing
7 Ridgmount Street, London WC1E 7AE
www.facetpublishing.co.uk

Facet Publishing is wholly owned by CILIP: the Chartered Institute of
Library and Information Professionals.

Phil Bradley has asserted his right under the Copyright, Designs and Patents
Act 1988 to be identified as author of this work.

Except as otherwise permitted under the Copyright, Designs and Patents
Act 1988 this publication may only be reproduced, stored or transmitted in
any form or by any means, with the prior permission of the publisher, or, in
the case of reprographic reproduction, in accordance with the terms of a
licence issued by The Copyright Licensing Agency. Enquiries concerning
reproduction outside those terms should be sent to Facet Publishing, 7
Ridgmount Street, London WC1E 7AE.

British Library Cataloguing in Publication Data
A catalogue record for this book is available from the British Library.

ISBN 978-1-85604-605-3

First published (as *The Advanced Internet Searcher's Handbook*) 1999
Second edition 2002
Third edition 2004
This fourth edition 2013

Text printed on FSC accredited material.

Typeset from author's files in 10.5/14 pt Bergamo and Myriad Pro by Facet
Publishing Production.
Printed and made in Great Britain by CPI Group (UK) Ltd, Croydon,
CR0 4YY.

>> Contents

› ›

‹ ‹

>> Preface

Welcome to *Expert Internet Searching*, which is based on the series of books that I wrote at the turn of the century called *The Advanced Internet Searcher's Handbook*. Looking back at the very first edition, which was actually published in 1999 and reprinted in 2000, it's almost impossible to recognize much of what I wrote. Probably the most shocking thing is that there was no mention at all of Google! Conversely, many of the search engines that I wrote about in that first edition (and come to think of it, the second and third editions as well!) no longer exist. I also paid a lot of attention to subjects such as USENET, mailing lists and the basics of HTML: subjects that would leave many of today's users of the internet looking completely blank. On the other hand, it's comforting to see that I still talk about the same types of search engines now that I did then. Owing to the number of changes, both in the *Handbook* but also in the ways in which we search now, 'Advanced Internet Searcher' didn't feel appropriate any longer; because many search engines do not have advanced search functionality as a separate feature – coupled with the fact that we're all advanced searchers now in many respects, because of what search engines will automatically do on our behalf – we can all become expert searchers by changing our habits and mindset. I hope that *Expert Internet Searching* will help you do exactly that.

The aim of this title is to help you make sense of the internet, and to give you the tools to find the information that you need more quickly and effectively than ever before. You may well puzzle over that sentence for a moment as the mantra of 'it's all on Google' starts chanting at the back of your head. However, as any librarian could tell you, this is very far from the case, and of course if you're a librarian yourself, you don't need me to tell you about how limiting just using one search engine can be! So if you're new to internet searching, or you just want to brush up on a few techniques, you should find some useful hints, tips and ideas in the book.

On the other hand, if you're already an expert searcher I'm confident that you'll still find information on a wide variety of search engines that you've never tried before and lists of tools and resources that will make you an even better searcher than you already are.

Perhaps the three biggest changes since the third edition of the *Advanced Internet Searcher's Handbook* was published is the unparalleled rise of Google, social media and the importance of mobile. Google strides the search landscape like the proverbial colossus and it affects everything that we do on the internet – and indeed in a very real sense in our day-to-day lives off the internet. Even if we don't use Google as a preferred search engine it's impossible to ignore it, since all search engines one way or another compare themselves to it. As for social media, Twitter and Facebook in particular, it has woven itself into the very fabric of what we do day by day. When we add in the third element, that of mobile, with our use of smartphones, which brings the availability of data and the mechanism for searching for information right into our pockets irrespective of our location, we can really see just how much the world has changed in a single decade.

However, we still need to search to find the information that we need, now more than ever. With the amount of information that's available to us increasing exponentially we need to find what we need increasingly quickly. Do we need a web page, or a fact? Is the information we need contained in a photograph or a sound file or video? And once we have that information, what do we do with it? I don't believe that searching has become easier; if anything it's becoming harder and more difficult to get what we need. The rise of Google, social media and mobile search complicates our lives, so in order to make any sense out of the world, the ability to find information effectively is less of a desire and more of a necessity. I hope that you'll find this title helps you make more sense out of the glorious chaos that we now take for granted.

Phil Bradley

» Acknowledgements

I am fortunate enough to work with some of the most interesting, committed, insightful, intelligent and helpful people in the world – librarians. Without going into hyperbole, I really do feel enriched by their company and I learn something new from them every day. I'm also honoured and fortunate enough to be able to work with librarians in training sessions, to talk with them at conferences and to listen to them speak – not just in the UK but around the world. They are a constant source of inspiration and assistance; several times when writing this book I reached out and asked questions and the answers were provided with lightning speed and with extreme generosity. So I would like to thank all of the librarians on the net, in Facebook, on Twitter, on Pinterest and everywhere else, not least of all in real buildings, for their assistance.

I should also like to thank the people – most of whom I don't know and have never met – who spend their time creating search engines, producing tools and resources and making apps that the rest of us can use. From those that I have talked to I know them to be an enthusiastic group of people who are keen to make their products work better – not just because of financial returns, but because it improves all our lives.

The folk at Facet Publishing and CILIP – the Chartered Institute of Library and Information Professionals – have also been a fantastic group of people to work with, in particular my editor, Jenni Hall, who has put up with a huge amount of hassle from me and has never complained once.

Finally, to my friends and family – to Bee for bringing me cups of tea and proofreading chapters, my brother and my sister-in-law Kay – all of whom have continually ~~nagged~~ encouraged me in the writing of the book. The *Expert Internet Searcher* is, however, dedicated to three little boys, Arlo, Ben and James, who really will be the first real digital generation, and to their Auntie Jill, who is watching over them.

❬ ❬

Every effort has been made to contact the holders of copyright material reproduced in this text, and thanks are due to them for permission to reproduce the material indicated. If there are any queries please contact the publisher.

Phil Bradley

CHAPTER 1

›› An introduction to the internet

Introduction

This is the fourth edition of the *Advanced Internet Searcher's Handbook*, and in the three previous editions I felt that it was necessary to include an introduction to the internet. I explained exactly what it was and how it worked in general terms. Looking back at the section headings it all seemed to be a wonderfully innocent time – 'both local and global', 'it isn't a single entity', 'it's difficult to say who is in charge', and so on. I was tempted to write a totally different introduction to this edition, but in actual fact the subheadings that I used are still in many cases apposite today. The internet is, if anything, even more local and global, and it's certainly not a single entity. Internet search is still very much centre stage, and while we have had (and to a limited extent still have) browser wars, a key 'battleground' is still being fought over search.

This may come as something of a surprise to anyone who thinks that Google has routed the opposition and sent them fleeing. However, this is most certainly not the case. While there's no doubt that Google is – at the time of writing – the dominant force when it comes to search, there is no saying that it will always stay there. Microsoft, Facebook, and to a lesser extent perhaps Apple and Amazon, are all keen on increasing their own market share. The war continues, but instead of the basic concept of 'largest search engine wins' the battles are now being fought across social media, in networks, on laptops and more importantly, on mobile phones. Internet search is not all about Google, and although I'll be talking about Google a lot in this edition (in contrast to the first edition, when it wasn't mentioned at all), I'll also be referring to the dozens of other search engines that are out there, and they also have an important part to play in the development of internet search into the next decade.

Consequently, I'll stay with tradition, to an extent at least, and have as my opening chapter a discussion of the internet, although my main focus will be on the way that search has infiltrated almost every area of the time we spend on the internet. I'll then start to look at search in more depth.

An overview of the internet

The internet is almost, but not quite, ubiquitous. The UK Office of National Statistics, in their 2011 release 'Internet Access, Households and Individuals' (www.ons.gov.uk/ons/rel/rdit2/internet-access---households-and-individuals/2011/stb-internet-access-2011.html) reported that 77% of UK households had internet access, and 45% of users have used a mobile phone to connect to it. People use the internet to communicate with friends either by e-mail or increasingly via a social network (or two!), purchase products, order their shopping, chat real-time face to face via video chat, complete official forms, obtain information from local authorities, consume news, watch television or films, or ensure the safety of their house while on a holiday that was booked and paid for via their online bank.

>> **Did you know?**
45% of internet users live in Asia, 22% in Europe, and 11% in North America (www.internetworldstats.com/stats.htm).

The two things that most people will do while using the internet however are e-mail and search. These activities have consistently been shown to be the most important things that we do on the net. Statistics from a Pew Internet survey from May 2011 show that both of these trend at about 90% or more and have done so since 2005 (www.pewinternet.org/Reports/2011/Search-and-email/Report.aspx).

We search for information all the time – and thanks to Google's web and trends history, which keeps tabs on me, I know that on average I run 1470 searches a month, which is about 48 per day. I search most on a Wednesday, least on a Sunday and my busiest search time of day is between 11 a.m. and 1 p.m. I suspect that these figures are not that untypical, and in fact may well be below average if I limit my sample universe to library and information professionals doing their jobs. Of course, that figure only takes into account the searching that I do via Google; there are the dozens of other search engines that I use, the casual searching that I will do once I arrive at a site using their own search engines, or the time that I spend on Facebook or using my iPad. Further interrogation of the figures previously mentioned

〉 〉

also show that internet search activity is not limited to particular demographic types – irrespective of race, ethnicity, age, education, income, everyone searches. To that extent, the internet has turned us all into researchers. However, due to the complexity of search and its paradoxical apparent ease, some people are rather better at it than others.

What the internet is and is not
It's not a single network

In previous editions of the book I took time to explain how the internet was created and maintained, and was actually created from the interlinking of different networks. However, the point that's worth making now, with respect to internet searching, is that data is still spread out into discrete units, hidden in databases that are only accessible via password, on social networks in walled gardens, kept private on closed wikis, found in social bookmarking systems, on photograph- or video-sharing websites, and so on. No single search engine can access all of this information and make it available, and in fact the hidden web is estimated to be thousands of times larger than the web content found by general search engines (http:// websearch.about.com/od/invisibleweb/f/What-Is-The-Size-Of-The-Hidden-Web.htm). Consequently, rather than search becoming easier to do, it's actually much harder. The cry often heard is 'it's all on Google, why do we need libraries or librarians?', when in actual fact it's hardly on Google at all, and we are in greater need of libraries and librarians to help us find the exact piece of information that we need. There's a quote on the net which sums this situation up perfectly, attributed to the author Neil Gaiman, and goes like this: 'Google can bring you back 100,000 answers, a librarian can bring you back the right one.'

Despite what the large search engines would have us believe, search has not become easier over the course of time – it's become much more complex and will increasingly become so as more and more data floods onto internet-based servers and in 'the cloud'.

It's both local and global

In 'the old days' (and how glibly that phrase rolls off the tongue) I meant that information was ubiquitous and it didn't matter where you were; if you had an internet connection you could get the information that you needed. I was of course referring to desktop use, but this is now an even more accurate statement than it was in the past. If I have my smartphone with me, not only can I access it to get the information that I need, I can simply speak to the search engine (as long as I'm using a Google app); it will know where in the world I am via a 'discussion' with the smartphone and it will bring me back information that I need based on where I am. If I'm in Manchester and I want hotels, that's what I'll get. If I'm in Liverpool and I need to find an excellent example of a football ground Google will happily direct me to Goodison Park, offering directions along the way. I can search for what I need by using Google Maps (http://maps.google.com), or I can seek out the information from a localized search engine, or check via Twitter's geographic search function. Not only is it now possible to go to anywhere in the world to get the most appropriate information that I need, but the most appropriate local information comes to me.

>> **Did you know?**
World internet penetration rates are highest in North America (79%), Oceania/Australia (68%) and Europe (63%) (www.internetworldstats.com/stats.htm).

It isn't a single entity

When I first wrote this I was thinking about 'the world wide web, newsgroups, mailing lists' and more besides. During the course of the last decade newsgroups and mailing lists became less important and the rise of the website became the pre-eminent focus for most people. The web was the internet, and the internet was the web. However, even back in the early years of the 2000s it was possible to discern the beginnings of competition to the HTML page, in the form of weblogs, where people were able to create their own spaces to say whatever they wanted, without having to author websites and buy domain names. These days, as well as newsgroups and mailing lists (which do still exist, although their popularity has dwindled) we have blogs, wikis, social network resources, photograph-sharing websites, Twitter streams, postings to Google+, social bookmarking databases, collections of books and forums on booksharing websites such as LibraryThing. We have sites that store and make available user-created videos, slideshow presentations, podcasts and more. If anything, the internet is more disparate in 2011 than it was in 2001 and search has evolved, and is evolving, to cope with that. With respect to search, the key thing to keep in mind therefore is that no one single search engine can do the job. If you wish to search the internet well then it is necessary to have a good grasp and understanding of a wide variety of different search engines and an awareness of their strengths and weaknesses.

It is possible to use a wide variety of hardware and software

Yet again, the accuracy of this statement has not changed, although both the content and concept have. As previously illustrated, an increasing number of people are using their smartphones to connect to the internet. However, it's also possible to connect via games consoles, televisions and many other devices, to say nothing of the traditional laptop or desktop. Finally, we must not forget the access that we can get to the internet via various tablet devices. Since we can use a variety of different types of software and 'the cloud' to store our data we must once again remember that no single search engine is capable of searching all of these different resources. As the amount of hardware and software options increase, so too do the places in which to store and find information, and consequently search engines have to become much more sophisticated and provide a much wider variety of options to allow us to find the information we need.

> **>> Did you know?**
> The top five languages on the internet are English, Chinese, Spanish, Japanese and Portuguese (www.internetworldstats. com/stats7.htm).

Moreover, unlike the early days of the internet, when it was necessary to produce your information in a standardized format or a web page, this can now be achieved using a wide variety of different file formats. An effective search engine must be able to not only index data but provide you with various options to enable you to retrieve it effectively.

It's difficult to say who is in charge

Publishing data onto the internet used to be a difficult task; it was necessary to understand the basics of HTML (HyperText Markup Language), then to obtain a website address, and to understand, or employ somebody who could understand, how to get a good ranking from search engines. One could, however, argue that even though no one individual or group was in charge of the internet various organizations could be in charge of discrete units of data. For example, a council, through the use of its website, could decide what information to make available, and if somebody wished to contact the council or to refer to the material that was available on the site or to discuss the services that were available, they would have to do it through the website. This no longer holds true, however, since with the increase in social media, and the ease with which it is now possible to publish your own data, it is now easier than ever for anyone to say whatever they would like to. If somebody wished to complain about council services they could do so easily via their own blog, on Twitter, or in a Facebook group. The importance of this cannot be overestimated, because the internet has now evolved from a resource where few published to the many into one where the many can publish to the many or to the few. As a result, the value of the website has decreased over time as the value of publishing via social media applications has increased. Not only has this meant that traditional search engines have had to adapt and to attempt to index that flood of data, it has also caused entirely new search engines to spring into existence to focus specifically on the information. Once again, therefore, if you wish to search the internet quickly and effectively, increasingly a single search engine will not do the job for you. Moreover, we have now moved to a situation where search is becoming real-time. By that I mean we are able to find information that was published not months or weeks or days ago but in the last few seconds. Consequently, our expectations of search engines have by necessity changed, for we not only expect a search engine to provide us with content from a wide variety of different types of resources but we also expect it to provide us with that data even if was only published a few seconds ago.

It's fast and effective

As previously mentioned, publishing information on the internet can now be done in seconds and retrieved as quickly. When searching for information we now not only need to consider the authority of the data, its accuracy and the context within which it was made available, but we increasingly need to ask ourselves 'how fresh does this information need to be?' That should also affect the choice of search engine that we use but it also brings into sharp focus that the information is even less trustworthy now than it has ever been in the past, because we are all publishers, journalists and authors. A good search engine must therefore not only retrieve information for us from a wide variety of types of data but it also needs to do so quickly and effectively, and have some way of checking the authority of that information. It is no longer acceptable for a search engine to return results to us based on simple algorithms of search terms in the title

repetition, links, and so on. We need much more by the way of authority –
and here search engines face a dilemma. If the traditional website becomes
less important, what takes its place? Given the rise of social media and the
ability of people to produce their own content, we must increasingly look
towards the authority of individuals, and the ways in which that can be
assessed, rather than that of the traditional website.

It's easy to talk to individuals or groups

In previous editions of the book I used this section to explain that it was
perfectly possible for people to use resources such as newsgroups and
mailing lists to share information backwards and forwards. That ability has
now increased exponentially as publishing on the web has become easier.
One only has to look at the popularity of resources such as Twitter and
Facebook to see that people enjoy communicating with each other, and
communicating a lot! That communication can also take the form of
documents being placed on the net or shared via social networks or stored
in resources such as Flickr. The difficulty of searching for and finding
information is therefore exacerbated by the ease and availability of
mechanisms for producing it.

It's not all hard work

I used to take this to mean that there were plenty of resources available on
the internet for people to indulge their hobbies. I think these days we can
take that as a given, but if we start to look at this in terms of internet search
and the effect that has we can very quickly see that people who have an
interest in a particular subject or hobby are able to produce content and
make it available on the web. Therefore, an increasing amount of
authoritative content may well be produced by hobbyists or skilled amateurs
and they will be making this information available in a variety of different
ways on a variety of different platforms. Effective search engines must
therefore once again be able to work out the authority and validity of
content not by the relatively simple means of assessing a website but by the
far more difficult method of evaluating the information provided by specific
individuals. So we can see that, once again, search is becoming inextricably
bound up with social media resources and if a search engine is going to
succeed it has to be able to take individuals into account at least as much as,
if not more than, traditional websites.

It's not just for 'geeks'

It used to be quite complicated to put information onto the internet, and there once was a concern that it would become more difficult, with complex HTML coding and markup. However, the exact opposite has occurred and it has become far easier to share content, photographs and images. Moreover, with the advent of smartphones people are able to add content to the internet quickly and effectively without even thinking about it. Not only are we all journalists, we are instant reporters and able to provide information on newsworthy items as they are occurring. The influence that this has on the development of search engines is therefore quite profound, since they have to weigh up the various merits of the immediacy of the data with the uncertain authority of the person producing it.

If we look at this subject from another angle we also have to take into account the fact that if anybody can produce content and make it available on the web anyone and everybody is going to want to search it. Search engines therefore are caught in a cleft stick, because on the one hand they want to make their engine as quick, as simple and as easy to use as possible for an unskilled and technically illiterate user, but on the other they have to be able to make it extraordinarily sophisticated, so that we can get exactly the information that we need when we want it. For search engines this is a major issue and the 'Holy Grail', because they want to personalize their results in order to make them appropriate for the needs and requirements of each individual. The danger is that they will create what Eli Pariser has termed 'filter bubbles' (www.ted.com/talks/eli_pariser_beware_online_filter_bubbles.html); by this he means that a search engine will give us the results that it thinks we want, without exposing us to different or alternative viewpoints.

A secondary consideration here is that the more search engines personalize results, the less a generic concept of search can exist. We are already seeing this, in effect, as an increasing number of companies will suggest in their advertising that we search for a specific word or phrase. It's also worth pointing out that companies will often point users towards their Facebook pages rather than their websites. As we shall see, the rise of Facebook and its 'walled garden' is a direct threat to traditional search engines, which emphasize their role in finding information on the web generally, on web pages in websites. If users are going to spend their time in Facebook (as they do) and run searches using Facebook's search option, why would they want to leave that environment to search elsewhere? As a result, it becomes more and more difficult to respond to an enquirer by giving them information couched in the terms 'do a search for so and so, and you will find that the result that you need is the third one down', since the third result down for the enquirer is not necessarily the same third result as seen by the searcher. There are, of course, many ways around this particular problem, such as using search engines which do not personalize results or logging out from those which do and then searching, thus ensuring that the engine doesn't know who you are, and cannot use that knowledge to affect the returned results. It is all too easy to forget this step, but skilled searchers will always keep in the back of their mind the fact that they are often searching on behalf of other people rather than themselves, and so the personalized results which they may receive are not necessarily the best results for the original enquirer.

It's not well organized

I don't think there can be any doubt about this, and indeed I would suggest that it is becoming less and less organized every second. This again means that search engines and well honed search techniques become absolutely vital. The more often people say 'it's all on Google', the more experienced searchers have to point out the dangerous fallacy in that statement.

It's growing at an enormous rate

Little did I realize when I first wrote those words just how quickly data on the internet is increasing. Twitter receives over 400 million tweets per day, Flickr users upload 3500 images per minute (www.digitalbuzzblog. com/infographic-the-growth-of-social-media-2011). There are 152 million blogs on the internet, 40 hours' worth of videos are uploaded to YouTube every minute and on English Wikipedia over 30,000 editors make more than 5 edits per month (www.bbc.co.uk/news/magazine-18892510). Around 1.4 million blog posts are created every day and 3.5 billion pieces of content are shared every week on Facebook (http:// visual.ly/internet-full). It is estimated that by 2014 users will create and replicate 5 zettabytes worth of data (1 zettabyte is 1 trillion gigabytes) and that by 2020 this figure will have risen to 35 zettabytes (www.economist. com/node/21553410?frsc=dg|b). While these figures are almost impossible to comprehend, one thing is for sure – by the time you read them they are going to be woefully inaccurate, such is the speed of growth of internet content.

Consequently, it is simply not possible for one search engine, or indeed one dozen search engines, to index, arrange and make available that amount of information. Unfortunately, however, it is the job of skilled information researchers to find as much appropriate information as they can out of that morass of data and to package it and make it available for their enquirers. So, rather than making things simpler and easier, the easy access to applications which make us all creators of content has in actual fact made it that much harder to find the information that we require. In order to solve this conundrum search engines have to improve, people have to help other people, and searchers need to explore as many avenues as they possibly can in order to do their job effectively.

Search engines

I have already broadly discussed some of the changes that have occurred with search engines and search engine technology in the last few years, but at this point it is worthwhile spending a few moments talking about another very important aspect of search engines, which is the understandable desire of their owners to create as much revenue as they can. So let me be clear right from the outset: the vast majority of search engines do not have at their core an interest in helping you find information – they exist in order to display as much advertising on your screen as possible. If there was no money to be made from advertising, there would be no Google and there would be no Facebook. A second and equally cynical point also needs to be made, which is that you are not a user of search engines; the users of search engines are the advertisers, and all of us are simply the fodder that is required in order to make them money.

Search engines do not have to be excellent at search; they merely have to be good enough for the vast majority of users. In other words, search engine developers will only introduce new functionality and techniques if and when they think it will increase their revenue streams. In the autumn of 2011 Google dramatically closed down a large number of experiments that they were running in the Google labs. Many of these experiments were interesting from a search standpoint but would have had little interest for the majority of users. Since Google wishes to develop a social network to rival that of Facebook many of their programmers were moved off projects that were interesting but were not likely to make the company much money, and onto the development of Google+, which is a central plank in the company's development of their revenue streams.

What does this mean for the searcher? First, it means that you should have no loyalty whatsoever to any search engine at all. Never forget that you are not a user of your favourite search engine, you are its cattle. The idea of brand loyalty with respect to search engines should simply not exist. You should exhibit the behaviour of a discerning shopper in a large mall; go from counter to counter to seek out the best bargains – or from engine to engine to seek out the best functionality that you can – and then move on to the next. Secondly, always remember that new search engines arrive on the scene (I am generally told about one new search engine per day, which is just slightly more than the number that close) and they should be explored to see what they can offer you as the searcher. Be ruthless in your approach and once a search engine fails to develop or give you what you need quickly and effectively, drop it and move on. Do not get attached to a search engine; it is in its interests to get you to go back to it over and over again so that it can show you more adverts, while it is in your interest to find the best resource for the query that you have. Once you start to rely on a specific search engine you will become a less successful searcher. That does not of course mean that you can't have your preferences, because we all do, but it does mean that your head needs to rule your heart.

Having said all of that, I really don't want to paint a bleak picture of internet search engines or to be overly cynical. Internet search is a vibrant and exciting area and one that is constantly changing. For the last 15 years I have run a course entitled 'advanced internet searching' and it is still as popular today as it has ever been. While the concept of the course is the same as it always has been, the content changes from month to month as I find new search engines or existing search engines develop new functionality. As we shall see in later chapters, there are many opportunities to explore different resources many of which are far more powerful than we would have thought possible even three or four years ago.

Failing resources

However, it should also be mentioned that many resources have declined in use and popularity as other resources have increased in value. There is no point in devoting entire chapters to resources such as USENET newsgroups, intelligent agents and mailing lists; these days they are worth little more than footnotes. The reasons for this are many and varied. While USENET newsgroups still exist, they are increasingly underutilized, because in order to get the most out of them it is necessary to use specialized software. Moreover, since they are almost entirely unregulated, they have fallen victim to the spammers and while several people made valiant attempts to save them they are quickly passing into internet history and have largely been replaced by resources such as Facebook groups. Intelligent agents first came to the fore in the early years of this century, and they were supposed to hunt around on the internet and find the information that we needed and bring it back to us. The term has since fallen into disuse, but the idea of news collation and curation on the other hand has developed and has been incorporated into other resources. Many readers will be familiar with tools such as Zite and Flipboard that they use on their tablets and these are the descendants of intelligent agents.

Mailing lists continue to exist, although I think that it is fair to say that they are in the main within the remit of academia rather than general use. They flourished in the past due to their use of e-mail, as it was very easy for people to disseminate the messages that they wished to larger groups of people and to have general discussions. However, with the increase in blogs, Twitter, Facebook groups and other social networks those discussions have generally migrated away from e-mail towards social media. We cannot and should not forget the existence of these resources, however, because, depending on the enquiry that we have, their archival value is still very important. The data on websites tends in the main to get overwritten but the archives of USENET and some mailing lists are still safely stored away.

The information mix

Effective internet searching is part science, part art, part skill and part luck. Most of all, however, it is an effective blend of different resources, different search engines and a willingness to look for information wherever it might be and for however long it takes. None of that should come as any sort of surprise to an information professional but the average internet user will probably not have the experience, knowledge, understanding or tenacity to blend those together in a successful search. Of course, in this book I am going to spend very little time talking about resources that are not on the internet, but we should never forget that traditional resources such as books, databases on CD-ROM, or even microfiche still have an important part to play. Therefore, please do consider their value and encourage your users to explore them because, after all, a successful search is one where you get the right answer, irrespective of where it comes from.

〉 〉

Summary

In this opening chapter I hope that I have at least in part laid down some markers that relate to where internet search is currently and where I believe that it will move to within the next few years. While it is all too easy to agree with the statement 'Everything is on Google', it is not only a fallacy but a dangerous one at that; I hope that this will not come as a surprise to anyone reading this book. In the coming chapters I will explore the different types of search engine that are available and their advantages and disadvantages. I will also provide examples of search engines within each category (full-text, directory, multi-search, and so on) and look at ways in which you can get the most out of them. Internet searching is a fascinating and enjoyable activity – in some cases almost a hobby – and I hope that you will be as excited, enthralled and intrigued as I am when I get the opportunity to explore a new search engine for the first time.

CHAPTER 2

›› **An introduction to search engines**

Introduction

I'll start this chapter by asking you the question 'How many search engines do you think there are on the internet?' The chances are that your immediate reaction will provide a figure in the region of perhaps ten or a dozen, or if you want to be wildly enthusiastic you may go up to several hundred or even 1000. In actual fact nobody has any idea how many search engines are available since ironically there is no central database that lists them. However, I have seen figures that suggest that up to 400,000 search engines may be available.

If you find that figure just too remarkable to believe, I'd ask you to hold back on your scepticism for a moment or two. While my question wasn't exactly a trick, I expect you're thinking of one specific type of search engine such as Google or Bing; that is say, a search engine that will attempt to index as much of the internet (i.e. web pages) as possible. If you answered my question by considering that type of search engine you could easily justify an answer in terms of a small handful. On the other hand, if your definition of an internet search engine was 'any search engine that's on the internet' then this would include search engines that were limited to searching a single site or small discrete unit of data; the large figure that I mentioned therefore may be quite an accurate one. If I had asked the same question but had referred to reference books instead I suspect that your answer would have been along the lines of 'nobody knows!' Of course that's true as well, but what we do find with reference books is that they can be divided into various categories, such as encyclopedias and dictionaries. Each of these types of reference book will exhibit their own behaviours and have their own set of defining criteria. Search engines can be viewed in exactly the same light; while we may have no idea of exactly how many search engines there are, it is nevertheless relatively easy to assign them to different types based on a number of factors: the type of data they find, the way the information is presented, how people can search, and many others besides. What I will do in this chapter is provide an overview of the different types of search engines that I see on a daily basis and will give you information on how they collect their data, how they return it to you, and the various advantages and disadvantages that they have.

Free-text search engines

Free-text search engines are very easy to describe. You can simply search for a single word, a number of words, or perhaps a phrase. You are not limited in any way as to your choice – you may search for the name of the company, a line of poetry, a number, a person's name, a word in a different language, or indeed just about anything. You are therefore *free* to type in any *text* that you wish.

This approach has both advantages and disadvantages, as you would expect. Free-text search engines are very useful if you know exactly what you're looking for or if you are looking for a concept that can be defined in a small number of words. They are less useful if you want a broad overview of the subject, or are searching an area that you don't know very well and consequently have no real idea about the best terms to use. There are a great many free-text search engines that you can use and we will look at some of them in later chapters, but now I'll simply give you a few examples: Google at www.google.com (did you really need that URL? I do hope not!); Bing at www.bing.com; DuckDuckGo at www.duckduckgo.com; Exalead at www.exalead.com/search/; and Ask at www.ask.com (or Ask Jeeves as it is known in the UK – you will be redirected to http://uk.ask.com).

The search functionality of these engines is quite varied; the key players will provide a reasonable amount of sophistication, but those search engines which are less well known do tend to be quite limited in the way in which you can search them. What you'll also find with the key players is that they will provide you with access to a wider variety of resources than just web pages – you will be able to search images, news, video, and perhaps other resources such as blogs. In fact it can be quite difficult to identify exactly what you can do with a search engine,

>> **Did you know?**
Dogs are allowed onsite at the GooglePlex, but not cats (www.stateofsearch.com/how-massive-is-google).

> >

since they all tend to advertise themselves on their simplicity and ease of use in order to encourage people to use them rather than bamboozle them with the kind of bells and whistles that would be more likely to attract information professionals.

How free-text search engines collect their data

In order to use the search engines effectively it is necessary to have some background knowledge of how they work. Most of them make use of 'spiders' or 'robots' or 'crawlers', which are utilities that spend their time looking at web page after web page, indexing the information that they find and then moving from one site to another. At some unspecified point in the future they return to the website and re-index or re-spider it and if and when they find any changes to the content on the page they will make that change in their own indexes. This is very much a movable feast and a search engine decides for itself when it will re-index either a site or a page on the site. Consequently, you may well find when you have run a search that some of the results may well not reflect the content that is on the page when you go and visit, and so when you are using a free-text search engine you are in effect searching through a variety of pages from the very recent to the quite elderly. The content of web pages is the responsibility of the organization or individual owning the site. It is therefore up to them to decide when to update the information they make available. Sites that are frequently updated tend to be visited more often by search engine spiders and sites that are seldom updated and so visited less often. Some search engines will provide you with a cached version of the page and so you can see when it was last updated. Figure 2.1 illustrates the kind of information that Google will return to you if you click on the cached version of a web page that is returned in its results.

As this process of crawling is entirely computerized and requires little if any human intervention, search engines in this category can list billions of web pages in their index. In the early to mid–2000s search engines in this category engaged in rather macho posturing, with each of them trying to outdo the opposition by claiming that their index was bigger than anyone

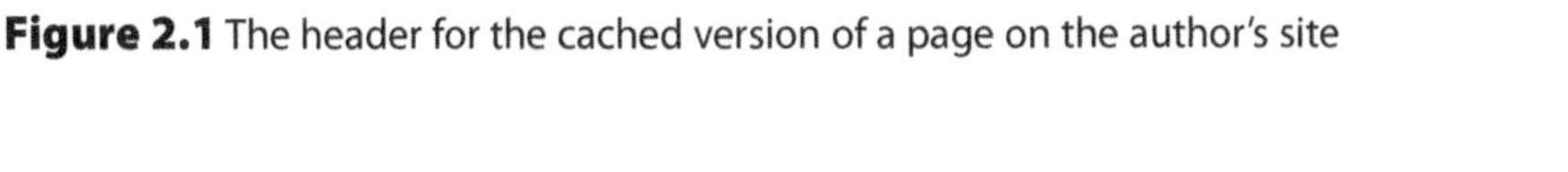

This is Google's cache of http://www.philb.com/. It is a snapshot of the page as it appeared on 10 Apr 2013 17:02:39 GMT. The current page could have changed in the meantime. Learn more
Tip: To quickly find your search term on this page, press **Ctrl+F** or **⌘-F** (Mac) and use the find bar.

Text-only version

Figure 2.1 The header for the cached version of a page on the author's site

‹ ‹

else's. However, they soon tired of this and so now we have no idea exactly how big a search engine's database is.

As an aside, it is also interesting to try to define exactly what we mean when we use the phrase 'web page'. In the old days it was quite easy to define, because a web page was, quite simply, a web page. No problems there! However, one could now argue that since each individual tweet, for example, has its own URL, that could be defined as a web page, however nonsensical that may appear. I personally don't think that there is much point in trying to define search engines in terms of the amount of data that they index because the vast majority of us never look beyond the first ten results anyway. Even if we do, we are unlikely to go beyond the first two or three pages of results and if we do we have probably done a search poorly.

> **›› Did you know?**
> 96% of American libraries have websites, and 68% use Facebook (http://open-site.org).

Relevance ranking

When the search engine runs a search for you it will obviously give you a series of results based on the web pages that it has found in its index. To state the obvious, if a search engine has not found, or does not know of the existence of, a particular web page or website it cannot return that page to you. That is a disadvantage that I will return to shortly. Search engines cannot simply return you a list of results in no particular order and so what free-text search engines do is utilize something called relevance ranking. This means that they will use a variety of different algorithms to work out why one page result is a better match for you than another. These algorithms may be numbered in hundreds and will differ from search engine to search engine. There are some obvious examples, however, that I can use for illustrative purposes. If the word or words that you have asked for are to be found on the title of a web page then clearly there is a good indication to the search engine that it has found a good match for you. The number of times that the word appears on a web page, its position (even down to position within a paragraph or a sentence), how quickly the pages load and the number of links pointing to a web page are all very common ways in which search engines will determine the relative value of a page and its relevance to your search. Of course, each search engine has its own methods of relevance ranking and if we add into that particular mix the fact that search engines find their own resources by using their own spidery programs we can very quickly see that there is not actually a huge overlap in the results that you get from different search engines. We can illustrate this by using a resource such as Thumbshots Ranking (at www.thumbshots.com), which compares the results that users get for searches made on Google, Yahoo!, Bing and AlltheWeb. Figure 2.2 shows an example screenshot from Thumbshots Ranking for the relative results from Google and Yahoo! for the search term 'Mars', with results from the Wikipedia website highlighted. The dots which are connected are web pages that have been found by both search engines (on the website you can mouse over a dot to obtain more details of exactly what page has been returned) and you can see for example that the second result at Google is the third result returned at Yahoo!, while the first result returned by Yahoo! (a Wikipedia page) is the sixth returned by Google.

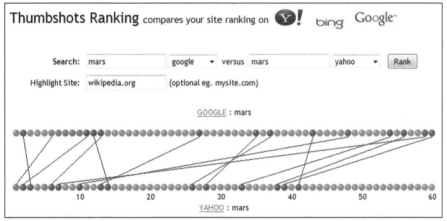

Figure 2.2 Screenshot from Thumbshots Ranking showing the results from two search engines (reproduced with permission)
Google and the Google logo are registered trademarks of Google Inc., used with permission.

There are a number of points that are worth making here. First, very few web pages are returned in the first 60 results by both search engines. Consequently, if you use just one search engine (and it doesn't really matter which) you will miss dozens of results that other search engines have found. Secondly, within the first ten results that are returned by both search engines only two are common to both engines – so, while each thinks that it has the best way of arranging the data that it returns to the searcher, it could be argued that they are poles apart in deciding what exactly the best results are. Thirdly, the Wikipedia site is highlighted in different shading

‹ ‹

(6–10 in Google, 2 and 4 in Yahoo!) and shows that Google makes considerably more use of the results from that website then Yahoo! does. In general terms it would be fair to say that Google does tend to pull a lot of its results from Wikipedia, whereas other search engines do not have that same level of reliance. So if anybody in the future says to you 'but it's all on Google', do please remember the Thumbshots Ranking website and give them a quick demonstration to show that this is very far from the case.

One final point to mention here is something that I've already referred to in Chapter 1, which is that search engine results are increasingly personalized as they try to encourage you to use their engine rather than the competition by giving you more targeted results. That's fine as long as you search for similar subject matter but if you are, for example, a reference librarian and your needs are constantly changing this can be less of a help and more of a hindrance. Finally, the results that you get may well also be affected by the location that the search engine believes you to be in. Consequently, the results that you get from searching a .co.uk search engine will almost always be different to those that you will receive by searching a .com version of the same engine.

In summary, free-text search engines are excellent to use if you know what you are looking for, you have some clear keywords or phrases in mind, you are happy and confident in using slightly more sophisticated search techniques and you want to search a large percentage (in relative terms) of the internet.

Index- or directory-based search engines

These search engines are increasingly being sidelined due to their inflexibility and small database sizes. They are best exemplified by referring to the Yahoo! search engine of the mid- to late 1990s. These search engines used a directory-based approach with major headings divided into subheadings divided again and so on until they displayed for you a list of websites that focused on a particular subject. A website about kittens for example could be found in the category Science/biology/zoology/animals, insects, and pets/mammals/cats. Search engines of this type proved very popular, since they were very easy to set up; one only needed to create a series of headings and subheadings and then invite web authors to add their website to an appropriate section. However this very method of data collection was fatally flawed and I believe this has led at least in part to the almost complete downfall of this type of engine. First, the web authors need to discover the search engine and be encouraged to add their own website. Secondly, human beings are required to act as editors for particular sections and oversee the addition of websites into their categories. Thirdly, this type of search engine can only ever act as a stepping stone. All that these engines can do is to identify a website – searchers must then visit the website themselves and re-run their search on the site's local search engine to discover the piece of information that they require. This is a rather time-consuming method of obtaining the information that is required and as such is not very attractive. On the other hand, search engines of this nature do provide a good subject overview, which can be useful if you do not know much about the subject you're searching for, and can provide ideas and suggestions on the best approach to take. They are also useful because they will give you an overview of a small number of websites that are focused on a particular subject area so it may in fact save you some time instead of forcing you to wade through pages of results. Finally – although I wouldn't want to push this too far – because sites are vetted by human beings they may possibly be of a more authoritative and accurate nature than you will find with the results from free-text search engines.

However, although these are advantages, they can in no way compensate for the slow growth in the number of websites in particular categories or the high level of maintenance required in their upkeep. Consequently, search engines such as Google that used to have a directory-based approach have in recent times chosen not to continue offering a directory-based search option. These days you will most likely find this type of search engine in very specific fields, such as a country-focused or subject-based search engine.

In summary, index- or directory-based search engines are increasingly looking very old-fashioned and worn out. While they still have a place and a role to play within the cadre of search engines, it would either be a very brave or a very foolish company that decided to start one.

Multi- or meta-search engines

The next type of search engine isn't really a search engine at all, since a multi-search engine such as Trovando (www.trovando.it) or a meta-search engine such as Ixquick (https://www.ixquick.com) doesn't search anything itself. Instead, it takes your query and passes it on to a selected group of other search engines. Once the results are coming in from the individual search engines a multi-search engine will display these on the screen. The more advanced engines will collate the results, remove duplicates and put them into some sort of sensible order; the most advanced ones of all will also allow users to display the results in a number of different ways.

There is, however, a second type of search engine in this category and it does not search at all. It will provide the searcher with a search box for them to input their term and underneath there will be a list of search engines that they can then choose to click on which will then run the search for them. When the search has been run the results will generally be displayed as a 'frame' in the existing browser window. It's then possible to simply click on one engine after another to very quickly flick from one set of results to another.

Multi- and meta-search engines are useful if you want to obtain a comprehensive listing of results without having to spend an inordinate amount of time visiting search engine after search engine. After all, why just search Google when you can search that and half a dozen other engines in about the same amount of time? Unfortunately, the advantage of these search engines – that they provide you with access to so many other engines – is also their downfall. The searcher is submitting his or her search to a number of different engines and consequently each engine needs to be able to understand the syntax being used. Therefore, searchers need to know that each engine used by the multi-search engine will understand what is being asked of it and as a result it's really necessary to run searches at the lowest common denominator without using any advanced syntax to focus the search more closely.

In summary, although these search engines do have the limitations that I have just mentioned, they are an excellent way for a novice searcher to quickly experience and explore the results that they will get from using a wide variety of search engines that they may previously have been unaware of. They are also a great way to keep out of the search engine rut and to keep your search choices fresh and varied.

Visual search engines

The vast majority of search engines will display the results on the screen for you in a text format. If you are lucky some search engines will also give you the opportunity of previewing a result either by displaying it for you on the screen within the search engine results themselves or with a mouse click that gives you the opportunity of looking at a thumbnail version of the page that is being returned in the results. There may, however, be times when

you wish to skim through a lot of results and this is where the use of a visual
search engine such as RedZ (www.redz.com) really comes into its own.
The results are displayed not in the usual text form but as a series of large
thumbnails that searchers are able to flick through with a simple mouse
click and drag until they find a result that they think is most appealing,
which they can then click to visit. This type of search engine does seem to
appeal to younger people and to students in particular.

Hidden, invisible or deep web search engines

Search engines are only as good as the data that they can obtain. Much
highly specialized data is contained in databases that can only be accessed
either by using a password or by running a search directly on a website, using
a search engine that is limited or restricted to a discrete unit of data. This
would, for example, include the data in genealogical databases, Yellow Pages,
and the databases of telephone companies. There is a huge wealth of data
that is therefore 'hidden' from the prying eyes of search engine robots or
spiders. You will also find this type of data referred to as the invisible or the
deep web. While access to this data may be as simple as inputting a search
and hitting Enter, the main challenge is finding the appropriate database in
the first instance. There are two approaches to overcoming this problem:
either do some lateral thinking and use a traditional search engine to identify
a website that may well provide you with access to the data that you actually
require (therefore if you need the phone number of somebody it may make
sense to run a search to find a specific telecoms company that would contain
and give access to such a database); alternatively, there are various search
engines and search resources that at the very least will identify a large
number of databases on different websites that you can then visit. These are
rather more like the stepping-stone variety of search engine that I mentioned
previously – the index- or directory-based kind – and exhibit a number of
similar characteristics to both index and multi-search engines. Unfortunately
there is no single listing of all of these search engines and no easy or fast way
to search them but this is where the skill of the information worker comes
into play, by first identifying appropriate search engines/databases and then
quickly working out how to get the best value out of them.

Multimedia search engines

One of the largest search engines in the world is YouTube; people use it not

‹ ‹

only to create and upload content but also to find information they require in a video or multimedia format. There are also search engines which are limited to retrieving images for you and others which will retrieve sounds or podcasts. Alternatively, you may find that some of the previously mentioned search engines, particularly free-text search engines, will provide researchers with tabs enabling them to search that type of data without having to go to the inconvenience of visiting other search engines. (As a rather cynical aside, it also means that as a result searchers stay on their site for longer and are consequently bombarded with even more adverts.) The important point to remember here, however, is that search results come in a variety of different formats and, although it probably shouldn't need saying, sometimes the best results that you can give an enquirer will not be in a text format. It's also worthwhile mentioning that a good search engine will provide researchers with the opportunity of searching for data in different file formats such as .pdf or .ppt. There are also a number of search engines that exist which are designed to find information specifically in different file formats, such as FindThatFile at www.findthatfile.com.

Social media search engines

With the dramatic increase in social media resources, such as blogs, wikis, microblogging services, social networks and so on, we have also seen an equally dramatic increase in the amount of data that is published via these resources. Not only is that amount of information extraordinarily large (as we have previously seen in Chapter 1) but it is created every second of every day and in the case of events of global interest can result in more information than any one search engine can handle. We have seen the publishing cycle go from months in the case of printed materials down to days with respect of websites, minutes when looking at blog postings, and seconds with Twitter updates. Real-time searching, therefore, is becoming increasingly important.

> **›› Did you know?**
> 3 million new blogs come online every month (http://go-globe.com).

The method used by traditional search engines when they are spidering and crawling web pages looks increasingly ponderous and old-fashioned when we need to find information that was published only seconds ago. Consequently, we are now seeing a new breed of search engines, such as SocialMention (www.socialmention.com); although, to be fair to the older search engines, some of those are also working hard to provide users with access to real-time data. We can consider this type of data contained within real-time search results in a rather different way, however; the vast majority of it will be produced by individuals who are expressing their own views or opinions or who are reporting back on situations which they may not fully understand. Even so, such data may well include links to other websites, news items, or other resources that will be of interest to the searcher.

Although this type of search engine may be seen to be indexing what we may call 'casual' information, it is nonetheless important that as information professionals we get to grips with search engines of this type and, moreover, start to use them. This will become clear later in Chapter 7 on social media search engines, but I have already hinted that as search is becoming more social we must get to grips with this form of search both as consumers of content and as creators of content.

Other search engines

Inevitably there is a miscellaneous collection of search engines or search resources that don't fit into the above categories, but we shouldn't ignore them or be tempted to sweep them under the carpet – they are often some of the most useful resources that we have at our disposal. Search engines which concentrate on one specific subject, such as the news, resources for children, applications that collect together the links that we create and resources that work specifically with smartphones or iPads all need to be considered when we look at the whole subject of search engines.

Summary

Despite the seeming omnipotence of Google, internet search is a vibrant and growing area. While it is fair to say that Google is by far and away the largest and best known of the search engines that are available, it is very far from being the only game in town. Indeed, the existence of other search engines which look to their own niche subject areas or which attempt to do things differently not only keeps Google on its toes but provides us, the searchers, with many different resources with which to do our work.

CHAPTER 3

>> **The Google experience**

Introduction

The seemingly unstoppable rise of Google is quite phenomenal and there are already plenty of books available which look at the company, both in general and in specific terms in much more detail than I will be able to in this book. A quick search of Amazon for the word 'Google' returns over 50,000 results: not a scientific study by any means, but it does help indicate that a wealth of material is available on various aspects of the company. It would therefore be very easy to devote the rest of the book to the best ways of searching Google, but that would be like writing a book about reference materials and only referring to the *Encyclopaedia Britannica* lists. In this chapter I'll look at both sides of the search engine, and indeed the company as a whole, because there are two very different ways of looking at it. On the one hand, it can provide excellent results very quickly, it is always innovating and making new resources available and it can be extremely responsive; after the Boston Marathon bombing it had a person search up and running within hours, before Bing was even telling people about the atrocity on its news pages. On the other hand, it's a company that is very focused on making money, and if they find that a product is not doing that for them – however good it may be, and however many people use it, such as Google Reader – they will close it down without any hesitation, despite protests from users. We therefore have a situation where there's an excellent product, but we rely on it at our peril, because the search experience may well change not only from week to week, but almost hour to hour.

> >> **Did you know?**
> The annual salary of Google's founders, Sergey Brin and Larry Page, is exactly $1, while their personal fortunes are estimated at $17.5 billion – each (www.stateofsearch.com/how-massive-is-google).

‹ ‹

The experience

I talk about the Google experience because we are no longer looking at just a search engine. It has evolved far beyond that even in the few years that it has been in development. We can use Google to search for information and to find images, videos or the news: we can use it to read books, research academic articles, find out who is blogging on a particular subject and more besides. We can use Google as a research tool, by finding out the time in different countries or what the weather is like there, we can use it to translate from one language to

> **›› Did you know?**
> The total number of Google servers is 900,000 and the percentage of worldwide electricity used by Google's data centre is 0.01% (www.statisticbrain.com/total-number-of-pages-indexed-by-google).

another, we can use it to run calculations and convert weights and measures. Gmail is the way in which many of us send and receive our e-mail communications, our houses have been photographed by Google for Street View and we store our data on Google servers so that we can share our documents with other people. We can use Google to chat real-time to people, both via voice and by video, and we can use their social network – Google+ – to keep up to date with what friends and colleagues are doing around the world. Many people and organizations rely on Google either to bring clients to their doorstep or, if they place Google adverts on their websites, to send them a cheque every month for the revenue they have earned by visitors clicking on them. While it is not entirely impossible to use the internet without also using Google, it can sometimes be very hard work to find good and useful alternatives. In addition, the more that Google knows about you the more it can personalize the whole internet experience in ways that you will find pleasing, but ironically which you may not even be aware of.

Serious researchers will use Google for a wide variety of different reasons and there's nothing wrong with that as long as Google is not seen as the only resource that they can use. One of the questions that we must all consider when we use Google is the extent to which we wish to become embroiled in the search engine. Regretfully I have to say that I think in order to get the most out of the search engine it is

> **›› Did you know?**
> There are over 2 million search queries per minute on Google (http://on.mash.to/1au1076).

necessary to have your own account and to make use of it. There are many sound search reasons for this, not the least of which is that if Google knows your search history it is therefore very easy for you to return to previous

> >

searches, either to re-search pages you have already looked at or, conversely, simply to search those pages which Google knows you have not already looked at. Google will happily give you an account with the associated e-mail address, web space for your documents, a photographic storage area and an entire social network. However, please also remember that Google is not doing this because it is deemed to be 'a nice thing to do' but because the more that you are using Google and associated services the more advertising it can place on your screen and therefore the more money that it will earn. You should also remember that Google will store the searches that you have run for several months and will make this information available to anyone who legally requests it. So perhaps we should give a slight twist to the old adage 'there's no such thing as a free lunch' by saying 'there's no such thing as a free search'. I would, however, always encourage everyone to regularly review their Google account and profile just so that you are happy and confident in the information that you are providing to the search giant. If this is a concern for you, don't log into a Google account before you search (or indeed don't have one at all) or consider using an entirely different search engine such as DuckDuckGo at www.duckduckgo.com, which doesn't track your searches. At the risk of being repetitive please, keep in mind that Google is not just a search engine, Google is an advertising company that uses search to make money and YOU are the product being sold to their advertisers. However, let's move on from that rather disquieting thought and look at the ways in which you can use Google to find the information you need.

Google search: the basics

I'll be brief on some of the basic search functionality of Google; I expect that you already know it and so I am only including it for the sake of comprehensiveness. The most basic search that you can do at Google is to type in a word or a number of words. Google will then search its index, find web pages that contain the word or words that you have searched for, apply relevance ranking algorithms, and then display the results on the screen for you. If I run a search on the two words '*search engines*' I am asking Google to find pages that contain both words, and it returns about 280,000,000 results. These are arranged by relevance ranking, where Google looks at a wide variety of different algorithms such as the positioning of the words on the page, their proximity to each other, whether the words are to be found in the title element and how many other pages link to the page(s) that it's checking. We don't know for sure how many of these algorithms it uses to rank pages, but it's in the range of 200–400, and they're constantly changing, as is the importance that is given to each of them. This in turn leads to a situation where you can run the same search on two different days and get different results – probably not major differences, but differences none the less.

It's worth noting that although the search that Google has just run has been to find web pages that contain 'search' and 'engines', if you actually try the search terms '*search AND engines*' you'll get a very different number – in the region of 550,000,000 – and will have an entirely different set of results. This is because Google, unlike many other search engines, doesn't recognize the use of the Boolean operator '*AND*', and so it's advisable to put the words next to each other and let Google make the assumption itself that you want to '*AND*' them together. If you don't, Google will look for the word 'and' as the word itself, not as a search operator.

Another common Boolean operator is of course '*OR*' and you can use this if you wish to find one word, term or phrase *or* another. You can also use the '|' symbol instead if preferred. A search for '*search OR engines*' gives us 19,640,000,000 results; a mind-boggling number. However, if we reverse the order of the terms, so we're searching for '*engines OR search*' we have 6,090,000,000, which is an entirely different number! There are two lessons to remember here – first, that word order matters, so make sure that you consider the importance of the terms and put the most important one at the beginning of your search, and secondly, Google can't count very well. You could argue that it doesn't much matter if Google gives widely differing results because most searchers are not going to look beyond the first 10 or 20 results anyway, and if they get the answer that they are looking for, is it that important?

I should also point out that the use of the Boolean operator '*NOT*' can also result in inconsistent results. (For queries that exclude terms, see below.) A search for '*moon landings*' returns 1,510,000 results, but if we then add in '*NOT hoax*' we get 8,110,000 results, and a search for '*moon landings -hoax*' (using the hyphen symbol for 'minus' as Google does) we get 35,200,000 returns! At the risk of name dropping, Amit Singhal, senior vice president at Google, discussed this with me some time ago, and his advice was not to get too hung up on the actual numbers themselves – as long as the results that are turning up in the SERPS (Search Engine Results Pages) gave good and consistent information, that's the important thing.

> **>> Did you know?**
>
> Google indexes over 1 trillion unique URLs and if these were typed end to end they would stretch 51 million km, or a third of the way to the sun (www.stateofsearch.com/how-massive-is-google).

What we will also find is that Google likes to think that it knows best. If I run a search for *'teaching search skills'* Google ignores my search terms and tells me that instead it has done a search for *'teaching research skills'* and if I want to search for *'teaching search skills'* I have to click on the option to run the search again. This is, to say the least, very irritating, because as the searcher I should actually know what I'm looking for – I'm all in favour of Google suggesting other terms or phrases, which is a helpful thing to do, but to completely ignore my search and to replace it with one of its own is, in my opinion, going rather too far. It can end up with quite surreal consequences. Karen Blakeman (a UK search trainer, blogger and consultant) did a search for the terms *'coots mating behaviour'* and Google decided that she actually wanted results for *'lions mating behaviour'*. Something of a difference in opinion, I'm sure you'll agree. Perhaps Google assumes that *'coot'* is a misspelling for *'cat'* and that the searcher would probably be more interested in lions than pussycats? You can read more about the experience at www.rba.co.uk/wordpress/2011/02/12/google-decides-that-coots-are-really-lions.

So, given that Google has a propensity for deciding to go off and run an entirely different search to the one that was originally requested, is there any way in which we can overcome this, right at the start? In the past Google, in common with other search engines, used the '+' symbol to good effect. Putting a plus sign directly in front of a word without any spaces told the search engine that it had to search for exactly that – no more and no less. However, when Google introduced their own social networking system to compete with Facebook – Google+ – they decided to change the use of the plus sign. If you use that now, the chances are high that you will be taken to the Google+ page that is associated with the word that you have emphasized. To make this a little clearer, if I do a search for *'pepsi'* then I will get the Pepsi web site as my first result. However, if I do a search for *'+pepsi'* then my first result will be their page on the Google+ social

〈 〈

network. In order to overcome this confusion Google originally suggested that users put double quotes around any words that should be searched exactly as given, but this could lead to far too many extra keystrokes, so they have now introduced a search function called 'Verbatim'. Once the search has been run Google will provide a set of results, with various options below the search box, as can be seen in Figure 3.1.

Figure 3.1 The search results screen after a search has been run
Google and the Google logo are registered trademarks of Google Inc., used with permission

By then clicking on 'Search tools' and then on the option which appears called 'All results', I can choose the 'Verbatim' option, and this can be seen in Figure 3.2. This does not initially save me any time or keystrokes at all, but the Verbatim option will remain as a default search option for future searches until I choose to turn it off or I close that particular search session.

We can already see that searching the internet using Google isn't quite as straightforward as it may at first appear, but to be fair to the engine there are other tools available that make life a little easier. Perhaps a better approach to searching Google is to use double quotes to indicate to the engine that you wish to search for a phrase. By telling Google that you want to search for ' *"search engines"* ' it will give us a smaller set of results, with the words in the right order, and therefore a more accurate result. Consequently whenever you can, it makes sense to do phrase searching. Try to think of the way in which the answer to your query is going to be couched rather than the way in which you want to write your query in the first place. Your phrase can be as long or as short as you wish, although obviously the longer the phrase the smaller the set of results will be returned. You can also include a number of phrases in your search, although you are limited to a total number of 32 words in any single query.

We can also exclude words or phrases from our searches by using the

> >

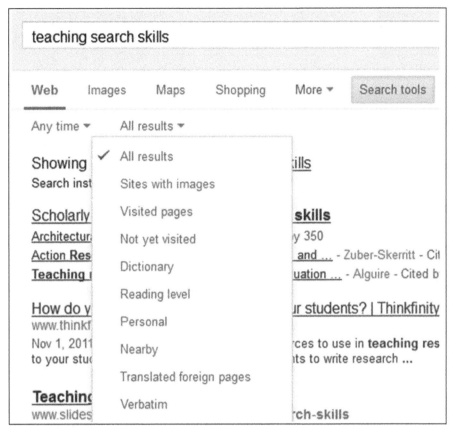

Figure 3.2 The 'Verbatim' option displayed
Google and the Google logo are registered trademarks of Google Inc., used with permission

minus or hyphen symbol '-'. If we use this immediately before the word or phrase that we wish to exclude Google will ignore any results that contain the term(s). If I'm interested in Google but don't want to see results that use the phrase '*"search engine"*' I can simply run the search '*google -"search engine"*' to achieve exactly that. However, since Google tends to plough its own furrow in search matters, if you are used to using the Boolean operator '*NOT*', you'll need to forget that, since Google doesn't exclude the word or phrase that you're not interested in, it simply adds in the word 'not' as another search term. This search function in particular should be used with some care, because it can result in perfectly acceptable pages being rejected. For example, if I wanted information on libraries, but none in London, if I include the search function '*-London*' then I would run the risk of excluding a page that started 'This page is about libraries, with the exception of those in London' which was actually just what I was looking for!

To summarize then, the basic search techniques that you can use with Google are:

➡ Simply type in words and hope that Google will be able to relevance rank them for you appropriately (which, to be fair, it can do in many instances).

➡ Do not use the Boolean operator *'AND'* – simply type in all the words you want.

➡ Use double quotes for a phrase.

➡ Use a hyphen (minus symbol) instead of *'NOT'* to exclude results with an unwanted term.

➡ Use the Boolean operator *'OR'* (which can also be expressed as a single vertical line, | , usually found sandwiched between the left shift key and the *z* key).

➡ To prevent Google from reinterpreting words in your search, use the Verbatim option, found in the search tools menu bar.

➡ Use the plus symbol only if you wish to find a company's Google+ page.

Google search: some advanced search functions

There are plenty of other ways in which you can run an effective search that are scarcely more complicated than the methods already shown.

Synonyms

When searching, it's important to remember the use of synonyms. When searching for 'car' it's always worth considering searching for 'lorry', 'automobile', 'truck', and so on. A search for 'beginner' is obviously useful if you're a trainer or teacher, but British searchers may not consider the American word 'primer' for example. Google used to have an excellent synonym search function which was the '~', or tilde symbol. A search for *"~beginner"* would automatically search on variants of the word, including plural and American/British terms. Unfortunately this was dropped by Google in June 2013, citing a lack of use and the expense in running that particular piece of code. Users now have to rely on Google's ability to do basic synonym searching; 'car tax' will also find results for 'vehicle tax' for example, but it's not as comprehensive as the depreciated functionality. In future, searchers will need to remember to use the 'OR' operator more widely. Personally I think this is a great shame, and illustrates a worrying tendency of Google to limit search functionality, rather than increase it.

Proximity searches

Another straightforward but slightly advanced piece of functionality is to use the asterisk symbol * between words. Google will interpret this as a request to run a search based on proximity with one or more words replacing the *. For example, a search for *'three*mice'* will return results which include 'three blind mice', 'three button mice', 'three strains mice', and so on. The search also returns the result 'three new blue track mice', so you can see that Google interprets the * symbol as meaning one or more words (and increasing the number of asterisks does not result in more words found between the *three* and *mice*). Google does, however, have a second proximity search syntax, which is the use of *'AROUND(x)'*, where *x* is the number of words between words in the search. Consequently, a search for *'three AROUND(5) mice'* would give us a set of results where the two terms that we searched for will be found on web pages where they occur within five words of each other. It should be remembered, however, that this is an undocumented feature (you won't find this in much of the search documentation that Google provides) and as such it's open to change and may well not always work in the manner that one expects.

Positional searches – searching in specific web page elements

While it is not exactly proximity searching in the strict sense of the term, Google does allow you to search for your term in specific elements of a web page. These are as follows.

You can type in the title of the web page with the syntax *'allintitle:'*. Thus, a search for *'allintitle:library success stories'* would return pages where all three words 'library', 'success' and 'stories' were to be found within the title of the page. It's worth pointing out that the title of the web page is not the one that appears in the main body of the screen but that which is to be found in the top left-hand corner of the page.

This option does not have a great deal of use, since one of the key ranking criteria that Google uses is 'all the words within the title element of the page'. The title of a webpage is normally displayed in the top left of a browser window, and this may differ from the title of the page in the main body of the screen. A search for *'allintitle: libraries birmingham'* will only return documents that have both words in the title element. When using this operator you cannot include any others.

A second search function is to get Google simply to return pages that contain the words that you have asked for within the URL of the web page. In order to do this, simply run a search with the syntax *'allinurl:'*. Thus, to move my example along, a search for *'allinurl:library success stories'* returns web pages such as www.netgear.co.uk/home/documentation-library/success–stories. This search function can be very useful if you wish to target a particular section of a website; the library pages, for example, may well be found in a subsection of the URL under '/library/' and while this is not always the case it is nevertheless a useful way to try a search. Another option that you might wish to explore is *'allinanchor:'*, which will restrict results to pages that contain all the query terms in the anchor text (the blue underlined hyperlink) on links to the page. A search for *'allinanchor library success stories'* will return pages in which the anchor text on links to the page contain the words 'library', 'success' and 'stories'. When using this operator, however, do not use any other search operators, since that

> ## >> Did you know?
> If you took one minute to look at each page that Google has indexed it would take you 38,026 years to look at them all. Google checks through them in 0.5 of a second (www.stateofsearch.com/how-massive-is-google).

merely gets Google confused, and it will sulk. You can overcome this slight problem by using the *'inanchor:'* operator. If you include this in your search Google will limit the pages that are returned to those that contain your query and which include your anchor term as a link from another page. So a search for *'success stories inanchor:library'* will return pages that contain the words 'success' and 'stories' and which are linked to by other pages using the word 'library' in the anchor text.

Site- and country-limited searches

An excellent way of focusing a search and limiting the number of results is to make use of the *'site:'* function. This can be used in a variety of different ways to instruct Google to limit the search to a particular type of website or to a country of origin. For example, if you just want to obtain information from one particular site, such as Microsoft's, the search would be *'site:.microsoft.com <search term>'*. You can obviously replace their site with

〉 〉

that of any other, as long as it's a site that Google has indexed. However, if that site also contains their own database (such as a telecoms site that provides access to telephone numbers) Google won't have been able to index that data, so it won't show up in a *'site:'* search. Please also note that *'site:'* has to be in lower case: if it's in upper case Google doesn't recognize the search syntax, and this is common to all operators. Finally, also be aware of the full stop in *'.microsoft'*, which is also a key component of this type of search. The function can also be extended – if you want to limit a search to country domains, the syntax would be *'site:.uk'* or *'site:.jp'*, for example; if you wanted to narrow further, a search through UK government websites would be *'site:.gov.uk'*. The value of this search operator really cannot be stressed enough. There is, of course, a huge amount of US-based content on the web and it's all too easy for Google to confuse e.g. the county of Essex in the UK with one in the USA. Limiting by country easily overcomes that issue.

Searching for related and linked pages

There's another page-related tool that Google makes available to searchers to help find material quickly. If there's a page (and indeed this works on site URLs as well) that a searcher finds useful, a search for *'related:'* and then the URL of that page will provide you with various other pages that Google thinks are related to it in some way. For example, a search for *'related:www.philb.com/whichengine.htm'* will return about 200 other pages that Google thinks are about internet search engines.

Finally, another useful tool to use is the *'link:'* operator. This will find pages that merely link to a particular web page or site that you already know about. For example, a search for *'link:www.philb.com'* will return a list of pages which link to my site www.philb.com. This can be extended to a specific page, and so in order to see which sites link to my page on web search engines (www.philb.com/webse.htm), the search syntax would be *'link:www.philb.com/webse.htm'* There are a few extra points to make here, however. First, it's necessary to get the link correct, as a search for philb.com without the preceding www. will return no results at all. Secondly, the number of results returned is not an accurate or comprehensive number; it's simply a collection of pages that Google thinks are particularly important. Finally, for particularly large sites such as Google.com or Microsoft.com you'll find a lot of the results are pages from the same site linking to other pages on the same site, which is pointlessly

‹ ‹

self-referential. In order to exclude these, simply exclude the URL of the website itself, using the minus symbol for exclusion. Therefore, in order to run a search to find pages that link to www.cilip.org but which don't come from the site the search syntax would be '*link:www.cilip.org -site:cilip.org.uk*'.

Searching for file types

As mentioned already, data is available on the internet in a wide variety of different sources and file formats. Not all search engines are able to index information which is not in a traditional HTML format, although to be fair most of the major ones can. The advantage of running a search like this is in the type of data that you can expect to find in a specific file format. For example, if you are interested in financial or statistical data it is reasonable to assume that a lot of authors will make that information available in a spreadsheet format. To take another example, many publishers wish their electronic versions to look exactly the same as their printed versions (this is true of official documents such as government papers, annual reports and, often, university prospectuses). Since this type of data is contained within a .pdf file format it makes sense to limit the search to that and no other. One final example is in the area of PowerPoint presentations, as these are often provided for an introduction to a subject area or, at the other end of the spectrum, as a way of indicating the research that has been done in a particular area: the .ppt format is not only useful for finding introductory texts but also for finding experts in particular subject areas. The syntax that Google uses for this type of search is '*filetype:*' followed by the three-letter abbreviation for the file format. Therefore, a search for '*filetype:ppt library success stories*' will return us results that contain the three words 'library', 'success' and 'stories' somewhere within the PowerPoint presentations the Google has indexed. Google currently recognizes ten different file types, ranging from the aforementioned to rather more esoteric formats, such as the Google Earth .kmz and .kml files, and also rich text format or .rtf.

We can start to combine these different search functions and truly see how powerful a Google search can become. A search for '*site:.gov.uk filetype:pdf library success stories*' will give us a reasonably small set of results which provide us with documents from various UK government departments which are at least in part formal and relate to success stories with libraries. Results can be narrowed even further by the judicious use of the phrase double quotes option.

At this point it is worthwhile issuing a slight caution. If you are

⟩ ⟩

particularly eagle-eyed you may well have noticed that there is an inconsistency in the use of some of the previous types of search syntax. Specifically, in the case of the *'site:'* option there is always a full stop before the variable, as in *'site:.gov.uk'* but when we use the *'filetype:'* format, as in *'filetype:ppt'*, we do not use a full stop. If searchers get this wrong they will end up with very poor results; if this happens to you please check that you are using or not using full stops in the correct place.

Search functionality via menu

When Google has run a search it will provide more functionality via the menu under the search box, as we can see in Figure 3.3.

Figure 3.3 The Google search tools menu bar
Google and the Google logo are registered trademarks of Google Inc., used with permission

There is a certain amount of duplication between this menu bar and the black bar at the very top of the page; image, maps and news are to be found in both, for no good reason. Clicking on the 'Search tools' option provides a very useful sub-menu of search options that we can make use of. These are 'Any time' and 'All results'. By clicking on 'Any time' we can limit search results to the last hour or the past day, week, month or year. We can also choose a custom range as well. The 'All results' options are slightly more interesting, however, so it's worth going through those in a little detail. 'Sites with images' allows searchers to limit results to those sites that contain images. Personally I've always found this a fairly pointless option, since images generally add to my understanding of a subject, and I'm not aware of any sites that don't have images of one sort or another, so I ignore this option. However, the next two, 'Visited pages' and 'Not yet visited' can be very helpful, particularly if you have to stop a search halfway through. When you come back later (sometimes days later) it's often difficult to remember which pages have been visited and which have not. These two options provide a really good way of eliminating that problem. 'Dictionary' is very straightforward – just type in a term that you need more information about and choose that. Google will return a definition of the term, pronunciation assistance and links to web pages that define the term in more detail. 'Reading Level' is a tool that is unique to Google, and it gives searchers an indication as to the reading level of pages, from basic to intermediate and advanced. These can simply be displayed so that searchers can see what percentage of results are in each of the three categories or can limit results to any of the three options. This can be useful if it's necessary to find basic level material on a complex subject such as subatomic physics, for example. It can also be slightly amusing to search for subjects or people to see the reading levels associated with pages about them. Reading levels for pages about Justin Bieber are Basic – 62%, Intermediate 37% and Advanced 1%, while comparable figures for Richard Wagner are 36%, 57% and 7% respectively. Perhaps not very useful knowledge, but internet search doesn't always have to be entirely serious!

The next search tool option that we are presented with is 'Personal'. This only works if you have a Google account and are logged into it when searching. If so, Google will limit results to those people who you follow on Google+, pages or information that others have shared with you on the social network, contacts on YouTube, and so on. It's Google's attempt to leverage the value of Google+ and to return search results to you from a network of people that you know and trust. It's worth pointing out that Google also shares this information at the top of the results screen; there is a toggle icon of a head and shoulders, which turns personal results on and off, and which also shows the search results number for a general web search and the rather smaller number of personal results.

'Nearby' is the next search tool that we can use. This works best if you are looking for a person, shop or service, rather than a rather more theoretical concept. For example, a search for *'comic shop'* shows me five stores in close proximity to where I live, *'dentist'* gives even more, but *'information literacy'* doesn't return any results. The 'Nearby' option can further be focused to city, region or state. Google will also provide a handy little map, addresses, phone numbers and Google reviews, pulled from the 'Local' option in Google+.

The penultimate search tool is 'Translated foreign pages' and this can be used to identify pages written in different languages, and these can then be translated into other languages, often with hilarious results.

The final option is 'Verbatim', which we have already looked at – it tells Google to run the search exactly as given, without giving the search engine an opportunity to 'think for itself'.

Each option can quickly be cleared by using the 'Clear' command. However, because of the way in which Google works you cannot use two options together – you can use 'nearby' or 'verbatim' but not both together. Incidentally, if you are wondering where search functions such as 'Timeline', 'Image swirl' or the 'Wonder wheel' are, Google decided that they were not important enough, or used to the extent that they hoped, and so have been withdrawn. It's entirely Google's right to choose what search functionality it offers of course, but there are very few functions that can absolutely be relied upon to continue to exist. Use them by all means, but keep in the back of your mind the possibility that they might not always be there for you, and have backup plans in place.

Google's Advanced Search functions

Google used to make it very easy to go to the Advanced Search functions page, since the option was placed right beside the search box. However, this has now been removed, and searchers either need to know that the URL for the option is https://www.google.com/advanced_search or they have to run a search. Once the search has been run, a cog icon is displayed to the top right of the screen; clicking on this gives Advanced Search as an option, or searchers have to scroll to the bottom of the page to find the same option available to them.

It is worthwhile spending some time looking at the Google Advanced Search page; don't get put off by that word 'advanced', because in fact I think search is easier using this page than from the so-called 'simple search page'. In fact, right at the very top of the Advanced Search page is a handy little box with options to simply type in words to get Google to search on. Options are 'all these words', 'this exact word or phrase', 'any of these words', 'none of these words' and 'numbers ranging from: to:'. This is, I believe, far easier for a novice searcher to grasp rather than remember the correct search syntax or keystrokes. The final option in this section is the numeric range, which allows you to limit a search to web pages that contain figures within a numeric range as defined by the searcher. For example, a search for *'blu ray player £100..£150'* will return web pages that should, at least in theory provide you with details and information on those gadgets within that price range.

Google then provides a second option to focus a search by allowing users to narrow results by 'language', 'region', 'last update', 'site or domain', 'terms appearing', 'safe search', 'reading level', 'filetype' and 'usage rights'. Most of these we have already looked at earlier in this chapter so I'll just focus on those which may not be so familiar, or which have a particular point waiting to be made. Google provides access to search results in many languages, currently over 30, and it has the largest number of languages that can be searched in. The region search option is really limited to countries, rather than specific regions, and while there is the chance to limit to, say, Germany, it's not possible to limit to Europe. Google's attempt at safe searching is unfortunately pretty disastrous. If safe search is in place, Google filters terms out of the search which it deems to be offensive in some way. Consequently, a keen ornithologist is going to find it very difficult to find information on the bird *Cyanistes caeruleus*, more commonly known as a blue tit. Google filters out the second word, leaving us with nothing appropriate at all. This is even more annoying in the image search function, because all that it's possible to see are images of blue-coloured things. Therefore, in order for children to be able to see images of the bird, they will have to turn the safe search function off, which rather seems to defeat the point of it. Google does, however, claim that even when safe search is turned off, sexually explicit results are not generally shown – a more specific search with further terms is necessary to bring up adult material. However, this seems to be a fudged solution at best. Other search engines are perfectly capable of working out the context of words to allow certain types of information or image through their filtering system, so it's strange that Google can't.

Google's usage rights filter in theory allows searchers to limit results to those resources that are available for people to use because the person who created the content or image have used the Creative Commons (CC) licensing system to allow people to use, modify or perhaps even sell material that they haven't created themselves. The creator of content can assign a particular licence and it's this that Google is attempting to search on. However, it's of limited value, because Google can only limit results to a particular page that offers material under Creative Commons. There may be many images for example on a page, with only one of them under CC, so the user still has to wade through the page to find out if the material that they are looking for is actually available. There's more information available on Creative Commons at their website at http://creativecommons.org/.

Google used to provide access to other search functionality on the Advanced Search page, such as the ability to find similar pages to one that you had already found. They have withdrawn those functions, although curiously provide a link to help screens that explain how to limit to similar pages.

〉 〉

Bracketed searching

Sometimes a search can become complicated very quickly if the searcher is using several variables in the search string. For example, a search for *London OR Manchester OR library OR librarian* could at first glance mean that the searcher wants one of two English cities, or the word library or librarian. However, it also might mean London or the word Manchester or alternatively the word library, or the search could be for any of the four terms. It's therefore helpful to group the terms by putting them into brackets or parentheses thus: *(London OR Manchester) (library OR librarian)*, which makes the whole search that much easier to follow.

'One-trick ponies'

There are a number of other searches that can be done using Google's search functionality which are either poorly mentioned in their help pages or are not mentioned at all. This is not a complete listing, since Google releases new search functionality on a regular basis and withdraws it almost as often. Most of these search functions have little professional value, although they can be quite useful for quick reference work.

If you have an interest in a particular football team (and by this I mean soccer) then you can simply type in the name of the team that you support into the usual search box. Google will give you the result of the last game that was played and will also provide you with the next opponent and fixture date.

Flight information can be obtained by providing Google with the name of the flight, such as *'BA123'*. Google will provide departure and arrival times as well as terminal details.

If you wish to know the time or the weather in a particular location simply type in time or weather and the place that you're interested in. Google will then provide you with local time and weather conditions.

Want to see what is on at the movies? A search for *'movies'* followed by a location will result in details of cinema showings, reviews, length, certificate and type of the film, and a link to a trailer if one is available.

Searchers can also use Google to perform a variety of mathematical calculations as well. The normal keystrokes can be used for basic arithmetic: +, -, * and / for addition, subtraction, multiplication and division. *'% of'* will give the percentage of something, as in *'45% of 39'* and a number can be raised to a power by using ^ or **, as with *'2^5'* or *'2**5'* for 2^5. Finally, it's possible to convert values from one system of units to another, such as *'300 Euros in USD'*, *'30 lbs in kg'* or *'30 in hex'*.

Searchers with an interest in stocks and shares can use the **stocks:** operator to view opening prices, high, low, volume and so on. Simply search for *'stocks:'* and the abbreviation for the company you are interested in, such as *'stocks: goog'*.

Searchers who need to know about a specific website can run a search for *'info:'* and the URL of a website, such as *'info:philb.com'*. You can put the entire URL string into the search, but you'll get the same result, so you may as well save yourself a few keystrokes. Please note that in this example there has to be no space after the colon and before the first character of the URL. This is another example of Google's inconsistency – sometimes the space between function and variable matters, and sometimes it doesn't. If in doubt, try both.

While we're talking about undocumented features, another one that you may wish to explore is what is generally known as a 'Google sinker'. It is a way that the searcher has of telling Google that it should pay particular attention to one of the words within the search. Let's say that I'm interested in comparisons between the elections of Presidents Bush and Lincoln. I could try and do a simple search such as *'President Bush Lincoln election'* but I very quickly can see that I don't get information of the type that I was hoping for; results might be about either president, or may focus on a specific aspect of a presidency, with little emphasis on elections. However, as odd as it may seem, if I start to repeat the word *'election'* the results that I receive change and become more focused on their elections. So a search for *'President Bush Lincoln election election election election election election'* can actually provide good results. I won't promise that it will work every time, but it's a useful trick to keep up your sleeve.

Google Knowledge Graph

In mid–2012 Google started to roll out a new search function, which we should all be familiar with now, called the Google Knowledge Graph which sometimes appears to the right of the results on the page, depending on the search that has been run. This tool connects your search query to Google's knowledge base of over 500 million people, things, events and places in order to display appropriate information in a sidebar alongside your search results. This information will include related facts for which Google has found a people search on a regular basis. For example, if you're searching for a famous author Google will display some of their book titles, date of birth,

〉 〉

spouse, children, films that have been made from the books and so on.

It's very useful if you need a quick piece of information, such as when a famous person was born. While you'll get that with a search, of course, with the Knowledge Graph you can just type in their name, and Google will do the rest for you. There's a very handy 'People also search for' option which could almost be used as a recommendation engine; the people who search for Charles Dickens also search for Arthur Conan Doyle, Charlotte Brontë and Mark Twain, for example. It's possible to delve quite deeply into information, just using the Knowledge Graph. For instance, if you are a fan of the science fiction series 'Lost', a search on the name will pull up the name of one of the writers, J. J. Abrams. Clicking on his name in the Graph box runs a search in Google for him, and pulls up a more specific Graph box on him, including the movies that he has coming out later in the year.

Searching for a specific location such as a theatre will instantly provide not only the basic address and phone numbers, but will link to the closest transportation facilities, upcoming events and reviews. If the location is a city, Google will link to points of interest, but then you can click on those to see a map, additional related places that are worth visiting, and so on – very handy if you are intending to visit for a few days. If your need is to find something in your current location, you can of course try Google Maps, but an equally quick solution is just to type in something such as *'post office'* to see the ones closest to you, with address and phone details.

One search point that does need to be made about the Knowledge Graph is that you have to be very precise with your search terminology. *'The Beatles'* pulls up the Knowledge Graph entry for the Fab Four, but *'beatles music'* does not.

Google has created a tool which is generally referred to as the Google Carousel, which is helpful, but seldom seen; you have to do exactly the right kind of search for it to come up on the screen. It's basically a visual listing across the top of the results, providing thumbnail access to data. For example, a search for *'downton abbey cast'* displays a listing of thumbnail photographs of the actors, their names and the parts that they play in the TV series. Clicking on a thumbnail runs a new search on that person, while pulling up a Knowledge Graph that relates to them. You can click a left or right arrow to see more cast members appear on the screen. The search has to be exactly right to call up the Carousel – a search for *'harrison ford'* doesn't bring the tool into play, but a search for *'harrison ford movies'* does. Similarly *'charles dickens'* doesn't trigger a display of his work, but *'charles dickens books'* does. While it's quite a nice function it's also slightly

‹ ‹

irritating, because it's not clear which are the magic terms that cause the Carousel to start.

Other Google search resources

Normally users will search 'the web' when using Google, but it's important to remember that Google does have various other databases available for use. These are either shown under the search box (once a search has been run) or across the top in the black ribbon.

Google Images

Google Images can be searched by either menu option or directly from its own URL at www.google.com/imghp and the database has in excess of 10 billion images. We have previously seen that Google relevance-ranks web pages using a variety of different algorithms such as title and links for example. With images Google uses a similar approach, by using the name of an image file, the alternative text that the web author can assign to the image and any words that are close to the image – working on the assumption that images close to specific words may well be images of those specific words.

There are various ways in which Google Images can be searched. If you look at the search box after clicking on 'Images' you will see a small camera icon. Clicking on the icon produces a dialogue box which allows users to either paste in the URL of a specific image that they are interested in or alternatively to upload an image from their own computer. This can be quite useful if a searcher wishes to find similar images to any he or she may already have, or perhaps in an attempt to identify an image on a web page that they have visited themselves. Reverse image searching (providing Google with an image to use as a search option) has a variety of uses. Some sites use 'paywalls', which require users to pay a fee to view content, such as newspaper or apartment listing sites. If an image is used in the free section of the site it might be possible to simply get Google to run a search based on that image to see if it's possible to obtain more information from some other site that doesn't charge a fee. If you find an image of an item that you're interested in purchasing, but don't have manufacturer details, upload the photograph of the item in question and Google may well be able to identify it for you. Google can help identify celebrities, and even the films that they have been in, simply by providing an image from a film or sometimes if you're lucky, from a photograph taken from your own television. Fake accounts on social networking sites will often use stock imagery in an attempt to hide behind the photograph of an attractive model; if you suspect this is the case then reverse image searching may well confirm this for you. A major problem in searching can be when trying to identify something that's very difficult to describe, such as a leaf, flower or insect, but this identification process can sometimes be made a little easier by taking a photograph of the item and uploading it. Google won't identify it every time, of course, but it's worth trying if you're really stuck. Finally, if you are an artist or photographer, it's an excellent method of seeing if your images are being used on other sites – either with or without your permission!

Alternatively, searchers can simply type in a word or a phrase and Google will try and find images as appropriate. As you may expect, you can look for one word, a number of words or a phrase, or use the Boolean operator '*OR*' to find a variety of images. Finally, words can also be excluded from an image search.

Images can be displayed and sorted either by relevance or sorted by subject, as defined by Google. A search for '*librarian images*' gives the searcher some related searches, such as '*librarians at work*' and the rather more distressing '*old librarian*' or '*mean librarian*' and some of these related searches are used by Google in the 'Sort by subject' option.

Google does provide the searcher with some excellent options for searchers. The image menu allows users to limit by size, colour, type or time period. The only option that isn't terribly clear from the listing is the 'Standard View/Show sizes' – all this means is that the size of the image in terms of pixels is displayed on each image. One particularly useful option is the ability to display images by subject, so a search for 'librarian' for example will display photographs of '*librarians at work*', '*male librarian*', '*old librarian*', '*librarian cartoon*' and so on. These options can be combined, so it's very easy to create a tightly focused search. Start by running a search for 'librarian', and then choose the 'Search Tools' option. Clicking on 'Type' will give an option for 'Face' and clicking on 'Color' will give various options, such as blue. Instantly you'll have results which either display the faces of librarians wearing blue, or which are posed on a blue background. As a result it may be possible to identify the book about which the user can only remember the subject and the colour of the cover. Google also recently (March 2013) provided us with the opportunity to search for animated gifs in image search. Simply run your image search as usual, then click search tools. A new option 'animated' has been added to the list of types of image returned.

Google video

Google has been involved with video for many years, firstly via their own offering but now more recently through their acquisition of YouTube. It's not easy to find, however, as it has been hidden at the bottom of the 'More' option in top black toolbar. The video search option does not, however, simply search YouTube, but a wider variety of video sites. Obviously, given the sheer amount of data that is added to YouTube every day, results from that resource tend to come up more often than any other. If you want to exclude the YouTube videos you could simply run your search and then add in '*-site:.youtube.com*' and that will do the trick. Many of the search options that we have already referred to are also available within the advanced video search option. So, for example, it's possible to search for a number of words, an exact phrase, to do an '*OR*' search or to exclude words from your search strategy. Furthermore, options are available to limit videos to those in specific languages, with short, medium, or long durations (less than 4 minutes, less than 20 minutes or longer than 20 minutes), within a particular timeframe, high-quality, from a particular site or domain, or only those videos with closed captions. Results can be sorted by relevance or date. All of these options are available from the advanced search screen at www.google.com/advanced_video_search or via the menu bar on the left-hand side of the page. One final point that's worth making is that there is a safe search option with three different options and, while it is good, it will never be perfect. You can learn more about the Google safe search filter at www.google.com/support/websearch/bin/static.py?hl=en&page=guide.cs&guide=1224171&answer=510&rd=1.

Google News

Google also provides us with access to recent news information, available as an option from the search bar at the top of the screen. It takes news from a variety of different resources but unfortunately they have chosen not to share all of those publicly. However, as well as national and international resources they do index a number of local newspapers as well, and also certain websites. You may find it is worthwhile exploring just to make sure that your favoured resource is contained within their database. Many of the search features are the same as those that have been previously described but obviously since this is a news resource there are some different functions available to searchers. There is an expanded date search function, the option of limiting news to specific news sources, news sources located in a particular country or state, articles written by specific authors, and finally the option of choosing to return results where the search terms occur in the headline of the article, in the body of the article or in the URL.

Google News does provide us with a very interesting resource, which is the option of creating an e-mail alert for a subject that is of interest to you. At the bottom of any news search results page you will see an option which says "stay up-to-date on these results:" you can then create an e-mail alert which means that Google will send you an e-mail whenever it finds new information for you on your subject of interest. Users can choose the type of information that they are sent, such as everything, news, blogs, videos, discussions or books, how often the alerts are sent, how many are sent; all results or only the best results (however that's defined), and the e-mail address the alert is sent to. There is also an option to manage your alerts at the URL www.google.com/alerts/manage?hl=en. Finally, there is also an option on the search results page for viewing the results in an RSS format but I will return to this in Chapter 15.

Other than current news, Google does have a partial index of hundreds of scanned newspapers from a variety of countries and a variety of time periods, some of which date back to the early 1800s. The scanning is of generally good quality and it does give a real feeling for history so it is still a useful resource even if Google has decided not to continue developing it. Unlike some of their other projects, however, it has not been deleted and is still viewable: it can be searched at http://news.google.com/newspapers.

Google shopping

I am simply making a reference to this option for the sake of inclusion, but it isn't one that I intend going into any great detail over. Search options include limiting to stock nearby, sites that accept Google Checkout or with free shipping or new items. There are price limitation and shop in particular stores functions. Finally, it is possible to compare prices from different stores. If you're keen to explore it, the option is available under the 'More' option in the toolbar.

‹ ‹

Google books

The Google books option (under 'More' in the toolbar) allows you to search the full text of books that Google has digitized. If the book is out of copyright, or the publisher has given Google permission, you will be able to see a preview of that book and sometimes the entire text. Furthermore, if it is in the public domain you can freely download a .pdf copy. Google has also created reference pages for every book in their collection, such as reviews, related books, selected pages, other additions, common terms and phrases, popular passages, references to the book, from other books, Google Scholar and web pages. Information about the author and bibliographic details are also given. You may also be able to buy the book from the Google eBookstore (although at the time of writing this is an option that is only available within the USA). The books that Google provides access to come from the partner programme and the library project. Further discussion on this is really outside the remit of this book but if you are interested you can find out more information at www.google.com/googlebooks/about.html.

Once again, search functions beyond the basic ones are available to searchers and these include the ability to search within the books, the preview or Google eBooks only. Search results can be limited to: any documents or books or magazines; material written at any time, this century, the 20th or 19th centuries, or a custom range; and results sorted by relevance or date. Finally, if you know either the ISBN or the ISSN a search can be limited to that specific title.

The value of this type of search to librarians and other information professionals is quite obvious. It allows searchers to quickly identify a few titles that may be available within the library, it provides access to data in a format that is familiar to everybody and it may be a quick way of being able to get the bibliographic data required in order to obtain the book via interlibrary loan. Finally, it may go at least some way to reducing the age-old request 'I need a book again; it had a red cover', although we have of course already looked at a possible solution to that problem by using Google image search!

Google Places

There will be many occasions when you want to find a resource or some information that is related to a specific location. You may wish to discover where to find a local library, for example, or you might need to locate a

> >

veterinary surgeon – any manner of different things related to a place. You can of course just do a straightforward search but the kind of information that you get may well be somewhat limited, which is why Google has introduced place search. Google has clustered search results around specific locations so that you can get comparisons of resources and decide where to go for supper or which vet to take your sick animal to. If you search for something and add in a location such as '*vet southend*' Google will do its best to work out exactly where you are, what you want, and then not only show you appropriate websites but also provide you with a local map. On the left-hand side of the screen Google displays results while on the right-hand side of the screen we have a helpful map of the general area together with an indication as to where each of the resources can physically be found. Clicking on any of the map locations will provide an enhanced view, provide details on the resource such as its address and phone number, there may well be reviews of the resource and also a Street view of the location. There is also an option to get directions from your current location, to search nearby or save to a map. Alternatively, if you click on the 'place page' link to the side of the results you will again get factual location data, a close-up map and you can also write a review or upload a photograph.

Google Maps

Another resource that is similar to Google Places is Google Maps. Access to this is via the black ribbon bar at the top of the screen or via the menu bar under the search box. Searches are similar to those for Places. It's worth noting however that the actual results that get returned from the two resources are quite different, so in order to do a really comprehensive search the wise searcher will use both. Google Maps is particularly useful for the Street View option, so you can see exactly where you will be walking or driving to, a Get Directions option and a rather sweet Estimated Fuel Cost resource, which you can change according to the price you're paying for petrol.

Google Street View is a powerful option that can be accessed via the Maps function. Once you have a map on the screen to the left is a plus and minus slider, allowing you to zoom in or out on an area, and above this is an icon of a person. Simply click and drag that onto the map (it works best if the map is zoomed into a point where you can see the names of the roads) and you can then view the streets and roads as they have been photographed

‹ ‹

by Google. It makes searching for locations much easier, and is an excellent way to search for details on a building, road, and so on.

Google Scholar

The subtitle of this resource is 'Stand on the shoulders of giants' and you can get to it at http://scholar.google.com. It's a simple way to search through scholarly literature, such as articles, theses, books and abstracts. These are from academic publishers, professional organizations, universities and other websites. Publishers can include their content, and libraries can link up with Google Scholar as well, by sharing holdings information. More details on this aspect are at http://scholar.google.com/intl/en/scholar/libraries.html. Searching is fairly straightforward, as you would expect by now, but there are specific search functions that are available – Articles (including patents) or Legal Opinions and Journals. The advanced search functionality filters by author, publication, date, collections (with seven subsections), legal opinions, opinions from different types of US courts and opinions by courts from different US states. It's worth pointing out that the advanced search function within Google Scholar is found in the search box to the right, as a down arrow. Unlike in Google websearch it's not available at the bottom of the page after a search has been run, or via the settings cog on the top right-hand side. Moreover, another inconsistency is that although most search filters and search options are available below the search box, Google Scholar still uses a left-hand menu, with the options (articles, time, sort and create an alert) running down the side of the screen. If you are interested in Legal Documents, this option is available below the search box prior to starting the search.

If you are managing your links and/or any citations in bibliographic management platforms such as EndNote, Refworks or BiTex, you can make use of this option by setting up Google Scholar to show links in a way that they can be imported into the package of your choice. This is very useful if you're creating a bibliography, for example. Google Scholar also shows library access links as well. Users can choose up to five libraries that they have access to: you may need to login with your library password, use a campus computer or configure your browser to use a library proxy – your librarian can help with any of these options in case you're not sure exactly what to do. It's also possible to set up an alert: run a search, choose the 'Create an alert' from the left-hand menu and then choose the exact search that needs to be run, and the e-mail address that results are to be sent to.

> >

Google Scholar provides access to useful information in the 'Metrics' option at the top right-hand side of the screen, labelled 'Metrics' oddly enough. This provides authors with a quick and easy way to see the visibility and influence of recent articles in journals. There are two columns; the larger right-hand column lists the top 100 publications ordered by their five-year h-index and h-median metrics. You can also explore publications via research area. Browse publications by selecting an area of interest in the left-hand column, click on the Subcategories link and then explore details on the publications as required.

Results are given in the form of title, author, publication title and publisher, summary, citations cites, related articles and access details – private individuals can purchase access to materials via the British Library, for example. Many of the articles are available as full text, and the sources tend to be rather more academic than those obtained via a standard search engine. However, results are not guaranteed to be current or comprehensive, and coverage has been said to be stronger in the sciences than the humanities. For a fuller discussion on the merits and disadvantages of Google Scholar it's worth reading an article on the subject at Indiana University Bloomington Libraries at www.libraries.iub.edu/index.php?pageId=1002229.

Google blogs

Weblogs, or blogs for short, have been around since the turn of the century. No one is quite sure how many blogs there are but some figures have suggested that there are more than 180 million. Of course, that isn't to say that all of those are currently being updated; very far from it. However, blogs remain a useful resource, for a number of reasons. They are a very good way to keep up to date with what is happening in a specific subject area. A good blogger will focus on a specific subject area and will do their best to provide a continual stream of information about that subject both in terms of news items and their own personal opinions. I will talk more about blogs in Chapter 7 but here I will briefly go through how they can be searched using Google's blog search option. This can either be accessed by using the menu below the search box or searchers can visit www.google.com/blogsearch directly. One of the things that a searcher will notice quite quickly when using this resource is that the information returned is often only a few hours or perhaps even only a few minutes old. Blog authoring software will quite often contact a blog search engine with

‹ ‹

details of the new posting rather than wait for days for the blog search engine to find the posting itself in the same way that spider or crawler programs locate updated web pages. Consequently, if you need recent material you may find that you get better results by using a blog search instead of a web search. The main disadvantage is, of course, that it's the right of the blog posting to have their own particular bias or opinion and this should be remembered. However, any good blogger will always link back to the original source of the information and so they are a very good way of locating original authoritative content. They can be very useful, because you are able to find experts and enthusiasts quickly in particular subject areas.

The Google blog search engine not only finds individual weblog postings but it can also identify blog homepages. Therefore, if, say, you need to find some key weblogs in a particular subject area simply type your keyword or phrase into the search box and Google will return appropriate blog suggestions for you to look at. As you would expect, all of the usual search functionality is still available to you but in order to make the most of the fast-moving world of the blogosphere search results can be limited to the past 10 minutes, hour, or 24 hours, as well as various other date or time ranges.

> **Did you know?**
> If you used one monitor to display all of the sites that Google indexes it would need to be about 6 million miles from corner to corner (www.stateofsearch.com/how-massive-is-google).

The blog search engine results page also provides you with an option to create an e-mail alert for your subject area of interest or a link through to an RSS feed according to your own preference.

Google discussions

In the early days of the internet a considerable amount of content was produced in the format of web pages but other resources were often used such as mailing lists or newsgroups. These would very often be rather more informal and give people an opportunity to have discussions that were rather more free-flowing. They were in many ways the precursors to resources such as wikis and Facebook groups. That is not to say that they have entirely fallen out of favour, since discussions may well be held in a variety of different formats. These may be things such as Google groups, discussions of photographs held on the Flickr photograph-sharing website,

〉 〉

or in various different forums hosted on websites.

The material that you find is unlikely to be located anywhere else; it is rather akin to grey or ephemeral data. As you will find with blogs a lot of the material returned reflects people's personal opinions, thoughts or ideas and so may well have a limited value for your search but on the other hand you will often find links through to more useful data or official websites. It can also be a useful way of seeing what people were thinking or saying about a topic at a specific period in time without the benefit of hindsight; another useful way of locating experts in particular subject areas, too!

Most of the search options are, as you will now expect, similar to those available for searching other databases but there is – in common with blogs – the option of searching through recent material but also discussions contained within forums or Q&A sites.

Google recipes, flights, patents and play

There are various other subject specific search engines that are offered by Google, but I think it is fair to say that they're quite specialized and will only be used by those people who are already using them, if that makes sense. However, in order to be comprehensive I'll briefly mention them.

➡ Google recipes provides some subject-specific search options, such as ingredients with a Yes/No tick box option, cooking time and calorific value.

➡ Google flights provides information on a relatively small number of flights from West Coast American airports to other American airports, with departure/return details, price and duration. Unless this is quite substantially boosted in quantity of data there's very little point in even looking at it, in my opinion.

➡ Google patents is rather better than its airborne colleague. Results include overviews (including abstracts and images), inventor details, classifications, citations and claims. Search functionality allows searchers to limit by filing status, patent type (utility, design, plant etc.), list or grid view and sorting by relevance or date.

➡ Google play is a link through to music, magazines, android apps and so on, which can be used in conjunction with a smartphone. There's very little here that's of interest to the searcher, so I'm including it for the sake of comprehensiveness.

Other interesting Google functionality

Because of the sheer size of Google it is not possible within the confines of this work to consider every single element of functionality that it provides; that would need a book in its own right. However, there are a number of other resources that might rightly come under the heading of miscellaneous that are worthy additions to the searcher's armoury. In this section I will briefly mention a number of them, which I think will make the searcher's life a little bit easier and provide them with access to information that they perhaps otherwise would not have.

Google trends

Google trends at www.google.com/trends allows searchers to see the worldwide trending of particular words or phrases. Search results will provide trending graphs, key websites, trending by region, city, and language. Google trends therefore provides searchers with an insight into broad search patterns and histories. Searches can be limited by region and the year to gain further insight into the search term or terms under consideration. An associated resource, Google insights for search (www.google.com/insights/search) allows users to compare search volume patterns across regions, categories, timeframes and properties. Google trends for websites (http://trends.google.com/websites) provides some basic data on specific websites, such as where visitors are likely to have come from, sites they were also to have visited, and terms they will have searched for.

> **>> Did you know?**
> Each day 20% of Google searches have never been searched before (www.youtube.com/watch?v=TXD-Uqx6_Wk).

Google also offers a 'hot searches' resource at www.google.com/trends/hottrends, although this is only available for terms searched in the United States. However, it is updated throughout the course of the day and searchers can see the 20 most commonly searched terms or phrases at any particular moment in time. This can be a good way of keeping up to date with what is of interest, although it should be stressed that the insights provided are only very broad search patterns.

Finally, in the area of trending data Google provides us with what it refers to as the 'Zeitgeist' for the previous year. We can therefore see, based on the aggregation of billions of searches, what people were interested in over the previous year. This data is broken down into such categories as fastest rising and fastest falling terms, fastest rising in entertainment, sports,

〉 〉

consumer electronics, fastest rising people, fastest rising health queries and so on. The data for 2012 can be found at www.google.com/zeitgeist/2012/ #the-world.

Google Ngram Viewer

The Google Ngram resource, at http://books.google.com/ngrams, is a database of words contained within books that Google has digitized from those published within the last 200 years. Searchers are able to research the popularity of terms and compare them with each other.

Google Translate

Google has a translation resource which is available at http://translate. google.com and translates between 60 different languages. The translation feature also works when Google identifies a web page that is not written in the default language as defined within the user's settings. While not perfect, it does provide a reasonable facsimile of the content available on a web page. It is useful to searchers since it allows some limited flexibility in finding information contained on foreign websites. Google also allows you to translate directly from the Google search box; all you need to do is start the translation with the word '*translate*' and then the text that you want translated and into what language, so an example would be '*translate librarians are wonderful into German*'.

Google calculator

Google has recently improved the calculator function. Now if you type in a calculation the result appears in a 34 scientific functions calculator. This has a large number of advanced features, where previously we only got the answer in bold. Unfortunately you have to do a calculation to bring the calculator up onto the screen.

Other Google functionality

For a nice quick and easy overview of some of the other things you can do with Google visit their page 'Find a new thing to do with Google today' at www.google.co.uk/landing/thingstodo. As previously mentioned, the sheer size of Google is quite daunting and I could fill the rest of this book with information on some of those resources, such as Gmail. While this is tempting, it is important not to get distracted from the main purpose, which is to look at search. However, if you are interested in further explorations you may wish to visit the FaganFinder page on Google (www.faganfinder.com/google), as this provides access to many more resources as well as a nice search interface. Furthermore, if you wish to experience Google advanced search within a friendly easy interface, or wish to introduce advanced searching to your clients and colleagues, I would suggest trying the Soople website at www.soople.com, which provides easy expert search.

Finally, there is another tool called MsFreckles at www.msfreckles.com/?lang=en, which allows you to 'frecklify your search' (no, I don't know what that means either). It's got a listing of search options such as normal search, keyword search, searching across types of sites, blog search, mathematic (calculator) searches, domain searches, file type, news, number and so on. In fact there are 16 basic options, plus translate, and a 'superfilter' option. It's really simple to use – just type in what you're interested in, and you'll be taken to Google with your information displayed on the screen. It's a really good way to introduce people to internet searching and showing them the search syntax that they'll need to use if they want to use Google directly.

The Google sense of humour

There's very little of any practical use in this section, so feel free to skip it, but I think that it's worth mentioning that Google does have a sense of humour. We're all familiar with the Google doodles that appear on the screen to replace the traditional logo for important events or celebrations, and if you want to see the entire collection it is available at www.google.com/doodles/finder/2013/All%20doodles. However, Google also has what are referred to as 'Easter eggs', which is to say odd things that happen if you manage to type in specific searches which trigger them. For example, if you type in the word '*askew*' by itself the search results page tilts off towards the right slightly, creating an example of the word that you're searching. If you run a search for the phrase (without quotes) '*do a barrel roll*' the results page does exactly that. Finally, if you run a search for '*define anagram*' the results screen displays the question 'Did you mean: nerd fame again'. If you're interested in these, perhaps to include as a light break in a training session, there's a very comprehensive list at Search Engine Land, 'The big list of Google Easter eggs', written by Chris

Sherman, at http://searchengineland.com/the-big-list-of-google-easter-eggs-153768.

The disadvantages of Google

There's no doubt that Google is an excellent search engine; it wouldn't be in its pre-eminent position in the search engine hierarchy if it wasn't. However, that's not to say that is perfect – very far from it. There are a lot of things that Google doesn't do very well or which other search engines do rather better. While I don't wish to be negative about any search engine it is also important to be realistic about both the advantages and disadvantages, particularly when so many people trumpet the claim 'but it's all on Google!'. Consequently, let's take a quick look at some of the things that Google does not do well.

Google generally thinks that it knows best. While in the main the answers that you get from Google are good and accurate, it can very easily get things wrong. Moreover, it doesn't always make it easy for you to put it right. I've previously mentioned the '*coots mating behaviour*' and '*teaching search skills*' in this chapter, but I'm sure that you can find plenty of examples of your own. To add insult to injury, Google will often repeat the original search on the page with the legend '*Search instead for*' which then requires another mouse click. While it may be beneficial for Google to make corrections to search terms and to a limited extent make assumptions about what the searcher wants, the fact that Google does this automatically without reference back to the searcher is a worrying sign of self-aggrandizement.

A more serious example of how Google can get a search completely wrong, or at least provide results that most people would regard as inappropriate, is to run a search for the US civil rights leader Martin Luther King. One of the websites that is listed close to, or indeed sometimes at the very top of the list of results is a website called Martin Luther King Jr, a true historical examination. This website has been produced by a US extreme right-wing party who have their own specific agenda. You should feel free to read into that whatever you think is most appropriate. Most people, if they were researching information on Martin Luther King, would not only find this website inappropriate and unhelpful, they would probably also find it upsetting. Google however does not care about this since it is not in the business of providing us with the best results possible. One could of course argue that it is almost impossible to define what 'best results' actually means and so one needs to have a certain amount of sympathy for the search engine. As far as Google is concerned the searcher wanted information on the three words '*Martin Luther King*' and the results that were returned match the search exactly. The reason that the right-wing website comes high in the list of results is partly because the three words are next to each other, that they are in the title of the page, and in the URL, but also that lots of other websites linked to that one. Some of those websites will be other right-wing organizations but many others will ironically be library and educational websites explaining that you cannot trust the information that you find on the internet. We therefore have something like a self-fulfilling prophecy; the more sites that link to it to say that it is not an appropriate site the higher in the rankings it goes.

While the personalization of search can be seen as a good thing, it can cause some searchers problems, particularly those who are always looking for different things. If the user consistently uses Google for his or her own personal searching it is understandable that personalization can be regarded as desirable, since it is possible to hone results according to oft-expressed interests. It can also be argued that this type of personalization creates a filter bubble which results in searches being skewed in favour of the searcher's own attitudes or opinions. It is of course possible to ensure that this doesn't happen, or at least happens to the bare minimum. You may find it useful to check your own Google dashboard at https://www.google.com/dashboard, so that you can manage your account, edit personal information, remove unwanted content, and manage your online identity. It may be considered appropriate to sign out of your account when searching, and/or delete your websearch history.

Google is also quite ruthless at dispensing with resources that it feels do not fit in with its overall offering. For example, in the past Google has had a very active Google Labs project in which searchers have been encouraged to explore various different search applications. While Google has never made any secret of the fact that these have always been in a beta test mode it is nonetheless still an annoyance when these useful resources are phased out. This is even more the case when Google has provided searchers with useful functionality which has been blended into the main search offering. It can cause considerable confusion when resources or search functionality disappears with little or no notice, and if a user relies on a particular resource this could cause considerable problems. Of course, Google can do pretty much whatever it wants to, but equally we have to remember that

〉 〉

Google is first and foremost an advertising company, and as such search functionality is not its highest priority.

Summary

There is absolutely no doubt that Google is an excellent search engine; it would be argued by many that it is the best search engine we have available to us. I do feel that it's important, however, to emphasis that if you don't see the same things on the screen that I do this is to be expected. Google runs a lot of tests on the way that search works and the functionality that they use, and they seem to choose random groups to run these trials with. I recently saw a situation where I was only getting four results on a screen, and then a division bar and below that more results that were referred to as 'Results for similar searches' and I had to click onto page 2 of the results to see more results based on the actual search that I'd run. The next time I ran a search this had disappeared. So when using Google, learn to expect the unexpected!

Plenty of other search engines are also available and they provide us with different results, different rankings, and different functionality. Since these other search engines are freely available and do not cost anything to use it surely makes sense to explore them and use them as appropriate. It is an unwise searcher who puts all of his or her eggs into the Google search basket. Within a library setting we never make use of one reference book, we make use of many of them, and why should internet search be any different? In the next chapter I will look at some of the alternatives to Google and this will hopefully tempt you to explore them and increase your internet search armoury.

CHAPTER 4

>> Other free-text search engines

Introduction

As we saw in the last chapter, while Google has many advantages, and while it could be argued that in many circumstances it is the pre-eminent search engine, it is far from being the only one that is available. There are many other search engines within the free-text category that are worth exploring, and using as well as, or dare I say in preference to, Google. This chapter will consider some of those engines, and in common with the approach used with Google, will look at how they can be used, as well as considering their strengths and weaknesses.

Bing

Bing is the latest attempt by Microsoft to wrest some of the searching public away from Google, and it's arguably their best to date. Previously it was known as Live Search, Windows Live Search and MSN Search. Much of the functionality is the same as that offered by Google, and the data collection method is the same; that is to say by spidering websites, copying the content of the pages and indexing them. Bing can be searched with or without logging into the service (a Windows Live account is required for logging in), but by being logged into it, searchers can see their previous searches, irrespective of the machine(s) the searching was done on. It's worth setting preferences once logged in, and these include Safe Search options, location, display, number of results shown, suggestions and search language. It's also possible

> **>> Did you know?**
> Google, Yahoo! and Bing together cover more than 95% of the US search engine market share (http://searchenginejournal. com).

to choose the country version used with Bing, or as they put it, 'Discover a search experience tailored to your part of the world'. This is quite an important point, as different country versions do provide radically different results. For example, a search using the India version for the term 'adult material' results in a response which states 'Your country or region requires a Bing SafeSearch setting, which filters out results that might return adult content' but the same search in other country-based versions gives very different results. It's fair to say that a similar result can be obtained if you are using another country version but have a strict Safe Search option turned on. However, there are some basic inconsistencies here, since searching for adult material in the video option while using India as the country choice does return material that some would regard as not safe for work.

Bing basic and advanced search

For anyone familiar with searching Google, Bing will offer no unpleasant surprises; the search results page is very similar, with results taking up the main section of the screen, a menu bar of options above the search box, and advertising above the organic results and also the right-hand side of the screen. Bing also does offer a 'related searches' option tailored to the search that's been run. In comparison to Google the advertisements can get in the way rather more and take up more 'real estate', but this does depend very much on the search being run – sometimes the adverts are only down the right-hand side of the screen.

Much of the functionality that you will be familiar with at Google is the same in Bing. Phrase searching will reduce the number of results returned, as will the use of the '*NOT*' or – (minus symbol). Searches can also be undertaken by using the '*OR*' option, of course. A *site:* search can be run, with the same effect as found with Google, although there is some inconsistency over the use of the full stop here. If you recall, with Google the syntax was '*site:.uk*' with that all-important full stop in place. In Bing, a search for '*library site:.uk*' results in 6,640,000 results, and '*library site:uk*' returns 6,730,000 results. Not a huge difference of course, but it's important to remember when running searches. Searches can also be run to limit results to specific types of site, e.g. government or academic sites using the appropriate domain qualifier, such as .gov or .ac.

As you will recall, Google provides much functionality under the search box, with quite extensive menus, but Bing is rather less forthcoming, since under a search the only options provided are to 'narrow by language' or

〉 〉

'narrow by region'. Unfortunately Bing doesn't provide access to an advanced search page in the same way that Google does, but it does have a number of useful advanced search functions.

The same inconsistency can be demonstrated when searching for filetype, as the preceding full stop does make a small difference in the number of results returned. The filetypes that Bing can search for differ to those available for Google, as they are as follows: .doc (Microsoft Word documents), .dwf (Autodesk drawing file), .feed (Rich Site Summary or RSS feed), .htm (Hypertext Markup Language), .html (Hypertext Markup Language – essentially the same concept as htm files), .pdf (Adobe Acrobat Portable Document), .ppt (Microsoft PowerPoint Presentation), .rtf (Microsoft Rich Text Format), .text and .txt (generic text), and .xls (Microsoft Excel Workbook).

Bing does have another filetype option which isn't offered by Google, and that is the '*contains:*' syntax. This allows you to find web pages that link to other documents and multimedia files such as music and video. So, for example, if you wanted to find out if there were any pages on the CILIP site which contained the word 'library' and linked to a Microsoft Word document, the search would be '*library site:cilip.org.uk contains:doc*'. This can be particularly useful if you wish to explore a particular site for one type of media, such as audio files (.mp3), compacted files (.zip), or executable files (.exe). Another very similar option is '*hasfeed:*', which limits a search to web pages that link to RSS feeds. Consequently, if you were interested in limiting a search to pages that contained information about CILIP and which had an RSS feed attached, the simple search would be '*cilip hasfeed:*'. If you're confused or uncertain about RSS feeds you'll find much more detail on them in Chapter 15.

While Bing doesn't have a 'Bing sinker' in the way that Google has (see p. 44), it does have something that is rather similar, but perhaps coded rather more efficiently, which is the *prefer:* option. This adds emphasis to a particular word, and so in order to find results that emphasize the elections of Presidents Bush and Lincoln, a good search strategy would be '*"president bush" "president lincoln" prefer:election*'.

Google dropped the use of the syntax '*define:*' for defining a word, preferring to use the dictionary option instead, but Bing still retains it. Therefore, if you really ever need to know exactly what a librarian does, a search for '*define:librarian*' (with or without space) will pull in answers from sites such as Wikipedia, Answers.com and so on.

Before moving on to look at more search functionality it is worthwhile just pointing out one particular option that Bing provides on the search engines results page, which is the 'fly-out'. This allows you to get a quick preview of a web page without actually having to visit it. It is very similar to the Google preview option but in all fairness it should be pointed out that Bing used this first with Google following suit shortly thereafter. Simply hover the cursor over a result and the fly-out will automatically work. Move the cursor off the result and the fly-out will disappear.

Positional searches

Bing has functionality to allow searchers to limit their results to specific places within a document, in much the same way that Google has (see p.35). Therefore, a search using the syntax '*inanchor:*', '*inbody:*' or '*intitle:*' will return pages that include the search term(s) in those positions. Stretching the concept of position a little, Bing offers a simple location option, which is to use '*loc:*' or '*location:*' followed by a region. Consequently, if it was necessary to find information on librarianship in the USA or UK, an initial search might begin '*librarianship (loc:GB OR loc:US)*'. As you can see, in common with Google, Bing allows for a logical or grouped search using brackets or parenthesis. Finally, Bing lets searchers find all of the sites that are hosted on a single IP address. This can be useful in some situations when trying to find out some background to a site, to see if it is authoritative, or why it might be blocked – sometimes filtering software will block an IP address rather than a specific site. A search for '*IP: 195.206.168.40:*' would return all of the sites based at that address, one of them being that of the author. Country, region and language codes can be found at http://onlinehelp.microsoft.com/en-gb/bing/ff808526.aspx.

Other Bing search functionality

As with Google, Bing has a number of what I have referred to as 'one-trick ponies'. A search for '*London weather*' will bring up a small dialogue box which will provide the required details. A search for '*London forecast*' will result in the same information. If you have an interest in films it's easy to find out what is showing in local cinemas simply by starting your search with the word '*movie*' followed by your location, just the same as with Google.

Bing also uses what it refers to as 'instant answers'. If you need to find out an area code in the USA type '*area code*' followed by the city and state or zip code. Bing will also run conversions for searchers and can convert units of measurement for distance, weight, time, volume and temperature. For example, some valid searches would be '*how many seconds in a day*', '*what is 50°F in Celsius*', '*how many kilometres in a light year*'. Bing can also provide searchers with basic mathematical operators as well as exponents, roots, factorials, percentages, trigonometry functions and mathematical constants. A full list of mathematical symbols used by Bing can be found at http://onlinehelp.microsoft.com/en-gb/bing/ff808576.aspx.

Bing does provide a link with Facebook, and has done so in one form or another for many years. Access to this functionality does depend on location and it is being rolled out very slowly; at the time of writing (April 2013) the latest evolution was not available in the UK. However, in the hopeful expectation that the situation will change in the not too distant future, I'll briefly describe it. If you are logged into your Bing account and you link it to your Facebook account, Bing can include a separate search results column that links to Facebook friends who have 'liked' a particular place, event or activity, who have written reviews, have shared photographs of a specific place, and so on. Searchers can then connect directly with their friends via the Bing page by clicking on their friend's name, and a box opens in which they can send them a memo. Bing also offers other social media options such as 'Friends who might know' and 'People who know', which pull content from public posts on services like Twitter. However, as this is a work in progress, please expect these options and the functionality to change over time.

Bing Images

In common with other major search engines, Bing provides access to image files and these are delivered as a set of scrolling results, rather than forcing the user to go from one page of results to another. Bing provides three settings for Safe Search: strict, moderate (the default) and off. However, I would not rely on this, since even with strict settings in place I was certainly able to see images that would probably result in your bosses asking questions if they saw them on your screen at work!

If you place the mouse cursor over an image this causes the image to 'pop out' of the results into a slightly larger size for viewing. The searcher can then click on the image to obtain more information, and to view the image in context, as well as see a full size version of it. You can also see a slideshow of images. However, if preferred, the searcher can click on the embedded link to see similar images, or further narrow down the search by size, layout, colour, style or people (faces or head-and-shoulders images) – very similar, in fact, to the offerings from Google Image search.

Bing Video Search

You will, I am sure, not be surprised at all with the options available for video search. Results can be limited by length (short, medium or long), screen type (standard or widescreen), and resolution (low, medium or high). However, Bing also offers the option of limiting results by source, such as MSN, MTV, BBC, YouTube or Daily Motion, and while this can be achieved within a Google search using the '*site:*' option, Bing's is perhaps a slightly simpler, more elegant approach.

The searcher is provided with the source of the image, time, and date of publication. This is almost exactly the same information as provided by Google, although Google also includes the name of the person who uploaded the video as well. However, Bing has one particular advantage over Google, in that videos automatically play in part if the cursor is placed over the static image. Furthermore, the entire video can be played within the search results page, although the option still remains for searchers to visit the originating page.

Bing News

Bing provides searchers with access to news stories via a variety of news sources, such as the *New York Times*, the BBC and Reuters. Results can be rearranged either by 'best match' or by 'most recent', although unlike Google it's not possible to limit to specific periods of time. Bing News does, however, provide a category approach in the form of business, entertainment, health, political and sport. An RSS option is also provided, although not an e-mail alerting service. For news junkies who want to see the headlines, the search engine has a 'top stories' section, with various links to UK news, politics, sci/tech and so on.

Bing Maps

In common with Google, Bing provides access to maps, as well as aerial views and a 'streetside' view, which is essentially a panorama of a street, although this is limited. Bing maps also provide various map styles, such as

〉 〉

Ordnance Survey. Nearby railway stations are given, as well as a directions option and some other nearby facilities. Although there are some nice features the Google offering does seem to be richer, more varied and much more functional.

Bing's Adaptive Search

All search engines want to be able to personalize results; one person's search for 'apple' will not be the same as another, and ambiguity is a search engine's biggest enemy. Bing is attempting to overcome this problem with what it calls 'adaptive search'. The more that you search on Bing, the more the engine is able to adapt to your search style and the type of results that you click on, although the search engine will also take into account your physical location. Bing does also make it clear that if searchers do not want their results based on previous search activity they can clear and turn off the search history at any point.

Bing or Google?

This is a question that is asked a lot, as people want to know which search engine is the best. However, while the question has merit, it's also a lot like asking if apples are better than pears. Google certainly has more search functionality than Bing, but Bing has introduced various improvements on search (such as fly-outs and scrolling results windows) before Google. On the other hand, Google Maps perhaps has better coverage than the Microsoft version. All of these are certainly ways in which the two search engines can be measured, but in the final analysis it comes down to the simple question – 'which results work best for you?' If one searcher feels that search engine X is better than search engine Y, they will naturally default to search engine X. However, why make a choice at all? Wouldn't a better solution be to take the best elements of both search engines and use them as appropriate? In all honesty, I don't believe that there is a simple answer to this conundrum, and in fact when we add more search engines into the mix it becomes even harder to come up with an answer. Bing has attempted to provide a way of answering this question: it's a tool called 'Bingiton' (www.bingiton.com), where you can take the challenge by running five searches and seeing the results in columns, and you choose which set of answers is the best for each search. At the end of the test, you will be told whether you prefer Bing over Google or vice versa. However, it would seem that Microsoft is only interested in its US searchers, since clicking on the link in Europe and elsewhere simply takes you to the normal Bing search page. This is disappointing, doubly so because for the first few days after its introduction the tool was accessible outside the USA. However, why limit ourselves to a simple choice between two search engines? Let's take a look at some more, to see what they can offer.

Yahoo! Search

Yahoo! has long been involved in internet search, and in 2003 became its own web crawler-based search engine, and it slowly changed from its original incarnation as an index/directory-based engine into the free-text search engine that you can find at www.yahoo.com. In July 2009 Yahoo! signed a deal with Microsoft that resulted in Yahoo! Search being powered by Bing. It is nevertheless still a search engine in its own right.

Yahoo! Search comes with the usual search box above, and a series of menu options below, for images, video, news and shopping with a 'more' option of minor search features. Search results are straightforward, with title, summary and URL available. Users can also view a cached version of each page in the list of results. Searchers are provided with a list of related searches, and a filter to limit by time (past day, week or month). The default search is for the web as a whole, but limits are available depending on country, so the UK/Ireland version will offer an option to limit results to only the UK or only Ireland. At the bottom of the results page is a related search option which is rather more extensive than the one offered in the left-hand side menu. Depending on the search which is being run, Yahoo! Search may well display some image results as default at the top of the results.

> **》 Did you know?**
> It is estimated that the US internet of 2015 will be at least 50 times larger than it was in 2006 (www.youtube.com/watch?v= ij5yC-moPCM).

Yahoo! Search offers an advanced search function, and if you're familiar with Google's advanced search (which by now I am sure you are) nothing will come as a surprise. Search options are all words, an exact phrase, any words, or none of the words, and this can further be limited to any part of the page, or just the title. There's a simple site/domain function with defaults for .com, .edu, .gov, .org, .co.uk, or .ie options, and the choice of limiting to a domain or site of choice. There are six filetype options, so it's quite limited, but covers the basics such as Adobe .pdf, Microsoft

PowerPoint and Microsoft Word. A safe search filter is offered with the usual three options (strict, moderate or off) and explicit content can be blocked for every search in the preferences option. Searchers can limit by country or language as well.

Blekko

Blekko, at www.blekko.com, is a relatively new search engine, which only launched in 2010, but it has already garnered a lot of praise. It provides search results in an entirely different way to the search engines that we have looked at so far, and uses the phrase 'slash the web' to indicate this. It has a small index in comparison to Google (but to be fair, which search engines haven't?), which focuses on what they term 'quality websites', by which they mean that they have eliminated spam, content farm and malware websites. The slashtag tool organizes websites around specific topics and is used to improve search results. Essentially this means that the searcher can use and create multiple custom search engines for themselves while using one generic interface. For example, a search on '*diabetes /health*' limits the result to a set of trusted medical sites. However, before looking at this concept in more detail, let's simply view how the search engine does its basic job.

As you would expect, the common search operators work, with single words being automatically '*AND*'d together, double quotes are used for a phrase and the minus symbol to exclude a term – although at Blekko the Boolean operator '*NOT*' does not work. The functionality of other operators is spotty, however – '*inurl:*' finds words chosen in the URL of web pages, but '*intitle:*' does not. Blekko does not use the '*site:*' command itself, but if that is used in a search, Blekko defaults to using results pulled from Bing. Blekko does not make use of an advanced search function, nor does it use separate databases for images, videos and so on. Search engine results are reasonable, in that they provide a title, short summary and URL. There isn't a preview option, however, but results can be shared on Twitter and Facebook. What the results do show is the cache of the web page with date of crawl, and what they term an SEO option. This shows how many inbound links there are to a page (both from US states and from other countries), duplicate content, crawl statistics, other sites that are co-hosted, outbound links, site pages, the source of pages and a wealth of other useful information about a specific site. This is very useful content for searchers who really need to drill down into a site to do some detective work on it, and a very simple way to see if another site has stolen content. Finally, if the user has logged in via their Facebook account Blekko will also show which of their friends has liked particular pages that are returned in the results.

I mentioned earlier that Blekko does not have options to search specific databases of images or videos. Instead it makes use of specific slashtags which do the same job. For example, in order to see results for the word librarian searchers simply have to type it in and if they wish to see images of librarians the search would be '*librarian /images*'. Similarly, if the searcher wished to see videos of librarians the search that they would run would be '*librarian /videos*'. It is using a variety of these slashtags that gives Blekko such wide functionality. The search engine has hundreds of these slashtags that can be used by searchers, such as '*/travel*', '*/recipes*' and '*/date*'. In fact, it is possible to search Blekko for specific slashtags using their own directory of tags at http://blekko.com/tag/show#tab3.

Each of these tags can be explored in more detail simply by clicking on the slashtag, which will then display the URL, title, and date added to the slashtag. Indeed, it is possible to comment on either the slashtag itself or any individual sites that have been added, if you feel passionately about a particular tag. It's also possible to apply to the person who created the tag – known at Blekko as the 'editor-in-chief' – to become an editor.

Blekko has approached the problem of finding information and personalizing it in a unique manner by giving searchers far greater control over the search process than almost any other search engine. Of course, if the searcher does not find the slashtag that is of interest to them they can create as many as they wish; I talk more about the process of creating search engines in Chapter 15.

In common with Bing, Blekko has an association with Facebook. If you log into your Blekko account you can connect your Facebook account as well. Run a search as normal, but then add '*/likes*' at the end of the search string. The results that are returned will be arranged with specific websites that have been liked in Facebook by your friends and colleagues. Blekko provides a brief indication of who these people are, but you can expand the view to see all of them.

DuckDuckGo

DuckDuckGo, at www.duckduckgo.com, is a general-purpose search engine just like Google or Bing. At this point in the chapter it is probably unnecessary to say that the search engine conforms to the general syntax

> >

that we have seen time and time again. However, for comprehensiveness, phrase searching is done using double quotes, words can be excluded using '*NOT*' or the minus symbol and the plus sign can be used to force the engine into only returning pages with the specific word. DuckDuckGo also allows the use of '*intitle*' and '*site:*' but not '*inurl:*'. Other syntax includes '*inbody:*' and '*filetype:*' and it also lets users '*sort:date*' to re-rank results and sort by date. Searchers can also use '*region:uk*' to cause results to focus on a particular region. It's also possible to run calculations, such as '*64*103*' or '*square root of nine*'; conversions can also be undertaken in a manner similar to Google, and the search engine gives examples such as '*5mph to km/hr*', '*100usd in eur*', '*5 fahrenheit in Celsius*'. Some searches can be done on regions, so '*time in London*' and '*weather in London*' will give answers in the form of a fact box as well as links to individual sites.

In common with Blekko, DuckDuckGo does not have an advanced function, but it does have its own unique way of providing access to a wide variety of advanced search functionality. The search engine results page provides basic information, starting with a fact box if possible, results in a standard format (title, summary, URL) an indication of an official site if possible, and links to try the same search on other sites such as Wikipedia or WebMD.

While Blekko makes use of the slashtag concept, DuckDuckGo uses '!bang syntax', which allows searchers to immediately retrieve results from specific sites. For example, a search for '*librarian !google*' will search Google for the search term '*librarian*', or '*library !slideshare*' will find presentations on the Slideshare website that contain the word 'library'. There are some obvious !bangs that are available, such as '*!images*' or '*!amazon*' but the complete list runs into hundreds and can be viewed at http://duckduckgo.com/bang.html. Alternatively, next to the search box is a down arrow that can be used to display them all alphabetically.

DuckDuckGo has now partnered with Zanran (www.zanran.com), a search engine that provides tabular, spreadsheet and statistical data to provide quick snippet answers to queries. A search for '*child poverty uk 2012*' provides very helpful quick links to statistical data, for example. Looking at the wider picture, if the search results would benefit from factual and statistical data, DuckDuckGo may well be a better choice to use simply in terms of speed and accuracy than another engine that requires an extra search to limit to spreadsheet data.

DuckDuckGo makes considerable play of the fact that it doesn't track its users. They state on their page at http://donttrack.us that when you search with certain other search engines and click on a link your search term is usually sent to that site along with your browser and computer information. This can often uniquely identify you and over the course of time a profile is built up about who you are, what sex you are, your location and what interests you. The result of this is that when visiting third-party sites that have advertising on them you may well find certain adverts will follow you around. Furthermore, this profile can then be sold, and you have no control over that. The point is also made that Google and certain other search engines save your search queries and these can be legally requested by an appropriate authority. DuckDuckGo doesn't send search details onto other sites and it doesn't store any personal details at all. Therefore, whatever you're searching for doesn't get shared. This means that results are not tailored or personalized in the way that Google's are, based on your search or click history. It also means that DuckDuckGo doesn't build up a profile and filter out material that other search engines would decide that you weren't interested in.

Polyfetch

Polyfetch (http://polyfetch.com) is another very new search engine, but it has some interesting functionality that may make it worth your time exploring. To start with, it's a straightforward search engine, with a rich variety of features. You have websearch, comparisons, shopping, maps and images. No advanced search, news or multimedia, unfortunately. The results page is interesting – you get the normal results in the format that you'd expect, with title, summary and URL, but there's also an image, which is pulled from somewhere on the page, which can be quite interesting in itself. However, there are a number of filters that you can try out with the results that you have. The default is to show all results, but you can limit to what is currently popular (which may or may not be new information), reviews, positive and negative information, 'how to' options or – the last filter – 'funny'.

The comparison search allows users to compare different things – products, football clubs, celebrities and so on, and gives a score out of 100 relating to positive mentions. Not quite so sure about this aspect, since it's going to rely on the written word, which is dodgy at best, but it's worth a look. Shopping is what you'd expect, with various subgroups such as Home or Electronics. The maps option allows you to choose a location, and then type in a search, and Polyfetch uses Yelp to try and identify appropriate

〉〉

resources. The images option is pretty much what you'd expect, although you only get a fairly miserly 18 images or thereabouts per page.

One other option that I liked in this search engine was that it was possible to keep a list of bookmarked sites together, using their 'bookmarklet', and then launch them later, in one go, on any device. Really helpful if you're doing some research or comparisons and want to get access to a lot of sites quickly and effectively.

The Internet Archive or Wayback Machine

Strictly speaking the Internet Archive (commonly known as the Wayback Machine), at http://archive.org/web/web.php, isn't a search engine of the type that we have looked at up to now. However, because it does find web pages and website information, I'm going to include it here. The search engine has been around for well over a decade, and it archives websites and pages. It allows you to browse through URLs that were produced from 1996 up to 9 December 2012. Not every single site or page has been indexed (crawls can miss them, and owners can request that their sites are not included), but rather a lot are. Recently the index has been updated and has gone from having 150,000,000,000 URLs to having 240,000,000,000 URLs, a total of about 5 petabytes of data. This database is queried over 1000 times a second by over 500,000 people a day, helping make archive.org the 250th most popular website.

It's extremely easy to use – just type in the address of the site that you want to check out the archive for, and you'll see a series of dates going back to – in theory – 1996, or whenever the site started. You can then choose your archived time, click on the link and view the site as it existed then. You won't find the entire site, and sometimes you'll find images missing, but it'll give you a fair indication of the content of the site.

There are as many different ways to use the Archive as there are users, but some basic ideas are as follows:

➡ Check to see the history of a site – has it always been owned by the same person/company, or has it changed hands over the years?
➡ Find out information about a company that's not currently on their site – e.g., who was the CEO five years ago?
➡ Compare attitudes towards different subjects then and now. Has the position of a person or company materially changed over a period of time?

➡ Initial responses to events – what was the first statement that a person or organization put out publicly about some event?

➡ See how web page design has changed over the years/months.

➡ View world events, such as 9/11, or national elections.

➡ Check out early pioneers of the internet – who was doing what when.

➡ Compare previous versions of search engines and their functionality with what they can do today.

➡ Cite specific examples of web pages, even when they have changed.

➡ Find archives for a site that has changed URLs.

➡ Locate a manual for an obsolete piece of kit.

➡ View a site that has been suspended for whatever reason, or which you cannot reach.

➡ Compare old and new prices.

➡ Find old predictions and see how accurate they have turned out to be.

➡ Content stored in the Archive has been used in legal cases.

That's a quick 15 examples, but there are plenty more valuable ways of using it. The Wayback Machine should be a really useful weapon in any information professional's arsenal.

Exalead

Exalead (www.exalead.com/search – the trailing /search here is important, or you will end up at the general site, which isn't what you want) is a European-based search engine, although obviously it is global in nature. In common with both Google and Bing it can be used either with or without creating and logging into an account. One nice feature that the search engine offers is the opportunity to use it as a very basic home or a start page by providing one-click access to websites of your choice. Simply provide it with a list of sites that you use on a regular basis and these will be included in a grid on the opening page. By making this your browser's home or start page you have immediate access to both a search engine and a list of bookmarked sites – very handy!

As you would expect by now, Exalead follows the common convention of search engine syntax. That is to say, it will automatically 'AND' words together, exact phrases can be indicated by the use of double quotes, the plus symbol (+) tells the search engine to search for that exact word, the minus symbol allows users to remove all documents that contain a specific word or expression from the search results, and it will also happily use

〉〉

advanced Boolean logic, such as '*(movie AND star) OR (famous AND people)*'. Furthermore, Exalead uses the '*site:*', '*intitle:*', '*inurl:*', '*link:*' and '*language:*' operators in exactly the same way as has been previously described.

Exalead does, however, have some functionality that other major search engines do not, and it is worth bearing this in mind, since these can help a searcher find information that the other major search engines would struggle with. Exalead uses an '*OPT*' command and this allows the search to specify a term without making its presence mandatory for documents to appear in the search results. The example given by the search engine is '*cow OPT mad*'. The results of this search provide pages that refer to mad cow disease, but there are also other pages that rank highly which relate to other uses of the term. Exalead also offers a prefix search, which allows users to find documents based on the beginning of a word. For example, a search for '*librar**' would find library, libraries, librarians and so on. Proximity search is also a strength of this particular search engine, as searchers can use the '*NEXT*' operator to find documents whether query terms are next to each other, and they can also use the '*NEAR*' operator to find documents whether query terms are all within a short range of each other. Exalead also offers two unique functions which are phonetic search and approximate spelling search. When you don't know how to spell a word you can write it as it sounds, and then use a phonetic search and the results will include words that sound similar to that which you typed, so for example, a search for '*soundslike:liberry*' will not only return results that use that particular word, but will also provide you with results using the word 'library'. Approximate spelling search works in the same way, only this time, if you are unsure about the spelling of the word, Exalead allows the use of the '*spellslike:*' function: for instance, '*spellslike:exlaead*'. Both of these options can be useful if you are searching for perhaps medical, scientific, or pharmaceutical terms and you are unfamiliar with them, but equally it could be used by students or other young people who have difficulty with spelling. Finally, Exalead has an interesting date search function, in that it not only allows users to search '*after*' a specific date, but also allows them to restrict a search to documents created or modified '*before*' a given date. Consequently searchers could search for '*library before:2008/05/21*' or '*library after:2005/05/21*' and this gives much more flexibility than we have seen with other search engines.

〈 〈

Exalead results page

The search engine provides users with a simple straightforward search engine results page; results down the left-hand side of the screen, with advertising above results, related searches below the search box, and news items as the first set of results. Each web page has its own thumbnail as well, so users have some idea as to what the page looks like. Summary information is quite sparse, with very short entries for each page and links to the Exalead cache and an opportunity to bookmark the result.

Exalead has bucked the trend by having its menu of options on the right-hand side of the screen rather than the left. Searches can further be filtered by site type such as blogs or forums, file types, related terms (and it's worth noting that related terms are not the same as related searches), languages or countries. Other options include an opportunity to limit by year as well as a directory search option. This last one can prove useful, particularly if for searchers unsure of what they need, or whose search is very broad. These search options can be used together simply by clicking on the filter as appropriate, or if the searcher is confident in the Exalead syntax simply typed into the search box. In either event Exalead could do a search on, for example, '*library category:Government filetype:pdf*' quickly and simply without having to visit the advanced search dialogue box. This dialogue box can, however, be called up when necessary and it appears directly on the screen rather than taking the searcher to a new page; the searcher can simply click on the option required, which is then automatically included in the search box. So for example, it is possible to take a basic search such as '*library*', see the results, click on appropriate filters from the right-hand menu, and then call up the advanced search box and choose an option, such as a prefixes search, and to be prompted by Exalead to add in the required prefix.

> **›› Did you know?**
> In 2012, 21 million households in Great Britain (80%) had internet access, compared with 19 million (77%) in 2011 (www.ons.gov.uk/ons/rel/rdit2/internet-access---households-and-individuals/2012/stb-internet-access--households-and-individuals--2012.html).

Exalead Image search

The Exalead image database is much smaller than that of either Bing or Google. A simple search for images for library returns 2,587,174 results from Exalead in comparison to 19,400,000 from Bing and a staggering 488,000,000 from Google. However, it can equally be argued that, since a

〉〉

user is unlikely to scroll through more than a few dozen images. It is not the
number of images that are returned, but their accuracy in being matched to
the search term, and this can only be assessed by the searcher.

Search results can be limited by size, to include or exclude facial images,
limited to graphics or photographs, file types, orientation, images that can
be used for wallpaper, or finally, images that are predominantly in one of
eight colours or black and white. The search functions previously
mentioned, such as the prefixes search, can also be included in image
searching but Exalead also offers searchers the ability to look for images of a
specific width or height with a search syntax such as '*width>1024*' or
'*height>300*'.

Exalead video search

Exalead searches across a wide number of different sources to return video
images and there is a menu option to limit to, or exclude from, any of these
sources when looking at results. One particularly nice feature is the ability
to sort video results by relevance, newest, oldest, rating, length, or view
count. The opportunity to re-rank results is quite rare; most search engines
assume that you will always just want to view the results in the order that
they give you, which of course is seldom the case. Videos can be watched
either while remaining on the search engine page or by clicking on the title
and visiting the video website concerned.

Exalead Wikipedia search

Exalead has incorporated a Wikipedia search option into their offering as
well. As you would expect, it searches the Wikipedia site and returns results
as appropriate. Nothing particularly exciting there, but the engine also
offers a text cloud as well, which is an interesting additional approach. The
text cloud comes in four coloured versions, Category, People, Location and
Organization, and these can be added into a refined search as necessary. The
cloud appears on the right-hand side of the screen, ensuring conformity,
and the searcher can click each option in turn to limit results. This is an
excellent way to quickly narrow a search down. For example, a searcher
could run a search using variables without knowing what they are, or how
the syntax works, just by clicking in the text cloud. A complex search such
as '*library category:"federal depository libraries" people:"martin luther"*' can
therefore be created very quickly and easily. As a result, Exalead can once

again be viewed as an easy alternative to Google or Bing for novice or unconfident searchers.

Exalead experiments

Google once had the Google Labs project until they streamlined their system, but Exalead continues to offer various experimental services. These services do change over time and cannot be relied upon to continue to exist or to move into general use, but it is always worth taking a look, just see what is possible. The Exalead experiments site is at http://labs.exalead.com and currently it's possible to explore resources such as Chromatik, which allows users to search by colour, Constellations, which groups websites and displays links between them, and Tweepz, which lets users manipulate data from Twitter and link it to individual users.

Ask Jeeves

The Ask Jeeves search engine has had a long and chequered career and, apart from one short brief period of time when it introduced a whole host of new features and an exciting 'triptych' three-pane results screen, it has – in my opinion – only just deserved to keep its place as one of the 'big' search engines.

Ask Jeeves search functionality

The search functionality provided by Ask Jeeves at http://uk.ask.com (if you're a reader from outside the UK you'll in all probability be looking at the Ask search engine; the company has decided that UK searchers would prefer the older version of the engine with the emphasis on the butler) is basic, with the usual options of double quotes for a phrase, minus and plus symbols to include or exclude work. Ask Jeeves also allows the use of '*intitle:*' and '*inurl:*' as well as '*site:*' and '*inlink:*', which searches for documents that contain the specific term within the anchor text. It's also possible to limit a search to any of six European languages or 21 different countries.

   The search engine results page is basic, with a large proportion of the results screen taken up with advertising. After that the searcher is provided with the 'Explore answers about' option, followed by traditional web page results. Ask Jeeves also provides a factual 'answers' section to its pages, so you will very often find a lot of factual information on the right-hand side of the screen. A search for '*librarian*' will link to quick answers about the Librarian of Congress, and popular Q&As. A search for '*dog*' will provide access to key facts, a link to find out information on particular breeds, and a 'helpful resources' section. A search for a film star will pull up a biography, links to searches for their films or spouses and so on. It's very similar in concept to the Google Knowledge Graph in fact, although I don't think that it's quite as comprehensive.

However, the rest of the information provided is disappointingly limited in comparison to the search engines that we have looked at in this chapter. No indication of the number of results, no preview options, no ability to add in filters such as date; the only other option is to restrict to the UK instead of global results.

Ask Jeeves media search

In common with most of the larger search engines, Ask Jeeves has an image search function, but in common with their web offering, it's fairly basic, with no advanced options, and just simple pull-down options for size and colours. Searchers can click to see a full-size version to supplement the image and file size, but the large advertising banners limit the number of images on the screen.

The video search option immediately loads a video into the search results and starts to play it, while the other video results are shifted to the right of the page. This can be quite irritating if the searcher doesn't want to watch the video that Ask Jeeves has assumed is the preferred choice, and it's necessary to be quite quick on the pause option. To be fair, users can also see video categories, a related search option and they do have the ability to sort results by relevance and date. However, other than that, this has little to recommend it.

Ask Jeeves also has a Reference section which is really a general index or directory listing of links to questions on various aspects of a subject, the content for which is very often pulled directly from Wikipedia.

Other free-text search engine options

It would be easy to write an entire book just on the direct alternatives to Google, but it would get very repetitive very quickly. In this chapter I have tried to highlight what I consider some of the major alternatives to Google, and also engines that have their own particular slant on search by offering something very different. In fact your own personal preference may not be one that I've mentioned, and that's absolutely fine – I'm not trying to list everything that's available, but simply to indicate choice and functionality. However, if you would like to explore further, you would do well to spend some time looking at engines such as Gigablast at www.gigablast.com, Kngine at http://kngine.com, Lycos at http://search.lycos.com or Quintura at www.quintura.com. For an even more complete list try my web search engines page at www.philb.com/webse.htm.

Summary

Free-text search engines are really the 'bread and butter' of the expert searcher, and because of the overall importance of Google they're the most common; if you show someone a page with a little white box on it, they're almost certainly going to try and use it to pop some search terms into. Free-text engines are by their nature the most flexible engines and it could easily be argued that they are the most powerful. However, there are limits to what can be done with them, and if the searcher isn't confident in what they're looking for they can be more hindrance than help. It's at this point that other engines come into play.

CHAPTER 5

Directory- and category-based search engines

Introduction

There are few aspects of search that have scaled so many peaks and then fallen so far than directory-based search engines. These search engines can really be considered dinosaurs of the world wide web, as they had their heyday in the 1990s when Yahoo! was one of the most important locations on the net, possibly even the most important. While Yahoo! is still a very important site for lots of reasons, I don't think that there would be any real disagreement with my describing it in slightly less glowing terms these days. The basic framework of index- or directory-based engines, while giving them a strong, rigid, systematic approach to providing data – has really proved to be their downfall, as they have been unable to adapt to changing patterns of use.

Category-based engines are slightly different – they are really a combination of a free-text search engine, allowing you to choose your own search terms, but they will also give you results based on different categories and they will attempt to group results together. Consequently, a search for 'library' will return pages that contain the term, but the searcher will also get responses grouped as 'public libraries' or 'academic libraries' and so on.

In this chapter I'll look at both kinds, why they are useful, and perhaps most importantly, where you can find them.

Background to directory-based search engines

The idea behind a directory-based search engine is quite simple – create an index of subject headings, with subdivisions under those and so on (rather like the Dewey Decimal System) and then invite web authors to submit their sites to appropriate headings. Individual editors will then assess the submissions, and if they decide that they are appropriate, will include them in the directory. We can already see that there are a number of key differences between these and free-text engines. First, they do not crawl the net; authors have to go to the directory and ask for inclusion. This means that the number of websites included is going to be far smaller than those trawled in free-text engines. Second, searchers will be directed to a site, rather than an individual page, so the engine acts more like a stepping stone on the way to finding the required information – searchers will have to identify the appropriate site, then leave the engine behind, visit the site and locate the precise data that they are after – presuming that it's there in the first place. Third, because individual editors choose to include or exclude sites the searcher may (and I stress the word 'may') find the included sites to be of a slightly higher quality than those retrieved by other types of engine. Fourth, they are not going to be comprehensive, or come anywhere close to it. Finally, directory-based engines can focus on a particular subject area very effectively – if searchers use a country-based engine, for example, they will quickly find out the type of governance used in the country – there will be a section for a Royal Family or not, depending on the history and background of the region.

> **>> Did you know?**
> There were 634 million websites in December 2012 (http://royal.pingdom.com).

Their advantages and disadvantages

There are many advantages to these search engines in comparison to free-text search engines. For example, since they make use of data in a structured format, it's much easier to drill down through headings and subheadings to find the information that is needed. If you don't know what you're looking for, a free-text search engine isn't going to be that much help. However, as long as you can define a fairly broad subject area, you can locate that with a directory-based engine, then get narrower and narrower until you get to the point that you need. A free-text engine is like having a map, and you have to work out where you are, and where you want to go, while a directory-based engine is giving you signposts at every step of the way.

On the other hand, because directory-based engines require web authors to submit sites directly, searchers will find that once they have identified an appropriate site, they will still need to visit the site in order to find the exact piece of information that they require – and so it is a two-stage process.

〉 〉

Searchers will also find that there are far fewer results – the further they drill down into subject headings, the fewer the sites they will find. This may, however, be seen as an advantage; sometimes people just want to find half a dozen or a dozen 'good' sites to look at. I wouldn't want to push this idea too far, but users of these engines are unlikely to find malicious or misleading sites, since a human editor will have looked at the submissions. Consequently, these engines are easier to use and they will appeal particularly to novice users, or those who are researching in an area that they are unfamiliar with.

One final disadvantage is that, as I mention below, there is no regional version, so the headings are biased towards the USA. 'Education' or 'Government' is actually US Education and US Government, and it's necessary to click on the top category, 'Countries', to find your own local information.

The Yahoo! Directory

Yahoo! have hidden their directory away, almost as though they are slightly ashamed of it, which is a pity, since it is how they first came to prominence on the internet. The URL to get you directly to the site is http://dir.yahoo.com (there are no local or regional versions – if you try dir.yahoo.co.uk you simply arrive at the basic UK Yahoo! interface). The interface is very simple – headings followed by some basic subheadings. These have hardly ever changed, and the ones that are available now are exactly the same ones that were available in the first edition of this book, produced way back in 1999! You could say that illustrates a lack of interest or development of the directory, or you could use the argument that they got it right first time. In any event, the headings are as follows:

➡ Arts and Humanities
➡ Business and Economy
➡ Computer and internet
➡ Education
➡ Entertainment
➡ Government
➡ Health
➡ News and Media
➡ Recreation and Sports
➡ Reference

➡ Regional
➡ Science
➡ Social Science
➡ Society and Culture.

There are two other sections – New Additions and the option of subscribing to sections via RSS. Below each of these headings there are appropriate subheadings, so under Arts and Humanities we have top categories of Artists, By Region, Design Arts, Humanities, Performing Arts and Visual Arts. There are also additional categories such as Art History, Booksellers, Museums, Organizations and so on. Yahoo! also lists some popular sites in each category as a type of quick reference approach. Sometimes a category will be listed in more than one place, so Booksellers can also be found in the Business and Economy>Shopping and Services> Books> Bookstores category as well. This is an important point which is not evident when browsing categories. If a site is commercial in nature, it has to be placed into a commercial category. For example, if you have an interest in baseball cards it may be necessary to check both the non-commercial category of Recreation> Sports> Baseball> Collectibles> Baseball Cards and the commercial section Business and Economy> Shopping and Services> Sports> Collectibles> Cards> Baseball.

Yahoo! Directory in use

Let's try one quick example to illustrate the value of the directory. Presume that you need a listing of UK newspapers. A search at Google for 'list of UK newspapers' brings up approximately 143,000,000 results, and almost immediately starts to rank specific UK newspapers. However, by clicking on the Yahoo! headings and subheadings thus: News and Media> Newspapers> By region> Countries> United Kingdom we very quickly have a collection of over 400 sites, which are then further subdivided by areas such as England, Northern Ireland and so on. We also have an immediate site listing by popularity of some of the leading papers. It's a fast and effective approach which takes a few seconds and saves a lot of time in comparison to wading through free-text results.

There is a free-text search option within Directory search, and this gives links directly to websites, but also provides users with the category that a website is listed in. A search for 'libraries' provides us with the Library of Congress as the first result, and this is also to be found in the category of

〉〉

Government> US Government> Legislative Branch> Agencies> Library of
Congress. It is also possible to filter by headings, time and related concepts.
Irritatingly, the ability to search the Directory is only available within the
directory section of the search engine – you will not find an option to
search it if you approach Yahoo! via the normal home page or URL.

Other Yahoo! functionality

Yahoo! is also a free-text search engine, and it works along similar principles
to the others in that category. In July 2009 Microsoft and Yahoo!
announced a deal that meant that the Microsoft engine Bing would power
Yahoo! Search. The value of searching the free-text version of Yahoo!
Search is therefore arguable, since Bing is readily available. However,
Yahoo! does have a variety of sites such as Sport, Shopping and Answers.
Most of these tend to provide up-to-date news, rather than acting as a
traditional search engine linking to different websites. Yahoo! has tried to
reposition itself as a news and lifestyle portal, with 'hot topics', news and
video picks being prominently displayed on the home page.

One resource which is worth mentioning in a little detail is the Yahoo!
Answers section, which can be found at http://uk.answers.yahoo.com. It's a
tool which encourages people to ask and answer questions, or to search
through previously asked and answered questions. Anyone can pose a
question and similarly anyone can answer a question, so the obvious caveat
of 'don't trust what you see' must be taken into account. A search on
'library' produced questions based on iTunes, but also ways to organize a
library for children, how to find a library with literary journals, and
different terms for library shelvers. In total, there are over 11,000 results. In
June 2012 the service reached 300 million questions, and it is regarded as
one of the larger social media networks.

The Open Directory Project

The Open Directory Project, otherwise known as Dmoz, can be found at
www.dmoz.org. It says of itself, 'The Open Directory Project is the largest,
most comprehensive human-edited directory of the Web. It is constructed
and maintained by a vast, global community of volunteer editors' (www.
dmoz.org/docs/en/about.html). It is developed and maintained by
volunteers who are experts in their areas of interest, unlike the Yahoo!
Directory, which is developed and managed by a small paid staff. Another

major difference between the two is that the ODP is entirely free, unlike the Yahoo! offering, which requires payment for an entry from a commercial organization.

Otherwise, however, the concepts are exactly the same. The ODP has 16 major categories, rather than 14, and they are slightly different and it proudly boasts a listing of over 5 million sites, almost 100,000 editors and over 1 million categories. If you like the concept of a directory-based engine, it's worth checking out both Yahoo! and the ODP to see which you prefer.

Other directory-based search engines

The structure of the Yahoo! directory is very appealing, both for organizations establishing web search engines and also for those people who are new to searching. However, as far as most users are concerned, they do seem to have gone out of fashion. Consequently, there are not a great many general directory-based engines, since there is quite a high overhead in terms of maintaining the directory. Many of the examples that I listed in the last edition of the book (AltaVista, AlltheWeb and Allsearchengines.com [that's just some of the As!]) no longer exist, or have been swallowed up by other engines. However, there are some good examples in this category, such as Beaucoup! Web Directory at www.beaucoup.com, with 15 main categories. Findelio at www.findelio.com has 16 different categories and also has regional quick links. Gigablast over at www.gigablast.com does have a directory, but it's based on that of the Open Directory Project. The 1Websdirectory at www.1websdirectory.com also has 15 main categories (there's clearly a theme coming out here) and it, too, has country-based access. This last point – country-based data – is interesting, since the majority of country-based search engines tend to fall into the directory category. There are a large number of regional/country search engines (numbering over 4000 in fact) and a reasonable (although slightly dated) list can be found at www.philb.com/countryse.htm.

Without wishing to denigrate any of these search engines I do feel that it's necessary to warn readers that they should not get their hopes too high when visiting these sites, as the majority of them only have a very small number of entries. However, to be fair, that might be exactly what is required in a particular situation.

> >

Category-based search engines

Just as a quick refresher, a category-based search engine is a hybrid engine – a cross between a free-text engine and a directory engine, exhibiting as it does characteristics of both. The categories will be created 'on the fly', which is to say they will be generated as a result of the query that is being searched for.

Carrot²

The Carrot² engine is an Open Source Search Results Clustering Engine. It can automatically organize small collections of documents (such as, but not only, search results) into thematic categories. At least, that's what they say about themselves (http://project.carrot2.org). What this means in practical terms is that users can use the free-text search box to type in a query as usual and Carrot² will return a top 100 results. These results are then broken down in folders, with similar results grouped together. So a search for 'librarian' returns folders such as Librarian Blog, Public Library, University, Library Services, Law Librarians and so on. You can see an example in Figure 5.1.

These folders can also be viewed in an interesting Circular format, or as a 'foam tree', as can be seen below in Figures 5.2 and 5.3.

This is a very different approach to that of the traditional search engine, quite obviously. It will certainly appeal to anyone who doesn't like a strict

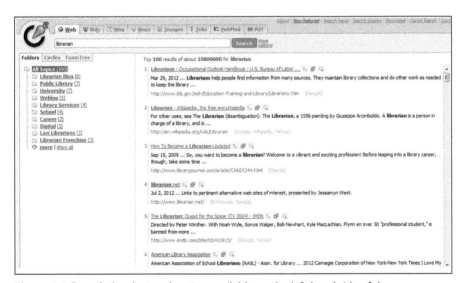

Figure 5.1 Carrot²: the clustered option available on the left-hand side of the screen as a result of a search for 'librarian' (reproduced with permission)

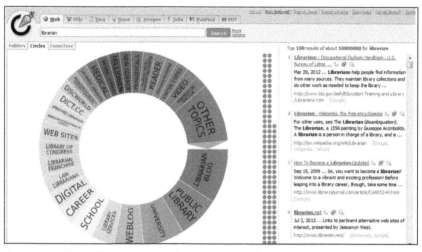

Figure 5.2 The Circles categories of 'Librarian' as defined by Carrot[2]
(reproduced with permission)

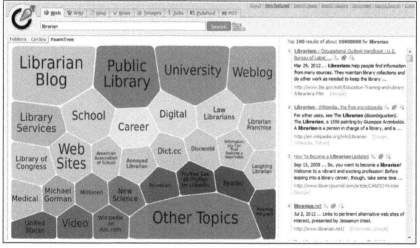

Figure 5.3 A 'foam tree' for 'Librarian' categories as defined by Carrot[2]
(reproduced with permission)

rigid and hierarchical approach. It also allows someone to explore a subject in a rather different way, so may appeal to students and people who don't really know a topic in detail.

Gigablast

The Gigablast search engine, at www.gigablast.com, which I briefly mentioned earlier in this chapter, produces results that are almost entirely category-based. My search for '*librarian*' produced collected results from sources such as Ask a Librarian, Internet Public Library, US Copyright Office and Librarian Action Figures. While it lacks the attractiveness of Carrot², it does nonetheless provide another approach to collating results into groups.

iSeek

The iSeek search engine, at www.iseek.com/iseek/home.page, uses the tagline 'Targeted Discovery' and it analyses the results of a search to identify themes, topics, people, places and more to better order the results for the searcher. This is a particularly impressive approach, since searchers can immediately start to link subjects together. For example, if you don't know the names of any librarians, but need to find some experts in a hurry, this would be an almost impossible job with a traditional engine such as Google or Bing. However, iSeek lists over 15 named librarians, 28 topics, a dozen places, various organizations, dates and times and abbreviations. My only concern about this engine is that it only returns a small selection of sites – the librarian search provided a fairly sparse 126 results, which did lead to a rather spotty collection of topics – Internet Librarian International 2009 was listed as a topic, but not 2010, or indeed any other year. However, that apart, it did give a very thorough breakdown of topics.

Other category-based engines

iZito, at www.izito.com, does a full text search, but the topics returned are fairly limited, with 10 groupings for Librarian, including the rather bizarre 'Judas' and 'Large Selection', which I didn't find to be terribly helpful. (In case you're wondering as well, there is a film called *The Librarian: the curse of the Judas Chalice*, which explains the link, but still doesn't give me any great confidence!)

Yippy (http://search.yippy.com) used to be known as Clusty. It promotes itself as a family-friendly platform 'protecting you and your children from pornography and more unseemly elements of the web.' The topic clouds are reasonable, but there is also an option to view categories based on sources, sites and time periods.

Zapmeta, www.zapmeta.com seems to pull up exactly the same type of content as iZito, with the same topic clouds.

‹ ‹

Similarity search engines

While index or directory search engines are becoming less fashionable, there is an almost direct replacement for them – the similarity search engine. A directory-based engine would take the approach of listing similar sites together in a single collection or category, while the similarity search engines work rather more dynamically, by requiring the searcher to input a suggested website or page, and then the engine would create a list on the fly to match the subject coverage. The idea of similarity search engines is reasonably new, although the concept of 'if you like this you will like that' is obviously an age-old idea. One of the first places where people really saw this concept in operation was on the bookselling website Amazon. Due to the sheer number of people looking at, and then buying, products it became very easy for the company to suggest to their users that if they bought a particular book or piece of music, it would be quite likely that they would like something similar by the same or another analogous artist. Of course, as this can be done for books and music, there's no reason why it shouldn't also work with websites.

> **›› Did you know?**
> Of the 5.2 million households in Great Britain without internet access, the most common reason for not having a connection was that they 'did not need it' (54%) (www.ons.gov.uk/ons/rel/rdit2/internet-access---households-and-individuals/2012/stb-internet-access--households-and-individuals--2012.html).

There are a number of different ways that something like this can be achieved. By taking the keywords from one site (from the title, URL, headings and so on) it's possible to map those across to other websites that use similar words in similar positions. Alternatively a similarity search engine is able to anonymously track usage, and if they discover that a lot of users will visit website B after looking at website A it's very easy to create a link. The value of similarity search engines should not be underestimated, as they are a tremendously useful way of researching a particular subject. I find myself being drawn to them on a very regular basis, especially when I need to create lists of alternative products, software packages and resources for example. They are an extremely fast and effective way to produce a 'top ten' listing of websites or other resources – of course, the researcher will need to spend time on each site checking that the similarity does exist, but having a list of resources already created for you is a great way to save time.

〉 〉

Similarpages

The Similarpages website (www.similarpages.com) has a very good
reputation for finding comparable pages and will often return up to 300
different suggestions. Users can simply type in a keyword or a website into
the search bar to see what the engine turns up. A search for '*CILIP*', for
example, returns a list of similar websites, together with a thumbnail of the
site in question, as can be seen from Figure 5.4.

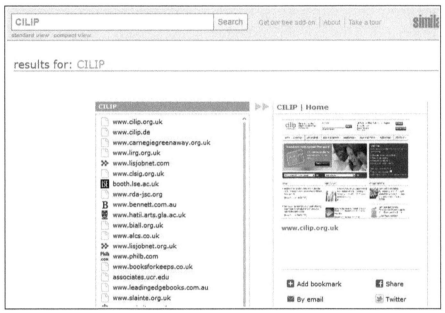

Figure 5.4 Search results for 'CILIP' from Similarpages.com
(reproduced with permission)

Similarpages returns a good collection of results from organizational
websites to academic sites to personal websites. Searchers are then able to
choose the site that interests them, or to further hunt for what interests
them in particular. For example, a searcher could then click on my website
and the engine will return details of it, but will also do a second search to
focus more closely on websites from individual librarians. Of course, this
isn't going to be an entirely comprehensive list, but then no list ever is!

Another way in which searchers can use Similarpages is to type in a
URL, rather than to run a keyword search. A search for '*www.ala.org*', for
example, will work in exactly the same way, and the searcher will be
rewarded with dozens of similar sites.

Finally, Similarpages has released a browser add-on for the Firefox browser. When browsing the web, if there's a page that the searcher finds interesting, they can simply click on the installed icon on the browser toolbar and the engine will instantly produce a listing of pages that are similar to the one currently being viewed. It is unfortunate that they have not yet produced a similar tool for other browsers, but this may well come in time.

SimilarSiteSearch

If you visit www.similarsitesearch.com you'll find SimilarSiteSearch, which badges itself as 'the best place to find alternative websites'. They explain that they are able to do this because they 'learned how to balance the following factors when computing similarity score: similarity in topics, website popularity, language and country match, user suggestions and ratings. We are constantly re-evaluating our scoring formula to save users' time by placing the most relevant results on top.' They also rely on users providing input by suggesting similar websites and by using a thumb up/down button, which provides useful feedback to the engine ranking system.

In order to use SimilarSiteSearch you do need to have a URL already available to you, unlike Similarpages, which allows users to do a keyword search first. However, once you have your URL to hand the engine will provide you with some useful information about the site that you have chosen to use as your introductory search URL, such as a description, popularity and site topics. Users are then given up to 50 sites which are similar to the URL. Searchers can then see the title, summary and URL of the suggestions, together with a grade bar indicating both how similar the site is to the original one, and how popular the suggested site is. Finally, there's that thumbs up/down option to indicate the level of similarity between the sites.

SimilarSiteSearch also provides a list of related searches and alternatives and an option to add details to favourite social media sites such as Facebook, LinkedIn and Twitter. Finally, users are able to click on the site topics option to get a list of top websites in the various categories. This makes SimilarSiteSearch rather similar to category- or directory-based search engines, which also rank sites by subject area.

Websites Like

You have, I am sure, got a clear idea of how this particular type of search engine works, so I can save us both time by not explaining it again, suffice to say Websites Like at www.websiteslike.org is no different. Simple provide a URL or a keyword, and it will attempt to find websites like the one you've provided. It will display site categories, titles, summaries and site topics of the alternatives, as well as an image of the website home page. It has listed over 1 million sites and will return up to about 50 alternatives, including thumbshots of the site or page if it has them available.

StumbleUpon

The StumbleUpon website at www.stumbleupon.com is slightly different from the previous sites that I've mentioned, in that it's less of a search engine in its own right, and rather more of an alerting service, or as they may like to put it, 'a content discovery site based on personal interests'. However, having said that, it's an accurate tool, and one that I've used myself with great effect. The concept is very simple, and akin to the Amazon model. Simply tell StumbleUpon what interests you have, and it will then go and find web pages, videos, photographs and so on which you probably wouldn't have found on your own. You can then provide like/dislike feedback to the service, which will then revise what it sends you.

> **>> Did you know?**
> The top five web hosting countries in the world are the USA, Germany, China, UK, Russia (http://royal.pingdom.com).

Since the user has to provide feedback, based on fairly random material that is initially returned, it's rather hit-and-miss. However, the more like/dislike feedback which is provided, the more the service can accurately predict what will be of interest. New 'stumbles' are e-mailed on a weekly basis, but it's obviously quite possible to simply visit the website and log into your account if you are in need of a serendipitous 'fix' of interesting material. There is also an add-on StumbleUpon bar that can be bolted onto to your browser. This has a nice interactive element, since users can like/dislike the page that they happen to be on, providing the service with useful feedback information to further hone its results. Finally, the add-on can be used to suggest other sites based upon the page that the user is currently on. There is of course a social element in the tool, as you can choose to follow individuals to see what they are looking at. It's also possible to comment on the sites that are viewed, in order to provide further information to other users of the service. StumbleUpon currently has over 25 million registered users, who between them have added over 25 billion 'stumbles'.

Alternative To

This again is a slightly different take on the subject of alternatives. The Alternative To website at www.alternative.to will, as the name suggests, find alternatives for you. However, in this instance, it's not looking for alternative websites, but alternatives to devices, singers, trainers and so on. For example, if I ask for an alternative to the iPad, I am provided with devices such as the Motorola Xoom2, the Asus Eee Pad slider, and so on. It's a very useful tool if you have a lot of enquiries about gadgets, cars and so on. I'm sure that you'll be relieved to know that when I asked for alternatives to librarians it wasn't able to offer me any!

Tastekid

Another example of the tools that provide you with similar material is the Tastekid website, www.tastekid.com. This is a site that is specifically focused on music, movies, shows, books, authors and games. It's about the only site that does have a particular section on literary figures – I asked for alternatives to Charles Dickens and was provided with Elizabeth Gaskell, Victor Hugo, Alexandre Dumas and so on. As well as suggestions, Tastekid provides some basic information about the e.g. person, place or band, culled from Wikipedia, and offers links to both that and to a Google-based search.

BookSeer

The site at http://bookseer.com looks quite formal, with a pen and ink drawing of a Victorian-looking gentleman, with a speech bubble that says 'Good Day. I've just finished reading ...... by ..... What should I read next?' The idea of course is that the user fills in the blanks of the title that they have just read, and the BookSeer will provide some alternatives. These are currently being pulled directly from Amazon – there is a link to LibraryThing but this is not being used to recommend titles at the time of writing. Interestingly, the BookSeer will not only work with fiction titles, but it can also be used to suggest non-fiction alternatives as well.

Other 'discovery' tools

At this point I think there is a danger of veering too much into the area of general discovery tools, so I will draw a halt at this point, but if you are keen on this type of resource, you may wish to try No Names, No Jackets at

> >

www.nonamesnojackets.com, BookFlavor at http://bookflavor.com or Whichbook at www.whichbook.net. These – as their names suggest – are all discovery tools for the written word. However, if you are more interested in the cinema, try Yournextfilm at www.yournextfilm.com/uk or the sister site www.yournextgame.com/uk for games. If music is your thing, take a look at Spotibot at http://spotibot.com, Melody Tubes at www. melodytubes.com or Finetune at www.finetune.com.

Summary

Directory and category-based search engines would appear to be an aspect of internet search that is quickly fading into history. While these engines do exist, their number does appear to be dwindling, and shows no signs of resurgence. At least, that's what I thought, but in researching this particular chapter I noted that a patent has been assigned to Google for 'Organizing search results in a topic hierarchy' which was filed back in 2008 but granted on 3 July 2012 (http://1.usa.gov/NBGsgU). The patent describes a system which, when you run a search, displayed a list of categories, or allows you to create your own. Searchers may then be able to vote up or down categories and associate their actions with a social media profile. At the moment this is of course merely conjecture, but perhaps the category approach isn't quite dead yet!

I do, however, think that we can now say with some confidence that the traditional approach of listing like sites together is now being done rather more successfully by the similarity search engines. They provide a greater variety of sites, since they are not limited to the few that the directory or index search engine is aware of, and people can add their own suggestions, thus crowd-sourcing more, and better content.

CHAPTER 6

≫ Multi- and meta-search engines

Introduction

No-one has any idea just how many search engines there are on the internet, and it really does depend on how you define them, since a tight definition (a search engine that searches for web-based pages) will give you a few hundred, while a broader definition (a search engine that will search anything and which is available on the web) will return a figure into the hundreds of thousands, if not more. Given that there are so many, it doesn't seem to make a lot of sense just to resort continually to using one, even if it is really effective. After all, any information professional who always first went to the *Encyclopaedia Britannica* every time they were asked a question would be looked at slightly oddly. However, to go from one search engine to another and then another is going to be time-consuming and confusing, so while we might all agree that it's probably not best practice just to go always to one engine, it's understandable.

There is a type of search engine that overcomes this problem, though; actually there are two closely related variants, multi-search engines and meta-search engines. A multi-search engine can best be described as a search engine that doesn't actually search itself, but provides searchers with the ability to search any number of engines from one page. A meta-search engine, on the other hand will take a query, pass it onto other search engines on behalf of the searcher, take the returned results, de-duplicate them and provide a single list of results.

There are plenty of advantages to using search engines like this. They can save a lot of time, since results are generally returned more quickly with a single mouse click instead of the searcher typing in one search engine address after another, and then retyping the search from scratch. Secondly, they're a good way to really highlight which results all search engines think are the best, rather than relying on the search algorithms of one. Finally, they're a great way to remind searchers that there are plenty of search engines available to them, and a good way to introduce them to new ones. A meta-search engine goes even further than that, of course, since it does all of the hard work for you and just presents you with a list of results.

> **>> Did you know?**
> Google accounts for 91% of all UK searches (www.factbrowser.com/facts/9918).

If these engines are so useful and valuable, then the question arises 'well, why don't we all use them all of the time then?' There are several reasons for this, not least that a search can really only be very basic – most engines will understand the use of the minus symbol to exclude a term, and double quotes to search for a phrase, but more complex (and useful) syntax such as '*site:*' will only be understood by a limited number of engines. Google knows that a searcher who types in '*site:.ac.uk*' wants to limit their results to academic sites in the UK, but another engine that doesn't use that syntax will assume the searcher is looking for web pages that include that string of characters on the page. Moreover, as we have already seen, lots of engines have very specific functionality such as the Knowledge Graph, news or video searching, and these features are not necessarily going to be available in a multi- or meta-search environment. Finally, in the case of meta-search engines, they all tend to pride themselves on how quickly they can get results back to you, and as such if one search engine is being a little bit tardy in sending a response they won't wait around but will simply display results on the screen from a reduced selection, which does rather negate the whole process.

> **>> Did you know?**
> 93% of teenagers (12–17) go online (www.pewinternet.org/Reports/2010/Social-Media-and-Young-Adults.aspx).

Consequently, if you are running a simple (in terms of syntax) search, and a comprehensive set of results is needed, it is worth considering this type of engine. If you're in a real hurry, and are happy with the engines that a meta-engine will use, it's best to use that, but if you want to take a little more time and search through sets of results, you're going to want to explore multi-search engines.

Multi-search engines

There is no obvious contender for the 'best' or most popular multi-search engine, and most of them will do exactly the same thing, so preference really comes down to the way that results are displayed on the screen, although that again is similar, with each engine result being framed below the search box. The second criterion is to look at which engines are available for searching, and in what areas: just web pages, or do they include news, video and images, for example? However, when all is said and done, it does come down very much to personal choice.

Browsys

Browsys (www.browsys.com/search) has a simple interface – a search box and a choice of tabs for Google, Bing, Mashpedia, Videos (provided by Bing), News (provided by Bing), Slideshare, (which is a site that allows users to upload and share presentations), Ask Q&A and Answers. Simply type the search term into the box and click on the appropriate tab. The results from each engine will display in the main pane below the tabs, so it's very easy to quickly click between them and look at the results. That's what it does, and that's all that it does, but it's fast and effective.

Fefoo

Fefoo (http://fefoo.com) is a neat little multi-search engine that provides access to over 250 different search engines. The searcher has the usual search box available to them, but below that is a pull-down menu that allows for various choices – web, images, news; all the usual suspects, but in total there are over 40 different options available, covering an extremely wide range. There are 12 different search engines available for search under the 'Web' option, but they are chosen individually, so it's not possible to combine results across engines. For each search option Fefoo provides access to an entirely different collection of engines, so under the 'Social' option there are another 19 engines. Once a search has been run Fefoo reduces itself to a single bar at the top of the screen from which users can continue to make selections as to subject area, choice of engine and search terms. It's a small but neat and elegant engine and far more powerful than it might at first appear.

Goofram

Goofram (www.goofram.com) limits itself to providing results from two search engines, Google and Wolfram|Alpha (see p. 186), and these are displayed on the same screen side by side, although this may require scrolling to the right or resizing the screen in order to see everything easily. This is a useful engine, in that Google gives users a listing of websites to visit, while the Wolfram|Alpha element of the search provides facts and figures about the subject. Consequently a search for a subject such as 'Jupiter' will really pay dividends very quickly.

Harvester42

Harvester 42 (http://harvester42.fzk.de/jss/Harvester42) provides access to rather more than the 42 search engines one may assume from the title of the engine. It displays results in a slightly different way to most of the other engines that we've looked at in this section, because it sends the query to each search engine in turn and creates a results page with one set of results following another, so that the searcher can scroll down the page looking at each framed set of results in turn. It's a nice, quick and simple way to look at a lot of results with ease.

Heapr

Heapr (www.heapr.com) riffs on the theme started by Goofram, in that the left-hand pane of results automatically loads results from Google. The right-hand pane gives the user the options of searching Twitter, Wolfram|Alpha or Wikipedia. It also has tabs for video search, with options from YouTube, hulu and Vimeo. It's an engine that's still very much in development, but once again it does the job simply and effectively.

Myallsearch

Myallsearch (www.myallsearch.com) gives searchers the option of Bing, Yahoo!, Google, Ask, Teoma, Lycos, MetaCrawler, Blekko and DuckDuckGo. This isn't immediately apparent, as there is only one search box on the home page, but when a search is run Myallsearch will display available search engine options. It provides searchers with the option to search the web, blogs, downloads, images, shopping, torrents and videos. For each of these Myallsearch has various engines at its beck and call, giving a total of 38 search options; a really nice set of tools that are immediately available for the searcher to get to grips with!

> >

Qrobe

Qrobe (which is pronounced Krobe) is located at http://qrobe.it. It has a
very simple search interface and searches the web using both Google and
Bing. However it also has some interesting powersearch commands
which look rather like the 'slash the web' options that Blekko supplies.
Consequently a search for the term 'flowers' on Google image search
can be run using the function '*flowers /gi*', while on Bing the search
would be '*flowers /bi*' instead. Various other options allow for searches to
take place on resources such as YouTube, Netflix, the Internet Movie
Database and Wikipedia. There is also an option to limit results to a
specific country as well.

Search!o

Search!o (http://search.io) is another engine that doesn't make it clear from
the outset exactly which engines it makes available to searchers – this is only
evident after a search is initially run. The web search element provides
access to nine different engines, such as Bing and Lycos, but several engines
that I would expect to be available, such as Google, DuckDuckGo and
Blekko, were missing. However, what Search!o loses in terms of search
engine variety, it certainly makes up for in coverage. Users can choose from
a total of 16 different categories, such as audio/music, blogs, images, fonts,
recipes and stock photographs, each of which uses a different collection of
engines. This results in access to dozens of alternative engines, several of
which even I hadn't heard of.

SearchBoth

SearchBoth (http://us.searchboth.net) provides users with the option of
comparing results from two different engines – there is a choice of Google,
Yahoo!, Bing, Ask, Dogpile, Metacrawler, looksmart and Websearch. It also
offers search categories such as images, video, shopping and news. It's a very
straightforward engine, but the chance to compare so many engines is good,
and would be an excellent way to indicate to a novice searcher that not all
engines are created equal – certainly not when it comes to their results!

Sputtr

Sputtr (www.sputtr.com – and I have no idea how to pronounce it) is quite

‹ ‹

daunting at first glance, since the home page is full of icons for a large range of different tools – not all of them search engines. There are options for variants of Google, Delicious, the Internet Movie Database, Amazon and eBay for example; 36 in total. However, if you set up an account with the service you can customize the icons on the page. Otherwise simply type in the search that is required, and click on an icon. Sputtr will open a new browser tab, taking the searcher directly to the site, and the search will run automatically. Simply close the tab and return to the search window to run more searches. This is quite simple and elegant, but it does mean that there is rather too much tabbing back and forth, particularly if a comparison of results is what's needed.

Soovle

Soovle (www.soovle.com) has yet another take on multi-search. It uses seven search engines – Amazon, Answers, Bing, Google, Wikipedia, Yahoo! and YouTube, and they are all circling the search box. As soon as you start to type in a search term, Soovle will present a list of options from each of the engines. For example, I started to type in 'do' and was presented with options as diverse as 'Downton Abbey', 'dozens killed in prison riot', 'dominos', and 'doctor of philosophy'. Once I'd typed out my query ('dog', just in case you were wondering) I could click on any of 70 different options (10 per engine). Because it was easy to see which results came from which engine it was a simple option to choose to view videos of dogs that I could watch, or dog collars that I could buy over at Amazon. Soovle is a refreshingly different engine and fun to use.

Trovando

Trovando (www.trovando.it) uses the tagline 'search different', and it's a long-time survivor in the search engine world, having started life back in 2005. It provides access to over 250 search engines across ten different categories – web, images, reference, tags, news, price, blogs, audiovideo, torrents and URLs. It also has a personalizable custom search engine where users can add engines from a choice of over 3300, and save the customization with a browser bookmarklet, without any registration. Trovando uses a very traditional multi-search engine approach, with a search box and list of engines underneath, which changes depending on what search category is being used. Choose keywords, run the search and choose the engine to get results from. Trovando will display the results in a framed window, while still retaining all of the search options at the top of the screen. Consequently users can simply click on the results and move swiftly from one set of results to the next.

Zuula

Zuula is an engine that can be located at www.zuula.com and it's another one which doesn't give you a choice of engine until you've run your search. It has tabbed options for seven different categories and provides access to most of the major engines, although once again DuckDuckGo and Blekko are missing from the list. In total there are over 50 search options for searchers to use. Unusually, compared to many search engines, it has an advanced search function with the normal Boolean operators ('*AND*', '*OR*', '*NOT*') with phrase searching, but it also has site/domain limit functions and a nice feature, which allows for results that were shown in the previous search to be minimized.

Meta-search engines

The number of meta-search engines has dwindled over the years, probably because they are technically much more difficult to program than a multi-search engine.

Ixquick

The best known in this category is probably Ixquick, at https://www. ixquick.com, which also prides itself on not tracking searches or linking them to IP addresses. Search is simple enough – type in a term and search. Results are then displayed on the screen in relevance-ranked order, with a number of stars next to them – the more stars, the more search engines used by Ixquick picked up that particular result in their own top results.

> **›› Did you know?**
> 71% of the UK population makes purchases online (www.factbrowser.com/facts/8386).

Irritatingly, however, Ixquick doesn't give users a list of the search engines that it used, and doesn't allow them to limit at all – it's very much pot luck. However, Ixquick does have some nice functionality – limiting by date for example. An advanced search option allows users to limit by word, phrase, the Boolean '*OR*' operator, by exclusion, with text in the title or field URLs, at a specific domain, or which links to a domain. Ixquick also has options for searching images, although it doesn't give very much indication of the engines that it uses for this process. Video search is powered by the Blinkx engine, and can be limited to one of six subject options. Finally the engine offers a telephone number look-up service, which offers a list of country options, but I didn't find this particularly effective.

Dogpile

Dogpile (www.dogpile.com) is one those search engines that has been around for so long it can certainly be considered a veteran of internet search. It provides access to web, image, video, news, local and white page results, and uses Google, Yahoo! and Yandex to create its results page. The results are arranged by relevance, and each result provides basic details, including which of the three engines found the result. Dogpile also suggests other relevant searches as well. It does have an advanced search function, but this is relatively limited to the Boolean operators, language and domain searching.

iZito

iZito (www.izito.com) works in the same way as Ixquick and again it doesn't provide users with a listing of the engines that it uses; a mouse-over of the star rating tells users, but otherwise it's necessary to hope and guess; not an ideal option. iZito does, however, do something slightly different to Ixquick, in that it offers a category option based on the search terms used. My 'community libraries' search resulted in options to narrow the search to e-books, public libraries, students and cities for example. It also gave me a suggested search feature as well. iZito has an image search option and a video search option, with the latter using various different resources and providing another category search option.

Mamma

Mamma, at www.mamma.com, styles itself as 'The mother of all search engines' and it has a certain right to the title, since it's been around since the mid-1990s. However, it also does not tell users which engines it uses to provide results in any of its search categories – web, news, image or Twitter.

PolyMeta

PolyMeta (www.polymeta.com) is 'the universal meta-search and discovery engine' and it searches across Google, Bing, Ask and Yahoo!. Once a search is run it passes the query onto those engines, collates the responses and displays them on the screen. However, that's just the basic results, and it does rather more than that since it provides a 'Topics' or category approach, news, images, videos, blog and Twitter links. It also tells users how many people on Facebook have liked a particular result, which is rather interesting in its own right, providing a limited social aspect to the results. PolyMeta also has search tabs for a total of six different areas, including news, Twitter and blogs.

Scour

Scour (www.scour.com) uses results from Google, Yahoo!, Bing and OneRiot. The main point of interest with Scour is that it's very easy to re-rank results based on any of the engines, so the user has the choice of seeing what each engine in turn regards as the best results, all culled from their first page of results.

Multimedia multi-search engines

We're in danger of 'multi' overload at this point, I think! However, I would be remiss if I didn't bring your attention to the fact that there are a variety of engines that tend to focus rather more on music, sounds, lyrics and video than they do on traditional web pages. Admittedly they are rather few in number, but when you're looking beyond the obvious these may be exactly the engines that you need.

Mundu

Mundu, at www.mundusearch.com, is an engine that searches the web, sounds, lyrics, music and video. Apparently 'mundu' from the Latin for 'clean, neat and elegant', and its search interface is certainly that. It combines results from its own search engine with meta-search results from other engines, although irritatingly it doesn't specify which – the only way that you can tell is by looking at the results screen, which does indicate the origin of each result.

Spezify

Spezify (www.spezify.com) is an odd tool in many ways. It says of itself that it cherishes serendipity over relevance, making no difference between different kinds of media. The results of this engine come from a wide variety of other resources, such as Amazon, Facebook and Vimeo. Results are displayed on the screen in a visual format, allowing the searcher to simply scroll through until they find something that is of interest to them. As a result, this isn't going to be an engine that will get a result quickly – or even effectively – but it may be worth using with an enquirer in order to get a better idea on exactly what they're interested in finding. While I wouldn't suggest that serendipity is the best approach to use when searching, it can sometimes help if you're really stuck!

Trooker

When looking for video-based results, it's worthwhile keeping Trooker (www.trooker.com) in mind. This is a search engine that searches some of the major video sites, such as YouTube, Dailymotion and Brightcove. When a search is run Trooker will provide results ranked by source, but this can be rearranged for relevance, upload date or title. A particularly nice feature of this engine is the ability to create an account and create sets of results which can then be shared with enquirers.

The hidden, invisible or deep web

Search engines will find whatever they can, although one could make the point that search engines can only find whatever they are allowed or able to find. There is a huge amount of information available on the internet that isn't immediately available to search engines. For example, data may be held on a website that is only accessible via a search engine on that site – the BT telephone directory is a good example, and genealogical databases are another. Search engines cannot get into the information because it's not arranged in a way that they can understand, they cannot interrogate the databases and even if they could, they wouldn't be able to recognize the type of information that's available. Consequently, the only way to access

> >

that information is to use a search engine that is on the actual website. Now, clearly, this is in many ways the exact opposite of a multi- or meta-search engine, but there are some tools available that will draw a lot of these individual search engines together into a listing of available resources, and although the searcher will still need to hunt through them individually to find the correct tool for the job, they do demonstrate some elements similar to meta-search engines. It's very easy to forget that these resources are available, so adding in a good engine that provides access to the hidden web to your search armoury is always a good idea.

Unfortunately, there are only relatively few engines which search the deep web – it's a very time-consuming job to create them in the first place and then maintain them after that. There's also very little reward for anyone doing so, as a deep web search engine is really only the starting point in a search – to identify a database to conduct the proper enquiry – so people will be unlikely to click on advertisements to make the developer much money. Moreover, those engines that are available are often regarded as academic or specialist in nature, and I have discussed those in detail elsewhere, so this is by necessity a fairly small selection. However, that shouldn't be taken to imply that they don't really exist – there are large numbers of databases that contain material that the other engines mentioned in this title simply cannot index. Whatever your subject area of interest, I can virtually guarantee that there will be specialist databases available to you – the only difficulty is in finding them. Consequently it's necessary to research here in a two stage process. First of all decide on the subject that interests you and work out if you are being too broad or too precise at this point. Then run some searches on a general engine and include search terms such as '*specialized database*' and '*(hidden OR deep OR dark OR invisible) web*'.

CompletePlanet

CompletePlanet, at http://aip.completeplanet.com, describes itself as 'The Deep Web Directory' and it lists over 70,000 searchable databases and speciality search engines. The engine has two elements – the normal search box, which helps users find databases that are relevant to their subject area of interest, and a directory or index approach with over 40 different subject areas, from agriculture to weather. When searchers click on a subject area they are presented with a listing of all appropriate databases, and this can be quite daunting – in the computing and internet section 1008 relevant databases are available. However, the subject is divided up into smaller sections, such as artificial intelligence, internet and software. In total CompletePlanet estimates that over 750 terabytes of information are available just in the top 60 largest deep web sites, with over 85 billion records or documents. Each database is very specifically focused, and has its own particular search syntax, so it can be a slow process to get exactly the information that's required, but generally you will find that the data comes from very reliable sources so it can be trusted.

CompletePlanet has a very sophisticated search structure, supporting Boolean operators, nested logic using parentheses, wildcards and stemming. If you are an 'old school' database searcher, and sometimes get exasperated because of the functional limitations of most modern search engines, CompletePlanet will immediately appeal. Consequently it will have no difficulty working with a search such as '*(movie OR cinema) AND (star OR celeb*)*'. Results will give the name of the database, a summary of what it covers, the URL, an estimate of relevance to the original query and when it was first added to the collection.

CloserLookSearch

CloserLookSearch (https://www.closerlooksearch.com) has a specific focus on medical and health subjects, and is particularly useful for searching for medical terms, procedures or conditions. The engine is able to take search queries, pass them onto a variety of other engines and pull back content, creating a helpful page of results. A search for hypothyroidism returned a definition from MedlinePlus, images from the same database, a general discussion of the subject from WebMD, causes, symptoms, conventional treatment, alternative treatments and further reading from various other databases.

Intute

Intute (www.intute.ac.uk) is a tool that was widely used, having been created by a consortium of seven UK universities working together with a range of different partners. Unfortunately the funding for the project ceased, and it closed in July 2011. However, although new resources are not being added, and no change is being made to existing content, the resource is still available for searching. It still contains a lot of very useful information, with links to many different academic subject areas, from agriculture to veterinary medicine with engineering and the physical sciences in between, to name just a few. Obviously as time goes on it will become less valuable as resources change their address or close and others open, but as long as that is kept in mind, it's a tool that is still worth considering for the time being.

Summary

Multi- and meta-search engines have a long and distinguished history in terms of internet search, and they continue to thrive to this day. They're relatively easy to create and programme, but they are often an intermediate step to getting the actual information that is required. They also piggyback off existing engines, which sometimes do not take kindly to this, as they lose the opportunity to make money from advertising clicks. It's therefore not surprising to see that engines of this type disappear almost as often as they are created. In researching this particular chapter it was sad to note that a lot of engines that were truly interesting, innovative and ground-breaking have simply fallen by the wayside, losing out in the bitter fight to their leaner and more streamlined single database cousins.

However, they should not be dismissed out of hand, as they continue to remind us of the existence of other engines, and that's never a bad thing. I would certainly recommend that it's worth keeping one or two of the ones that I have listed in your searcher's armoury to pull out when you're stuck for ideas, or simply need to be comprehensive in your searching. If nothing else, it's always a good idea to show them to your enquirers to illustrate just what engines are available, and how skilled you are in being able to find just the right one to answer their questions!

CHAPTER 7

>> Social media search engines

Introduction

Before we can start talking about the search engines which trawl through social media content we first need to come up with an acceptable definition of what exactly social media is. It's one of those terms that gets bandied about quite happily, and most people have a rough idea of what it means, but a 'rough idea' is not really acceptable in the context of expert internet search. A recent Wikipedia entry for 'social media' provides us with the following:

> **Social media** includes web-based and mobile technologies used to turn communication into interactive dialogue. Andreas Kaplan and Michael Haenlein define social media as 'a group of internet-based applications that build on the ideological and technological foundations of Web 2.0 and that allow the creation and exchange of user-generated content.' Social media is media for social interaction as a superset beyond social communication.
>
> http://en.wikipedia.org/wiki/Social_media

Well, that's probably useful for some people, but I have to say that this doesn't exactly answer the question! There are some key elements there – social media has grown out of the concept of Web 2.0, which includes such resources as weblogs and wikis, and there's also the mention of 'user-generated content', which covers the creation of videos on YouTube, posting photographs online for people to share, content on social networks such as Facebook and Google+, and a myriad of other resources. There are some very helpful infographics that demonstrate how much is now happening on the internet every second, minute, hour or day, which help to clarify exactly what user-generated content means, and I was tempted to include one in this book.

However, the disadvantage is that these infographics are instantly out of date. By the time that you're reading this chapter I would estimate that there are going to be over 150,000 tweets per minute, 50 hours of video uploaded to YouTube every minute, 550,000 comments posted to Facebook and over 4000 photographs uploaded to Flickr. For an up-to-the-minute counter I would suggest taking a look at Gary Hayes' social media counter at www.personalizemedia.com/garys-social-media-count, which provides a second-by-second update on the production of new information.

When we look at social media one thing is certain – it is produced in numbers that are close to unimaginable, and which are certainly outside the scope of traditional search engines to index and make available quickly and accurately. The old method of data gathering – visiting web pages, updating them in an index and making them available to searchers does not scale, to say nothing of the fact that much of this content is not held in a traditional format. While websites and web pages are still central to the dissemination and curation of data on the internet they do not command the same importance that they did even three or four years ago.

> **>> Did you know?**
> The average Facebook user has 130 Friends (http://go-globe.com).

Traditional search engines do not provide searchers with the information that they need when it comes to this form of data, and this has led to the rise of a new type of search engine – the social media search engine, which concentrates on providing access to this ever-increasing flood of data. You could ask 'If they can do it, why can't existing search engines?' and it's a good question. To be fair, some search engines are attempting to do just that, as we'll see shortly, but it's a little bit like asking an oil tanker builder to start producing submarines – both are water-based transportation vehicles, but entirely different in nature.

The difference between social media and other data

The amount of data and speed of production are only two aspects of the difference between social media and more traditional media. There is a third, very important difference, one that the searcher always needs to keep in mind, and that is the producer of the content. With websites it's generally fairly easy to see who, or at least which, has produced information. Any good web authoring team will ensure that both the author and the date of publication on the web will be clearly indicated, so that it is a relatively simple job to assign a level of authority to content. Unfortunately, this does apply to social media. While there have been a number of high-profile cases in which people have been in court over what they have blogged or tweeted, this is far from the norm. Anyone can say whatever they like (technically, at least, if not legally) and in most instances this will not be checked, and worse will often be repeated and reamplified, so that an incorrect message takes on a life of its own. For example, on 2 January 2012 Twitter was alive with the rumour that Fidel Castro had died, and there were over 50 tweets per second repeating this information: it became one of the most trending subjects on the microblogging site. It turned out that this was an entirely incorrect rumour, and as with most rumours it wasn't possible to find out who started it.

> **>> Did you know?**
> The average Twitter user has tweeted 307 times (http://istrat.gy/huffpo100).

Consequently, while information may be produced very quickly, and in vast amounts, that alone does not mean that it is accurate in any way at all. Before those who carry a banner for more traditional media get too smug, we should remember the many examples when the newspapers and media reports get things wrong as well. However, social media is created by individuals, and while it may be quicker to access, its very nature means that it's going to be unchecked and personal. Authority checking, therefore, becomes even more important: double-check your information and take note of your sources.

Having said that, we are beginning to see the rise of the individual as a news or information source in a way that we have not seen before. When we use social media resources, be they Twitter, Facebook or any one of dozens or hundreds of others, we are beginning to see search results which show that a friend may have 'liked' something using the Facebook 'like' button, or they may have used the Google equivalent of +1 or even that they have blogged about a subject or website. For example, if I run a search at Google (when I'm logged into my account) for CILIP a subsection of the results looks like those in Figure 7.1.

Various colleagues have shared this information, and this acts as a personalized recommendation system for me. As time goes on the importance of individuals marking, sharing and liking resources becomes far more important to me than automated results using algorithms that I don't know or understand. We are slowly moving to a situation therefore where experts – real live human beings – become increasingly important in helping us check the authority of what the engines retrieve for us. At the

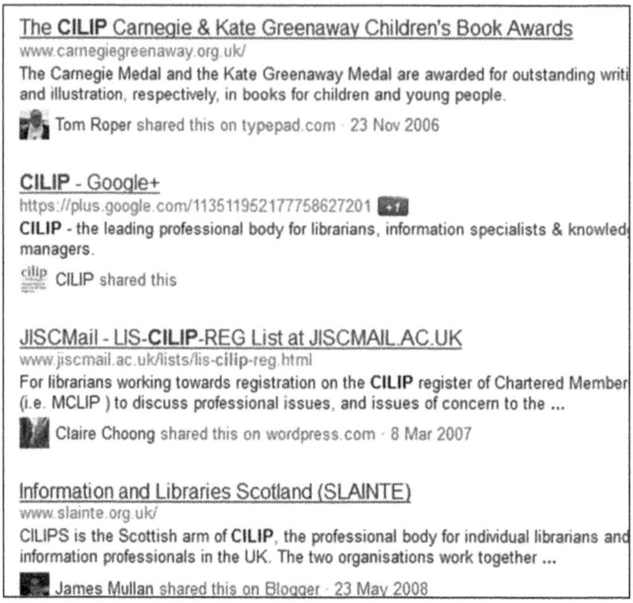

‹ ‹

The **CILIP** Carnegie & Kate Greenaway Children's Book Awards
www.carnegiegreenaway.org.uk/
The Carnegie Medal and the Kate Greenaway Medal are awarded for outstanding writi
and illustration, respectively, in books for children and young people.

 Tom Roper shared this on typepad.com · 23 Nov 2006

CILIP - Google+
https://plus.google.com/113511952177758627201 ·+1·
CILIP - the leading professional body for librarians, information specialists & knowled
managers.

cilip CILIP shared this

JISCMail - LIS-**CILIP**-REG List at JISCMAIL.AC.UK
www.jiscmail.ac.uk/lists/lis-cilip-reg.html
For librarians working towards registration on the **CILIP** register of Chartered Member
(i.e. MCLIP) to discuss professional issues, and issues of concern to the ...

Claire Choong shared this on wordpress.com · 8 Mar 2007

Information and Libraries Scotland (SLAINTE)
www.slainte.org.uk/
CILIPS is the Scottish arm of **CILIP**, the professional body for individual librarians and
information professionals in the UK. The two organisations work together ...

James Mullan shared this on Blogger · 23 May 2008

Figure 7.1
Personalized results
for a Google search for
'CILIP'
*Google and the Google
logo are registered
trademarks of Google
Inc., used with
permission*

moment, many people derive their authority from the organization that
they work for, but perhaps we're heading towards a situation where the
opposite holds true.

Engines to search for social media content
Socialmention*

Socialmention* (www.socialmention.com) describes itself as a

> social media search and analysis platform that aggregates user generated content
> from across the universe into a single stream of information.

(As an aside, please don't look at the bottom of the page for the asterisk
reference; it's part of the name of the engine!)

> It allows you to easily track and measure what people are saying about you, your
> company, a new product, or any topic across the web's social media landscape in
> real time. Socialmention* monitors 100+ social media properties directly,
> including: Twitter, Facebook, FriendFeed, YouTube, Digg, Google etc.
>
> www.socialmention.com/about

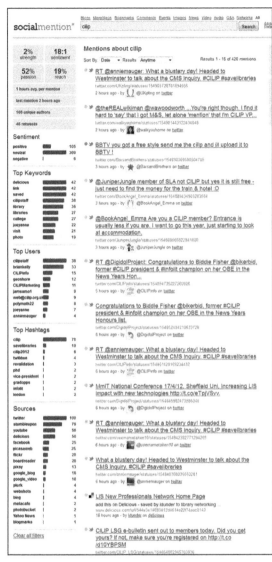

Figure 7.2 Search results from the Socialmention*
search engine (reproduced with
permission)

Searchers can either search across all categories in one operation or can choose from blogs, microblogs, networks, bookmarks, comments, events, images, news, videos, audio, questions or specific social media sources on an individual basis. Data is pulled from a variety of resources for each of these sections, but such is the fast-moving world of social media there is little point in trying to list these in detail; suffice it to say they include sites such as Twitter, YouTube, Diigo, Flickr, Netvibes, Wordpress, Blogger and Facebook. Figure 7.2 shows the results page for a search on '*CILIP*'. As you can see, the searcher is presented with a rich variety of information. In the central element of the screen are results drawn from appropriate resources, and these can be arranged by date (as illustrated) or by source. They can also be time-limited by the last hour, last 12 hours, day, week or month. Searchers can also create an RSS feed for the search or an e-mail alert, or the data can be exported as a CSV or Excel File.

On the left-hand side of the results page, the engine provides searchers with a unique set of data. The first element is a cube of four criteria – strength, sentiment, passion and reach. Strength is the likelihood that the subject or brand is being discussed in social media. This gives searchers a better 'feel' for the extent to which the subject that interests them is currently in the news. This is worked out using a simple calculation – the number of mentions in a 24 hour period divided by total possible mentions. Sentiment is the ratio of positive to negative mentions. Passion is the measure of the likelihood of individuals repeatedly talking about the brand or subject. Finally, reach is a measure of what they call the range of influence. That is to say, the number of unique authors referencing your brand, divided by the total number of mentions.

Below this cube the searcher can see the average number of mentions per hour, the last time the subject was mentioned, unique authors, and the number of retweets. Next, one can see more information based on sentiment, top keywords (very useful if searchers need to go into more depth for a subject), top users (useful to identify key experts in an area), top hashtags and key sources.

Socialmention* has an advanced search function, which allows users to limit by words, phrases, excluded terms, sources, time periods, results per page, language and sort by. Users can also limit results to specific geographic locations, and they can also choose not to show results from specified users.

A useful function provided by the engine is a 'Trends' section, which shows the top 35 trending topics, aggregated from numerous sources. There is also a 'real time buzz widget' which allows users to create a dialogue box that they can place onto their website or blog to constantly monitor and update references to a subject of choice.

Socialmention* is one of the earliest social media search engines and was established back in 2008, but really only came to prominence in late 2009. It's a particularly useful tool for searchers who need to get some general indication of the way that people are currently feeling about a particular subject, but the ability to create RSS feeds and e-mail alerts is also very valuable and an easy way to keep on top of a fast moving subject area.

Icerocket

Icerocket (www.icerocket.com) is another search engine that has been around for several years and has slowly reinvented itself to focus directly on social media content. Icerocket has search options for Blogs, Twitter, Facebook, and 'Search All'. In the 'Search All' category results are arranged by type: Blogs followed by Tweets, and then Facebook mentions. Icerocket has a reasonable selection of search syntax – phrase searching, (+) and (-) to ensure that certain words are included or excluded, Boolean query operators are supported (but must be in all uppercase) and parentheses can be used to group terms and operators together to form more complicated queries. It's a fast, simple and easy-to-use search engine which gives a good selection of results across the range of social media. While it does not cover as much as Socialmention* it's a good choice if you just need a quick overview of a subject or only need to do a bare bones search.

Addict-o-matic

Addict-o-matic (http://addictomatic.com) takes a refreshingly different way of providing access to social media-based resources, in that it can instantly create a custom-built page on any topic that is of interest to the searcher. It searches 25 live sites for news, blog posts, video and images, providing the latest headlines in a search results dashboard. Users can then personalize the layout of the page, deleting results that they don't like and adding different sources from those available. The user is in control of the resources used, since a pull-down menu of sources is available and it works on a toggle basis, so different sources can be turned on and off as necessary. News items are displayed in small news boxes which can be moved around or even deleted as necessary, thus creating a very personalized version of the news, which can then be shared with other people if required. The page can then be bookmarked and returned to in the future as a type of alerting resource, and shared with colleagues. A page of results from Addict-o-matic shows various modules or widgets displayed on the screen showing results for search from, for example, Twitter, Bing News, Google Blog search, YouTube and Flickr. If you want to see a live version, the search that I ran for CILIP is available at http://addictomatic.com/topic/cilip. There is more discussion of Addict-o-matic as a news-based search engine on p. 203.

48ers

In a world of unusual names, this search engine (http://48ers.com) certainly ranks high. It explains its choice thus: 'Some of the earliest fortune seekers were known as the "49ers", but the very first pioneers were known as the "48ers". These gold-seekers uncovered nuggets of gold worth thousands of dollars. We named our service after them as our aim is to help you find nuggets of gold from conversations across the web.'

It's a fairly basic search engine in that it doesn't have a huge amount of search functionality, but what it does do, it does well. While it doesn't support a '*NOT*' operator, it works quite happily with the (-) option, but confusingly it does work with '*AND*' as well as '*OR*' (and also the '+' and '|' alternative symbols as well.). It pulls data from Twitter, Facebook, Digg and Delicious, and searchers can filter by any one of those options.

The results pages are clear and easy to read. Links are active, so it's easy to follow a story or individual quickly and easily. However, it's rather limited in scope, so in its current form is not one that I would immediately turn to.

WhosTalkin?

The WhosTalkin? search engine (www.whostalkin.com) describes itself as

> a social media search tool that allows users to search for conversations surrounding the topics that they care about most. Whether it be your favorite sport, favorite food, celebrity, or your company's brand name; Whostalkin.com can help you join in on the conversations that you care about most. Our goal is to deliver the most relevant and current conversations happening in the world of social media.
>
> www.whostalkin.com/about

In common with Socialmention* it's been around rather longer than most people think – since 2008, in fact. It concentrates on blogs, news, networks, videos, images, forums and bookmarks, and over 50 different resources (such as Twitter and YouTube) within those major categories. The interface is very simple, without any advanced search functionality. However, it does index Facebook entries that are public, and it returns content that is only a few seconds old, so its level of currency is high. Due to its lack of sophistication it wouldn't be one of my first choices as a search engine, but it's a useful backup.

Twitter-specific search engines

Twitter is a key resource when it comes to social news and information, with thousands of tweets per second, news updates, information on conferences, and so on. In a relatively short period of time it has become one of the key resources that a searcher will use in order to find out exactly

〉 〉

what is going on in the world at any given moment. While some search engines include tweets in the data that they return this isn't always the case, and there are a number of specialist search engines that are worth considering when trying to keep up to date with the firehose of information.

> **〉〉 Did you know?**
> Since Twitter began there have been over 163 billion tweets (http://istrat.gy/huffpo100).

Twitter search

Twitter provides users with both a basic and an advanced (refine) search function. The location of the search option depends on the interface that you're using to access Twitter, and the version of Twitter that you're using, since they are prone to change the look and feel of the service on a regular basis. The best suggestion I can make is to simply look around the page until you find the search box! There is an option to save the search, which means that you can simply click on it again at any time in the future to re-run it, although in order for this to work you do need to be logged into the service. The advanced search option is available via the 'Refine results' link or directly from the page at https://twitter.com/search-advanced. The search options are generally not particularly exciting and you could probably predict most of them without ever looking at the page yourself. All the words, exact phrase, any words, none of the words, a specific hashtag and language are all standard. There is, however, an option of searching for people, which could be very useful if a searcher is trying to find an expert in a particular area, for example, or trying to track down a particular individual, since the options available are searching 'from an account', 'to an account' or 'mentioning an account'. There is a links filter option, which means that users can limit tweets to those that contain a specific word or phrase and which contain a link to a URL – '*library filter:links*' There is a geographical option to search 'near' a particular place, and finally a miscellaneous 'other' section, which makes use of the positive and negative emoticons of J and L as well as a question mark. The major disadvantage of Twitter's own search options are that it's not possible to go very far back in time. Searchers are usually limited to about a week's worth of content. This is a disappointing and frustrating omission, and for any serious search work, other engines, such as the previously mentioned Socialmention*, which goes back months, are actually preferable.

Wefollow

The search engine 'Wefollow' (http://wefollow.com) takes a rather different approach to searching Twitter, in that it focuses on subject areas (in a directory format) and individuals, rather than specific tweets. Search is simplicity itself – just start to type in what you're interested in finding and Wefollow will make suggestions as you do. A search for '*librar*' will return matches for 'librarian', 'library', 'libraries', 'librarians' and 'library2'.

As can be assumed from the previous statement, most people (that is to say non-celebrities) have to register with Wefollow themselves, and it is up to them to decide which subject areas are appropriate for them. Having identified a subject area that is appropriate for the search, users will then have two options – displaying individuals by the number of followers they have, or how 'influential' they are. While it's easy to see how the former is computed, the latter is rather more difficult to work out, particularly since Wefollow don't explain their algorithms, but it can be assumed that this would include similar functionality to Socialmention*, such as their reach, the number of times they are retweeted and the extent to which they engage in conversations. Once a page of results is displayed searchers can then click on a link for an individual to discover basic information such as followers, following and updates, as well as interest rankings.

In summary, Wefollow is a useful engine to identify individuals on Twitter, but searchers should remember that it's up to users of the service to add themselves, so it shouldn't be regarded as an entirely comprehensive service.

Snapbird

Snapbird (http://snapbird.org) is another tool that goes back far beyond Twitter's self-imposed search/time limit. It also allows searchers to sign into the service and identify themselves so that they can then search their friends' tweets, direct messages and users' favourites. This can be tremendously useful if you can recall seeing something on Twitter – with the likelihood that it was one of your own contacts who tweeted it – or to check something that you can recall having tweeted, but are having difficulties finding again.

Other Twitter search engines

Backtweets, at http://backtweets.com, is an engine designed to allow users to check links to specific sites or pages. Simply type in a URL that is of interest and Backtweets will find links regardless of their form – shortened links, URLs with or without the www prefix and so on. It's a great tool to check what people are saying about a particular company, site, web page or person.

Hashtags (http://hashtags.org) allows you to search for specific hashtags, such as #librarian or #cilip, and shows you a trend by time line, with user, message and when it was posted.

Monitter (www.monitter.com) is a real-time Twitter search tool that enables you to monitor a set of keywords on Twitter. It also allows you to narrow the search to a particular geographic location, allowing you to find out what's going on in a particular part of the world.

PicFog (www.picfog.com) shows pictures from Twitter *as* they're posted, in real time. You don't even need a Twitter account to enjoy the benefits – and you can filter by keyword, location or user. PicFog does have a real-time live flow of images, but this is unfiltered, and may contain images that you do not wish to view.

PostPost (http://postpost.com) is a Twitter search engine with a difference, as it is designed to search your own Twitter stream for brands, products, references to usernames and hashtags. It also pulls up topics from your timeline so that it's easier to find them without searching.

Topsy (http://topsy.com/tweets) is a general social media search engine, but it has a good Twitter search option. It gives results that provide latest results, tweets in the last hour, day, week, month or all time, and allows searchers to re-rank their results by date or relevance.

Twellow (http://twellow.com) is a search engine to find useful individuals on Twitter. It's broken down into various categories, such as Health, News and Media, Computers and Technology and so on. Each category has various subcategories, so it's a fast and simple way to find some subject experts to follow.

Other Twitter search engines are available, and there is a more comprehensive listing at www.philb.com/twitterforlibrarians.htm.

Facebook Graph Search

At the time of writing, Facebook is rolling out the Graph Search option very slowly, and it may well take months, if not a year or more before you are able to make use of it, depending on your location. However, there is already much to be said about it, based on demonstrations. It's still very basic at the moment, but the thrust of where Facebook is taking search is very clear. To start with, it's *not* a web search engine. You can't use it to find all the pages on the web where there are references to a particular football team for example – it's designed to leverage the huge amount of content that's contained within Facebook. That itself is a really big reason why librarians and other information professionals will need to have access to Graph Search (as well as the rest of Facebook, of course), because it's a huge information resource. To deny access to Facebook is to deny access to an extremely large portion of the internet experience – I'm not going to replay all the figures associated with Facebook here; you can check out my Pinterest collection of social media statistics or run on over to Visual.ly and do a search for Facebook Statistics; either of these resources should give you the information you need.

Graph Search is starting out around the Ps – People, Places, Photographs. The idea is that you'll be able to do a search to find out what your friends like, so you could find out which board games your friends like, or which board games your married friends with children enjoy playing. You could locate a dentist based on recommendations from friends, or the restaurants in a particular area that you'll probably enjoy eating at based on trusted (i.e. friend's) recommendations. You'll be able to explore particular areas and see the photographs that friends or colleagues have taken, so you might decide to grab photographs of London that friends took on holiday, or pictures that work colleagues took of conferences that took place in London, and so on.

Don't worry – privacy will still be a big thing, and the information that you can get will be based on whatever settings people have chosen, but you'll also be able to get data on information that people have shared publicly, and that's still a large number of people – about 25% of the Facebook community. However, Facebook does have a very patchy record when it comes to privacy issues, so this is something that you'll need to look at when it comes to using the service yourself – or when your friends do!

Up until now, Facebook has been about you and your friends. There's certainly an element of leverage here, in that the Graph Search will collate a lot of that information in new and interesting ways. Does this make it a stalker's toolbox? I think that's going to be down to the settings that you choose for yourself, but it's going to make us think really hard about why we want to use Facebook and importantly how we use it. Is it just for 'friends' or are those friends actually 'colleagues'? In a promotional video Facebook produced (which can be viewed at www.facebook.com/about/ graphsearch), one of the engineers makes a really interesting point: that in future we're going to be able to use Facebook not just to find our friends and colleagues, but to find people that we perhaps should know, or who can help us do something that we currently can't.

This is where the value and importance of Facebook Graph Search starts to come into play, and hopefully you're already seeing how a library could utilize this. I would suggest that every library (public, private, corporate, academic, etc.) needs to be on Facebook. Your library needs to be found. Now of course, it can be found when people are doing generic searches on Google and the rest of the search engines, but the important point here is that if people are already logged into Facebook, they're more likely to use the search option in the future – particularly if they've found that it works well for them. So if you're not there, you won't be thought of by the searcher; it will be as if you don't exist. In exactly the same way a few years ago I would have argued that a library or business needed to be on the internet, because who uses the printed Yellow Pages any more? If you're not on the net, you don't exist. If you're not on Facebook, pretty soon you won't exist either – it really is that simple.

So – the library needs to have a Facebook presence; it's becoming vital. However, that's only stage one. Stage two is that library and other professional staff also need to be on Facebook, so that they can be found. For example – I have an interest in American History (the Civil War to be precise) and if I'm going to the USA to speak at a conference, I'm going to be keen to see if I can fit in some visits to places connected with the Civil War that will interest me. Yes, of course, I can do a general search and get some stuff, but that's still very clinical. However – if I can see who is going to the conference, and they're friends of mine, I can use Graph Search to find out if any of their friends are into the same interests, or work at a useful library, and maybe I can get an introduction to hook up to an expert quickly. Because of the friendship element, I suspect that I'll have a much richer experience than if I just wander into the local museum or library. However, for this to work, that person with the Civil War interest needs to be actively talking about it on Facebook – they have to be engaging, writing about it, mentioning the really great restaurant at the edge of a battlefield that's worth going to, or particular sites, and sharing their photographs. So we're going to have to have an entirely new level of engagement with Facebook for that to work well, and we're also going to have to change – to an extent – our concept of privacy, yet again. If that friend of a friend keeps their interest private, I'm not going to have a chance to make that connection. However, if their information is public, it's a great contact for me. This doesn't mean that everything you do on Facebook all of a sudden has to be public – not at all. However it does mean that we're going to have to think very carefully about what we keep private and what we make available to all and sundry, or indeed if we should have different Facebook accounts for different purposes (which Facebook doesn't like of course, but hey, why should they have all the fun?)

If you – as a professional – have expertise in a particular area, you probably want to share it. You want to help people, or to promote your organization or your library. You want to be able to reach out into a wider community, and Facebook is offering you a chance to do exactly that. If I'm going to a particular part of the country and I have an interest in local history, wouldn't it be great to be able to see a collection of old photographs or prints of that area which have been shared on Facebook by the librarian in the local public library? If I have a few moments I may then decide to pop into that library to look and see what other stuff is available for me to use. Simply by doing what it is that we do – preserving and presenting information, and working with communities to get more stuff available, we're getting out to that wider audience, and increasing our profile.

This also has an advantage for Facebook as well, of course. The one thing that Facebook can't cope with is inertia. This isn't so much a problem for Google, because there are always new things happening that it can index and make available to us, but if we're stuck at six Facebook friends that's not really adding that much to the Facebook universe, because you're not sharing content widely or making new connections. However, if you're active on Facebook, and doing more, sharing more and contributing more content Facebook is growing. So, if we move away from the concept of 'friends' and more towards the concept of 'colleagues' there's an entirely different option for Facebook to grow, as we make more friends and share more stuff.

Make no bones about it though, there's a huge impact in other areas as well. If we're moving away from an organizational presence to a personal presence (and I've argued that point well enough in the past, as it's the way that we need to go), how does an organization respond? Sure, someone can still be responsible for putting up the local history photographs but someone needs to decide to do that, at some level. If we're going to encourage professionals to share their expertise for the benefit of both the organization and the community, we have to let them do it themselves. This is not going to go down very well with the web development team or the people who produce the council guidelines on internet use. I would argue that it's our role as information professionals to point out that Facebook is not what it once was, and that it needs to be regarded in a completely new way.

Does this require us all to sit glued to Facebook at the expense of other methods of communicating? No, I don't believe that it does. It's perfectly easy to share content across social media with a quick click of a button. As we are looking for information, then finding it, we can do the next thing, which is to recommend it. However, it does also mean that yes, I believe that we need to spend more time using social media, and that has to move further up the list of priorities. I think we'll be seeing social media (or real-time media) roles within information centres, and it should be part of the role that everyone has, not just a few people. We cannot escape it, nor should we – in fact we should be actively embracing it. For a library and its staff to flourish we cannot expect people to come to us in the building. We have to go to them, and they are on Facebook, Twitter and the rest.

So, in summary, Graph Search is important for the profession because:

➡ It gives us access to more information to be able to do our jobs better and more effectively.
➡ It will quickly put us in contact with people whom we can contact for information, and who we may have a link with.
➡ It's a way that we have of promoting our library to both existing and new members.
➡ We can use it to provide more information than we've been able to do in the past.
➡ It's a very positive way to demonstrate our own skills and abilities.
➡ It gives us more control over the information that we have and how we demonstrate it.

There's another way that's now available to us, which means that we can virtually leave the buildings behind us, and connect directly with our members. How Graph Search will develop into the future is the subject of much speculation at the moment, but in truth, unless you are one of the developers at the company, there's no real way of knowing. However, there's no doubt that this is a subject area that we shall really need to take notice of in the coming months and years.

Google+ search

Google is very aware of the threat that Facebook poses, so it is doing its best to counter that by creating its own social network. It's had two attempts at this already, Google Wave and Google Buzz, but for various reasons both of these failed quite spectacularly. Google has now established Google+, which is being heavily integrated into all of their other offerings, such as Gmail, YouTube and, of course, search. We have already seen that if you are logged into your Google account the engine can return personalized results based on what your friends and contacts are looking at or blogging about or '+1'ing' – which is a horrible contraction, but essentially means the same as 'liking' something on Facebook. This time though, Google may well have got social networking right, since it now has over 340 million active users and is the second most popular network behind Facebook (www.zdnet.com/google-moves-up-to-second-place-in-social-networks-7000010372).

There are various ways that Google+ can be searched. When logged into the system users are presented with a menu down the left-hand side of the screen, allowing access to things such as their profile, photographs, events and communities for example, the main body of the screen is taken up with posts that people in their network have put up, and an opportunity to link with more suggested people on the right-hand side of the screen. At the very top is the ubiquitous search bar. When typing in a search Google automatically adds in suggestions based on the characters keyed in, and these will commonly include people's names, Google+ pages and communities. Once the search has been run Google will display a list of posts in the main body of the screen, a right-hand side bar of 'people and pages' with an option to add any of them to the searcher's own profile, a list of communities that match the subject area of the search, and a list of trending words or phrases. Finally, if people have +1'd a particular site this will also be listed as well.

The results can be filtered; Google provides an option to search for 'Everything' or various other more focused searches, and this is available after the initial search has been completed. It's therefore possible to limit a search to People and Pages, Communities, Google+ posts, Hangouts (video chats that have been recorded and made publicly available), Photographs and Events. Finally, there are options to limit a search to people that are in the searcher's own social groups (generally referred to as 'circles'), posts from or to the searcher, or those which were sent from a particular location.

Searchers can also locate specific communities that are of interest to them by clicking on the 'communities' menu option, and then searching for subjects of interest. For example, a search for *'library OR libraries OR librarian'* will return communities such as the UK Library Community, Library

〉 〉

Technology, Australian Teacher Librarian Network, Libraries and Librarians and several dozen more.

Surprisingly, the search options in Google+ are not terribly exciting or efficient, since they only provide the searcher with very basic information – almost like a stepping stone, in fact. Consequently, it may be better to try other tools to find the information that's needed, rather than Google+'s native search interface.

Search Google+ with Google

Perhaps the easiest way to search Google+ is to actually just use the normal Google interface. Since Google+ has its own site at http://plus.google.com, the '*site:plus.google.com*' option works well. Consequently, if you needed to find librarians who have lived in London and work at the British Library a search such as '*site:plus.google.com "lived * london" "librarian" "works * british library"*' would work well.

FindPeopleOnPlus

If you need to find people on Google+ the FindPeopleOnPlus tool at http://findpeopleonplus.com is an excellent search engine. The home page displays the usual search box, and you can type in your preferred keyword, or alternatively choose search options such as brands, schools, countries, places lived, occupations or employers. A search for the keyword 'librarian' returns over 13,000 people, with their name, biography, a summary of their location, school and occupation and a thumbnail shot of their avatar or profile picture. Results can then be filtered by profile type (brand or person), relationship, age range, education, employer, and so on. The main disadvantage that I found was that there didn't seem to be any real way of ranking the results – my 13,000 librarians were displayed in a seemingly random order, so the filtering option becomes very important very quickly! Finally, only about 45 million Google+ users have been indexed which – while it's a lot of people – not exactly comprehensive when compared to the total number of users.

Other subject-specific social search engines

Not all social media search engines will search across all platforms to pull data back from a wide variety of sources – some will only search a very small number of resources, and indeed others will limit themselves to a single resource. That should not be taken as meaning that they are of less value, however – in fact it can be argued that because they only pull data from one specific source they are able to do so more effectively than the 'jack of all trades' engines previously discussed. There are a great many of these engines, and I don't intend to even try and cover them all, but I will highlight several that I think are particularly useful, and also link to several others as well.

Qwant

Qwant (www.qwant.com) was launched in January 2013, having been in development for a couple of years. It's an interesting engine, because it really tries very hard to do a whole range of different things. It says of itself

> QWANT offers the first web and social service, where you can dynamically use the power of your own brain to refine search in classic Web, Live, Social, Media and Shopping verticals so as to reach exactly the information and the people you are looking for, those that answer your exact query of the moment.
>
> www.qwant.com/about

What this means in practice is that you run a search and get six datasets to play with. These include an image set, web-based results, live search results, which are website-based, but which only pull in recent updates, social content from Twitter and Google+ and shopping-based results. It's a helpful engine in that it does pull in a great deal of content very quickly and although the page of results is very cramped it's a good tool if you want to start with a range of data from a multitude of different resources.

Lanyrd

Lanyrd (http://lanyrd.com) is a social search engine that focuses on conferences and professional and hobbyist events. It also includes workshops, unconferences (an unconference is an event which is informal in nature, with content and sessions being decided on the day by the participants themselves), evening talks, conventions and so on. Lanyrd is geared towards knowledge-sharing events with sessions and participants.

Lanyrd works in a manner similar to Wikipedia, in that anyone can add a conference, list speakers, sessions, events and so on. Other people can then

〉 〉

edit the information as necessary. While this does at least in theory open the resource up to vandalism a track is kept of all changes, and any inappropriate information can be quickly deleted.

Anyone can search the social conference directory, but in order to add or edit content it's necessary to log into the service using a Twitter account. Search is simple – just type in a subject of interest into the search box and retrieve matches. For example a search for '*library*' will return information on the topic of libraries, with details of both future and past conferences. Searchers can filter in a number of different ways – by time (past or future events), type (sessions, people, topics, venue and so on), place (country, state and city), topic, person, coverage, year and specific conference.

Each entry has fields that can contain information on specific talks, timings, speakers, links to speaker profiles, access to slides or files used in presentations, links to publications produced by speakers and Twitter session hashtags, as well as other information, such as short URLs and related books. Lanyrd is a unique resource which has a wide variety of uses for the ambitious searcher, enabling them to find speakers, subject experts, publications, events by tweet, and resources by date, location and subject matter. The archival nature of the resource is also very valuable, providing access to content that might otherwise be deleted once the event has finished.

Openbook

The Openbook search engine, at http://youropenbook.org, searches through publicly available Facebook updates. The engine uses Facebook's own search service, so to that extent it doesn't offer anything that Facebook doesn't already provide, but the value of the system is that it's not necessary to log into Facebook in order to search. Furthermore, because of the particularly complex and confusing nature of Facebook privacy options, this engine allows you to see exactly what everyone else can see. Unfortunately Openbook is not being currently maintained, but it's still a useful tool to have available, if for no other reason than to check that your own updates are private!

Likebutton

If you use Facebook on a regular basis you will be used to seeing your friends and colleagues 'liking' or recommending a wide variety of resources. You'll also doubtless have experienced the frustration of knowing that a friend liked something but you're unable to find it again, or you may simply wish to keep up to speed with all of those recommendations, particularly if you follow hundreds or perhaps thousands of people. This is where the Likebutton site, at http://likebutton.com, comes into play. You can login using your Facebook credentials, and the search resource will then pull together recommendations from your friends across a wide variety of different subject areas, such as Popular resources, news, apple, tech, style and so on. It doesn't have a search option, but it does refresh every few minutes and it is possible to go back in time to view more results.

Summary

It never fails to both amaze and depress me when I see people – including some in the information profession – who seem to think that social media (and by implication searching social media-based content) is somehow trivial, unimportant and a waste of time. I cannot express strongly enough that this is absolutely not the case. What we are now seeing is a fundamental change in the way that search works.

Traditional engines such as Google focus on web pages, and that's not a surprise – that's what they have always done. However, while web pages are still vitally important, that's not where the development is taking place any longer. A website is increasingly the place where people and organizations put the 'facts and figures'. If I need to know the phone number of an organization, I'll go to the website, and if I need to know how to get there, or want to see their most recent reports, that's also where I'll go. If you want to read any of my articles on search then again – off you should go to my website. However, if you're more interested in my views on the most recent search engine that I've reviewed, you're better off visiting my weblog, and if you want the latest news from a company, or you want to see if a library is open because there's heavy snow, visit their Twitter feeds or Facebook pages.

We're already seeing the effect of the rise of social media and real-time search – Google is increasingly putting its own Google+ pages into search, Bing and Blekko are incorporating Facebook content, and Facebook is producing its own search engine to keep people on its website, as we've already seen. The future of search has its own chapter later (Chapter 16) and

〉 〉

I'll go into more detail there, but suffice it to say – any searcher is going to ignore social media results and search engines at his or her peril, since traditional search methods are no longer enough.

CHAPTER 8

>> Visual searching

Introduction

In Chapter 5 we saw that clustering search engines such as Carrot² were able to display results in a non-linear form, by the use of folders and grouping like results together. There are various advantages to this approach, such as allowing searchers to stop thinking that the first result is in some way 'the best'. A logical next step on from this category is to be able to see the websites themselves directly in the search results, rather than having to click on a link to go to them. This chapter will look at search engines that use this approach to display results. However, that's only one side of the visual search coin – rather than seeing search results portrayed in a visual format you might actually just want to search for images themselves (which of course has a very visual component in the way that results are displayed) and this chapter will also look at some image search options in detail.

Traditional search engines

As you might expect, traditional search engines were quick to start offering the ability to view web pages directly from the results page. Google provided a 'fly-out' option which a searcher could simply click on in order to obtain an advance view of the page. Bing used to supply something similar – in fact their offering predated that of Google – but it's currently not operational, although it may return at some point in the future. Exalead incorporates thumbnails of results pages directly into the organic results that it returns, although, since they are rather small, they are of very limited value. None of the other major engines is currently providing this type of 'look ahead' functionality, unfortunately.

Free-text visual search engines

Some of the lesser-known free-text search engines are providing access to screen previews, however, so before we move onto those engines that work solely by displaying visual results, let's take a look at a few of them, in case you want to dip your toe in the water.

Slikk!

Slikk! (www.slikk.com) formerly known as SearchLion, has the display of web pages right at the heart of its results. Users are able to click on an 'open' icon, to view the returned result directly on the Slikk! page of results. Futhermore, users can open up a series of tabs and flick between them in order to compare page results. The tab view can be moved around the screen, enlarged or shown below results or as a quarter screen. This allows users to neatly and easily navigate around other sites while still remaining at the search engine.

WebNocular

The WebNocular search engine, which is located at www.webnocular.com, works using a combination of Google's fly-out option and Exalead's thumbnail approach. Each result has a thumbnail displayed to the left of the result, with a 'Quick Look' option that a searcher can click on to open the web page on the WebNocular screen. This is displayed in a fully functioning scrolling frame, allowing the user to explore the returned website result directly from the search engine.

Simploos

The Simploos engine, at http://beta.simploos.com, is a tool that allows searchers to obtain results from Google or Yahoo!, so it's acting almost like a go-between. Rather than loading a list of web results, Simploos immediately starts to display results on the screen for the searcher to view. This can be viewed simply by moving the mouse around the screen. At the top of the page small thumbnails are displayed and the user can easily scroll through the results extremely quickly. This is a very elegant solution and is a superb way of very quickly going from result to result.

〉 〉

Visual search engines

Readers can be forgiven for being slightly confused at the outset by the difference between free-text search engines and visual search engines. The free-text search engines just mentioned have a very visual component in their search results; rather than just providing a straightforward text listing of web pages the searcher is encouraged to look at thumbnails of pages that accompany the text about a page. A visual search engine, however, as we shall see in the examples below, is an engine that extensively or entirely uses visual information, perhaps just in the form of web page screen shots that the searcher can scroll through.

RedZ

The RedZ search engine (http://redz.com/home) icon is a red zebra-like creature, but I'm not sure if the name came before the icon or if it was the other way round! Suffice it to say that RedZ has been available since 2007. It provides results in the form of an arc of web pages, as can be seen in Figure 8.1.

Figure 8.1 The RedZ search results page

Searchers can click to go from one page of results to the next. Unfortunately it's not possible to maximize the thumbnail, and clicking on it takes you directly to the web page in question. It's also not the current version of the page, but is instead a cached version; the engines mentioned above do draw a current version of the page directly from the site.

Searchers can also use RedZ to find images, but there is no real way of limiting to size, colour, format and so on. Moreover, when an image is clicked on, RedZ takes users to a framed version of the page which includes the image, which isn't terribly helpful. Finally, there is a video option that displays a screenshot from a YouTube video, with the link taking users directly to it.

Spacetime3D

The Spacetime3D search engine, at http://search.spacetime.com, is very similar in concept to RedZ in that it provides searchers with an arc of images, and these can then be flicked through by clicking and dragging with the mouse. Results are pulled from Google, with a maximum of 30 pages to scroll through. Spacetime3D is rather more effective when it comes to images, however – although searchers are limited to a total of 19 results, they load quickly and are much larger than the thumbnails provided with engines such as Google. Spacetime also offers results from Wikipedia and YouTube in the same format.

Search-Cube

While visual search engines do provide access to results in an non-textual format obviously, they can often still be very linear, by showing one image or result after another. However, Search-Cube, at www.search-cube.com, works in an entirely different way and can truly be described as a visual search engine. It presents results in a three dimensional cube interface, previewing up to 96 results, be they websites, videos or images. A search for the word '*librarian*' for example will result in a cube being displayed on the screen, with each side of the cube displaying a 4 x 4 collection of images which relate back to specific web pages, giving the searcher 96 results.

The cube can be moved along all planes by the use of the mouse and keyboard. There are limitations with the engine of course – the 96 results limit may be considered one, but the greater issue I think is that it's almost impossible to tell if the result you look at is simply an image, or an image from a web page or a video. However, apart from that, it's an intriguing and different way to look at results, and may well appeal to students and children in particular. The results themselves are drawn from Google, so searchers can rely on comprehensive results.

〉 〉

Oolone

The Oolone search engine (www.oolone.com) also uses a display of pages similar to those of RedZ, but instead of an arc of pages, Oolone uses a figure-of-eight display, and searchers work their way around the display simply by pressing left and right options on the screen. I can see no real purpose to this and it has no effect on the results. The results screen provides a thumbnail of the page that's been returned and basic details such as the URL and the title of the page. Clicking on the image of the page loads the result into the browser window. It's an attractive search engine, and has some advanced search functionality such as '*site:*', but irritatingly there is no advanced search option, so searchers are forced to guess functionality, rather than having it displayed for them.

TouchGraph

This is an experimental search engine, but it has been around for several years and shows no sign of disappearing, so I thought it was worthwhile including. You can find this engine at www.touchgraph.com. Search results are pulled from Google and displayed in a two-pane screen, with the right-hand side being reserved for a mind map approach, the search term in the middle and website results coming out in spokes from that. Users can zoom in or out of the results and change the spacing. They can also export the data or the graph itself and can make the image full screen. Searchers can also click, drag and pull the image around as necessary, so it would be a good option to use if an information professional used it while discussing results with a member of the library. TouchGraph has another interesting search feature, in that it remembers previous searches and if possible will link them together using the concept of the spokes and wheels.

The left-hand pane has three tabs, for related searches, search results in a linear form and a listing of top domains, which are clickable and can provide the searcher with extra information. Consequently, what TouchGraph really excels at is allowing people to explore the connections between related websites, using Google's 'related sites' search option.

Cluuz Search

At first glance, Cluuz (www.cluuz.com) does not appear to be much of a visual search engine, since it provides straightforward linear-based results. However, once you start to explore the results you will notice that some of them have a magnifying glass next to them (usually the results on the right-hand side of the screen) and if you click on this, the result opens up into a series of 'spoked' links. These can all be clicked on, and the screen enlarged in order to see quite a complex pattern of links between different websites, as can be seen in Figure 8.2.

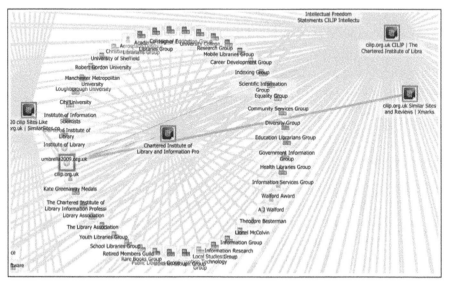

Figure 8.2 A set of visual results from Cluuz for the search 'CILIP'
Reproduced with permission of Sprylogics International

The links are sensibly sorted out – so from Figure 8.2 you can see that CILIP groups are found on the right-hand side of the 'wheel' while all of the university links are in the top left-hand quadrant. Clicking on the link allows users to discover more about the site in question. As with TouchGraph, this isn't so much a search engine that finds specific web pages that match your search query, and more of a search engine to identify and explore websites. Consequently it's useful if you are exploring a subject area of which you have limited knowledge, or if you were conducting a reference interview with a member of the library and were using this as a basis for discussion.

Quintura

Quintura (www.quintura.com) has the tag line 'see and find', and says of itself 'Visualization becomes the center of user experience replacing antiquated listings and Boolean strings'. However, having said that, it still uses a linear, numbered set of results, but at the very top of the screen there is a word cloud of other related terms. Placing the mouse cursor over any of these terms results in a small dialogue box being displayed on the screen detailing results of the original search term, plus the term chosen from the word cloud. It's a fast and effective way of seeing sets of results very quickly. For most users I suspect that the main drawback to Quintura is that it emphasizes Russian sites and terminology, which is a little offputting if you cannot speak the language.

Yometa

A final search engine in this category is Yometa (www.yometa.com), which provides yet another spin on the idea of visual search. Yometa presents the most relevant search results from Google, Bing and Yahoo! in a visual Venn diagram approach. Consequently users see all the top results from the three engines simultaneously, showing four results at a time in order of relevance. Therefore, any result(s) in the very centre of the diagram are especially relevant, as they have been found by all the engines, while results further away are less relevant. Users can, if they wish, simply display results from a combination of engines (such as Google and Bing or Yahoo! and Google) by clicking on the appropriate section of the diagram.

> **>> Did you know?**
> There are more than 227,230,423 Creative Commons licensed photographs available (http://creative commons. org/licenses/by-sa/3.0).

Image search engines

Many search engines – certainly all of the major ones – provide access to images as part of their search offering. However, there are a number of resources that just work with images, so in this section I will cover the traditional approach and also look at a number of engines that specialize.

Google Image Search

Perhaps the best of the general search engines is Google, particularly due to its innovative approach of providing the ability to search by using an image provided by the searcher, using the camera icon in the search box (see p.46). Alternatively, and more traditionally, simply type in the search term(s) that are appropriate and Google will return images for you. Search syntax such as

‹ ‹

'*site:*' can also be included to limit results in the way that was previously discussed in Chapter 3. Google provides results based on the filename of the image, the alternative HTML text tag, which can be used to describe an image, and any image that is physically close on the page to the search term. Results are displayed in a scrolling format, rather than page by page, and can be explored by positioning the cursor over them. The image will then be presented in a small dialogue window, with opportunities to see the title of the image, the URL, the size and a brief segment of text. There are options to search for similar images, or for the same image in different sizes.

Google Image Search provides a variety of extremely helpful ways of narrowing down the millions of results that get returned. For example, searchers can limit by subject or personal. A search for 'librarian' and limited by subject returns images of librarians at work, male librarians, old librarians, funny librarian and so on. Images can be limited by size, colours (full colour, black and white or specific colours), and by type, such as face, photograph, clip art or line drawing.

There is an advanced image search option, but in common with general Google policy it's quite hard to find. Either visit the URL https://www.google.com/advanced_image_search or click on the small cog wheel in the top right-hand corner, and choose the Advanced search option. Searchers are then in a position to limit by image size in more detail – both by pixel and file size, aspect ratio, region, limit by sexual content, file type and by usage rights. This latter option is based on the Creative Commons licences and more detail can be found on them at http://creativecommons.org.

Bing Image Search

Bing Image Search is very similar in concept to that of Google, although it should be pointed out that Bing introduced the concept of scrolling images instead of pages, and Google subsequently adopted it as well. There is little to choose between the functionality of the two rivals, as Bing also has options for searching by subject, size, colour, style, layout and people. However, the final option does include the ability to limit by head and shoulders or just faces. In common with Google, searchers can find out more about an image by placing the cursor over it, in order to view title, size (pixel and file), URL, and different sizes of the same image.

Yahoo! Image Search

The search function is somewhat hindered if users have the safe search function turned on; as we have already seen in the context of Google searches, a search for 'blue tit' did not return any results at all, since they 'may contain adult-oriented content'.

Images are displayed in individual squares, which often cuts off part of the picture, which isn't helpful. Once the image is highlighted by running the mouse over it, it will pop out, providing title, size (both in pixels and kilobytes) and the URL of the originating site. Yahoo! provides a small variety of image filters, such as time, size, colour and usage rights, but in comparison to those of Google and Bing they are very limiting and quite disappointing.

Other traditional search engines

Most of the major web search engines offer an image option. There is in all honesty very little to choose between them. Scrolling results are favoured by most engines, and a dialogue box is a common standard. Obviously if you have a personal preference for a search engine you will in all likelihood use that, rather than chop and change between engines. However, there may be times when you want to really explore the availability of images, and consequently it is worth taking a look at some of the many image search engines that are available.

Flickr

Flickr is a resource that is designed to allow its users to upload, tag and share the images that they have created. They can be added to different groups and notes can be added to them, and they can also be made available to other users via the Creative Commons options. Flickr has over 6 billion images and the vast majority of these can be searched; users do, however, have the option of restricting access to specific images if they so wish.

> **>> Did you know?**
> 20 million photos are viewed on Flickr every minute (www.mediabistro.com/alltwitter/internet-minute_b38168).

Search is very straightforward – simply type in the term(s) that are appropriate; there is limited use of search operators, so it's usually best to be as simple and straightforward as possible when choosing terms. Results are displayed with a number of different options – they can be sorted by

‹ ‹

relevance, currency or 'interesting' (Flickr uses various arcane methods to work out what makes a photograph interesting, often based on the amount of activity it inspires in users). Photographs can be viewed small or medium-sized, or with details, such as title, views, comments, notes, locations and tags. Flickr also provides access to photographs based on groups, specific photographers and tag clusters. A search term such as 'librarian' will return over 135,000 images, links to the 'Libraries and Librarians' and 'Libraries from around the world' groups, a user called the Food Librarian photographer, and the option of searching on tag clusters such as library, books and libraries and librarians.

Searches can also be made to directly identify groups that Flickr users have created to share their images and to discuss them, and you can also search for specific individuals in order to see the photographs that they have publicly shared. There is an advanced search option which allows users to restrict their searches to tags or full text of the image description, and searches can also exclude terms as well. Searching can be limited in a variety of ways, depending on if you have an account to Flickr (which is free) or if you're searching without one. Searches can be limited to safesearch, and this is something that I would generally advise; safesearch is automatically turned on by default if searchers are not searching via their own account, and while there is a lot of adult material on Flickr it is generally well contained behind a Flickr firewall. Once you have your own account, however, you may accidentally find material that is objectionable. Content can also be searched by content type – photographs, videos, screenshots and screencasts, and illustration and animation. It's also possible to break the first option down further, to just photographs or just videos. Flickr includes a date search function, with photographs taken or posted before or after specific dates. Finally, there is a Creative Commons option, to limit the search to licensed content. This is a tremendously valuable option, as it is possible to find images that you can reuse without seeking specific permission. If you need images for a PowerPoint presentation or to include in a report, this is a fast and effective approach.

Flickr-related search engines

Flickr is an extremely popular site and a number of other search engines have been created to provide access to the wealth of data that is contained on it. While the actual images are exactly the same, the interfaces and search

〉 〉

options will differ. Behold (http://behold.cc) emphasizes Creative
Commons search options, as does the FlickrCC engine, at http://flickrcc.
bluemountains.net/flickrCC/index.php, and the Flickr Storm engine at
www.zoo-m.com/flickr-storm works in the same way. However, Phrasr
(www.pimpampum.net/en/content/phrasr) is an interactive web-based
application that uses Flickr images to illustrate the phrases that users submit.
Finally, Tag Galaxy pulls images from Flickr and creates a 'solar system
galaxy' concept, with a central sun (the original search term) with planets of
related terms around it. Clicking on a 'planet' calls images from Flickr,
which then cover the surface of the 'planet'. While it is rather a novelty, it is
a quick and effective way to scroll around a lot of images very quickly in an
enjoyable way.

Reverse image searching

As already mentioned (p. 46), with Google it's possible to upload an image,
or to provide an image URL in order to use that as the basis of a search.
There are lots of good reasons for doing this – while a picture speaks a
thousand words, if you don't know what any of those words are going to
be, it's not terribly helpful. However, by uploading an image of a plant, for
example, or perhaps a photograph of a work of art, you may quickly obtain
the thousand words to provide you with the information that you need.

TinEye (www.tineye.com) is a reverse search engine that has been
designed for exactly this purpose. Upload an image, drag and drop, or
provide a URL, and the search engine can begin its work. It searches over 2
billion images in less than 2 seconds to provide the searcher with results
based on best matches, most changed (in terms of colour, aspect, inclusion
in other images and parts of an image) and size. To that extent, it's a far
more useful engine than Google's reverse search, the 'most changed' being
an extremely powerful way of identifying how images have been used.

RevIMG search engine, at www.revimg.net, finds images according to its
matching algorithm based on shape, dimensions and colour resemblance.
The resulting links are listed by matching percentage. The unique selling
point of this engine is that search results can be limited to various
categories, such as flags, logos, symbols and so on. This provides a neat and
effective shortcut that other engines are missing.

Finally in this category there is Macroglossa (www.macroglossa.com),
which has five different subject categories; animals, biological, panoramic,
artistic and botanical. It works in the same way as the previous engines –

simply upload an image, choose the category and it will return related images for you.

Multi-search image engines

There are a small number of search engines that will trawl through a wide variety of different sites to return information and images to searchers in exactly the same way as traditional multi- and meta-search engines (see Chapter 6). For example, Spezify (www.spezify.com) searches through sources such as Amazon, Instagram, Twitter, Facebook, eBay and Flickr looking for images that match search queries. As you may imagine from such an eclectic mix, the engine makes little distinction between media types, so a search will retrieve images, tweets, eBay sales and so on. The results screen is a scrolling display and, while it's excellent for browsing, focused, accurate search is very difficult. Oskope (www.oskope.com) lets searchers browse through images culled from a variety of sites such as Amazon, eBay, Flickr, and Fotolia. Results can be viewed in a grid format, as a stack, a pile, graph or a list. The images can then be moved around the screen, allowing searchers to group them as they feel appropriate.

Geographically based image search engines

There may well be times when you need to find images of a certain place. It's certainly possible to search traditional engines, or even to run a search via Flickr, but as there are several engines that focus on this specific aspect of search it makes sense to investigate them. For example, Ookaboo, at http://ookaboo.com/o/pictures, covers a wide variety of countries, structures, museums and artefacts from different locations. Panoramio, at www.panoramio.com, works in the same way – simply type in the place that interests you, and it will then display a Google map, dotted with photographic images of the surrounding area. Additionally, however, there are displays of popular images, recent images, specific places and interior shots. There is a social element to the engine as well, since you can register and comment on the images that you find, as well as adding your own of course.

Royalty-free image engines

When an image is published on the internet, in most instances, the copyright to that image is owned by someone. In many cases it's possible to find the image that you need via a Creative Commons search, but not always. Therefore it's necessary to search further. A number of engines list images that are royalty-free, and may simply require a link back and attribution to the photographer. It doesn't always mean that the image will be free, however; commercial use may well incur a cost, or if you want an image with a high resolution there may also be a fee. It's always worth checking through the small print of these sites in order to be clear and confident of what you can legally do with an image.

Everystockphoto is a 'license-specific photo search engine' and can be found at www.everystockphoto.com. It indexes and searches millions of freely licensed photographs from a wide variety of sources, including Flickr and MorgueFile, for example. Users are encouraged to visit the site which contains the image in order to see exactly what licence is being applied to any particular image.

Freefoto (www.freefoto.com/index.jsp) has over 125,000 images in 183 sections with 3640 categories.

MorgueFile, at www.morguefile.com, allows free use of the images on its site, although you are encouraged to make a donation.

Pixabay (http://pixabay.com) was created as a repository of outstanding public domain images. You can freely use any of the images from the site in a digital or printed format for personal or commercial use without any attribution to the original creator. There are currently over 70,000 images available in photographic and clipart format.

The Wikimedia Commons at http://commons.wikimedia.org/wiki/ Main_Page is a database of 13,399,959 freely usable media files to which anyone can contribute. As well as images, this includes sounds and videos as well. The database can be searched by topic, location, type, author, licence and source. Each result provides a good-quality image (some going back well over a century), description, source data and, very importantly, copyright information, including where the image is copyright free and for what reasons. It's an excellent resource, making available public domain and freely licensed educational content. As the name would suggest, everyone can edit and add material to the database, and can copy, use and modify any of the files freely, as long as they follow the terms specified by the author.

Specialist image search engines

This section is by way of a miscellany; there are so many different types of images that fulfil so many different functions that there are many that simply refuse to go into a specific category. So I apologize for the random nature of this final collection of engines, but as you read through them I hope you'll understand why!

The IconArchive, at www.iconarchive.com, and IconFinder, at www.iconfinder.com, are two excellent engines that will assist users in finding appropriate icons to use on web pages, in presentations or in a printed format. Between the two they list over 500,000 icons in various categories.

The Vintage Ad Browser (www.vintageadbrowser.com) is a fascinating engine which has over 100,000 vintage advertisements to explore, with categories ranging from airlines to Xmas. This is a sister site of the CoverBrowser site (www.coverbrowser.com), which has over 450,000 covers of comics, books and DVDs.

Karen's Whimsy, at http://karenswhimsy.com, was an interesting find. The site says of itself 'On the following pages you will find hundreds of beautiful images gleaned from my collection of old books, magazines, and postcards. They are all from material printed prior to 1923 and are in the public domain.' It certainly is a whimsical collection, and one that it would be easy to spend a lot of time hunting through. There's a basic category arrangement, and my feeling is that it's a collection that would suit crafters and hobbyists, rather than people who needed images for reports and presentations. No library images, but six clipart images of books.

Niice is a 'search engine with taste' at www.niice.co. This is a search engine for designers. It pulls in image content from a very small selection of sites at the moment, but some of the images it finds are unique and high-quality. It's not clear from either the engine or the page that you land on what the copyright situation is for each image, but if you're looking for inspiration, this is a great idea.

Twicsy (http://twicsy.com) is often referred to as the 'Twitter pics engine'. Apparently, there are about a million pictures uploaded onto Twitter every day. Twicsy is one of the ways of searching for them. Simply pop in your preferred search term, and see what it comes up with. It's a fairly random collection, as you might expect, and results often have little to do with the term you input, so it's not brilliant. You get results from the past hour, past day, and so on. Please be aware that images which are NSFW (Not Safe For Work) do often turn up as well. It has a particular value in that it highlights images that are related to trending words, phrases or hashtags in Twitter at any particular moment in time. So if you need to grab some images quickly about a big sporting event, volcano or politician,

› ›

Twicsy is certainly worth having on your list.

If you take a lot of pictures and put them up on the web, sooner or later someone may well 'borrow' one in order to use it themselves. They may mean to steal it, they may not, but either way, it's out there and out of your control. You could of course use one of the reverse image engines to look for rogue copies, but there is another approach that you could take. 'Who stole my pictures?' (https://addons.mozilla.org/en-US/firefox/addon/who-stole-my-pictures/#) is a Firefox browser add-on that you can use to try and identify use of images elsewhere. Simply find your image, right mouse-click and choose the 'Who stole my pictures?' option. The resource will then search through five different image search engine sites trying to find it. What you do then is up to you of course. However, if you think laterally, it's a very good way to identify sites that are using specific images, and it's likely that they will be covering the same kind of subject area.

> **>> Did you know?**
> The total number of internet users in the world (approximately) is 2,293,851,258 (www.realtimestatistics.org).

The internet is home to an increasingly large number of 'infographics'. These are images that provide factual data in a visual format, making it much easier to understand or visualize the subject under discussion. They are particularly useful to include in reports or presentations but they are not easy to find – a basic image search for the subject of interest plus the word infographics may help, but it's certainly not a way to guarantee success. The **Visual.ly** engine is a good solution to this problem. If you point your browser to http://visual.ly you will quickly learn that the engine is 'the largest data visualization showcase in the world'. (It can also be used to help create your own data visualizations as well.) I ran a search for the term 'librarian' and it returned several useful graphics for me – how much librarians are paid, the 'anatomy of a librarian' and the evolution of librarians being just three examples. Search is quite primitive, but the time spent researching is usually well paid in terms of the value of the images that get returned.

Summary

Hunting for photographs or visual data is a fertile field for the researcher. There are not only a large number of image search engines available, many with their own databases, but they provide filters in a way that traditional text-based searching simply cannot manage. Furthermore, with visual search engines, results are turned into images which can be browsed, shared and used as discussion points with enquirers. The sensible searcher will however always be aware that NSFW images may pop up every now and then, even with the strictest search engine, so it is as well to warn enquirers or, if demonstrating, try your searches out first. This is particularly true in my case, since I am unfortunate enough to have an American namesake who had a long career as a gay porn star. Needless to say I have to be very careful if I ever demonstrate image searching using personal examples!

CHAPTER 9

)) **Finding people**

Introduction

If you talk to people about the internet, and specifically ask them what they think that it is, you will get a wide variety of answers. Information professionals will talk about the rich range of data that is available at our fingertips, sales people will tell you how much money can be made from product placement and online shops, technical folk will wax lyrical about the intricacies of the programming that goes to create the resources that we use, and so on.

However, many of them will not think of saying that when it comes right down to the basics, the internet is about people. People provide information for other people to use, it's people who buy the products and yet others who put the programs to good use. If you look at statistics for Facebook, Twitter or Google+ one of the main metrics that is always referred to is the number of people who use each resource. So – if the internet is all about people, it would be reasonable to expect that it's a great resource from which to be able to find them. However, this is unfortunately very far from the truth. It's extraordinarily difficult to find particular people – not least because there are so many with the same name. Added to that is the fact that genealogy is a major interest with internet users and you find that you're not only searching for people who are alive today, but those who have been dead for hundreds of years. This problem has further been compounded by the explosion of social media, and people who would never have thought of being available electronically are suddenly tweeting, blogging and connecting with friends on social media sites such as Facebook.

There are different approaches that can be used to try to identify specific people. The first is obviously to use standard search engines in the hope that the person that you are looking for is active on the internet and is referenced on web pages. You can use specific e-mail search engines that will attempt to identify them, try a 'people finder' to look for individuals, or try a small number of social media tools that will try and find where specific names are used. Then, of course, there are the times when you want to find someone and you have absolutely no idea who they are, because you're just looking for an expert in a particular subject area. It then becomes necessary to consider where and how such people will be identifying themselves on the internet, and then find key tools to track them down. Finally, one should also consider the unpleasant aspect of internet stalking, and the ways in which we should all protect ourselves – this is something that I'll address in more detail further in the chapter.

Standard search engines

An obvious first port of call is the usual suspects, engines such as Google and Bing. There's no magic to this type of search – just type in the person's name and see what comes up. I'll use my name as the example here – not particularly out of an attempt at ego boosting, but simply because it would be unfair to put any friends or colleagues under the spotlight! A Google search for Phil Bradley returned 33,600,000 hits, and 480,000 when searched as the phrase '*"phil bradley"*'. Out of interest, the results for this search when I ran them for the 3rd edition of the *Advanced Internet Searcher's Handbook* were 250,000 and 5400 respectively – something of a jump! Bing provided me with 16,300,000 and 21,200 results – a considerably smaller set to work from. Both engines, however, gave similar information – websites, blogs, Twitter accounts, Flickr feeds, LinkedIn accounts and so on. It is interesting to note the sheer amount of social-based data that turns up in searches, in comparison to even a couple of years ago.

Of course, a search like this is not very effective – a quick tour of the results shows me that my namesakes include a porn star, a country and western singer, a basket weaver, a baseball star and so on. The search also ignores the fact that in some places people will refer to Philip or even Phillip and then there are also the times when middle initials are included as well. It's possible to use the asterisk in a Google search which will result in something such as '*Phil * Bradley*' or even '*"Phil * Bradley"*', which will return a different set of results again. Now, while this search may well catch instances of my name where it is included as Phil W. Bradley or even Phil W. H. Bradley (I know, I know, my mother had a thing for

〉〉

middle names), it's not going to catch Philip Bradley, and it will also give me results such as Phil and Mary Bradley. In the past it was possible to use the tilde symbol, and '*~phil*' would return phil, Philip and Phillip, for example, but this has now been discontinued by Google. In order to search comprehensively, then, the search starts to become rather unwieldy quite quickly. One possible option that is worth considering is the use of the @ symbol – Google has recently started to index this, so if you have an idea about the type of e-mail account someone has, it might be worth trying a search for '*philipbradley@gmail.com*'. However, this itself has complications, because the e-mail address of philbradley at gmail.com has also been taken – a very polite and patient gentleman owns it and he kindly forwards e-mail to me on a regular basis, and I have been known to forward mail onto him as well. So the wise searcher will view the results that are returned from a search of this nature to see the context within which they are being used. The other obvious search element to add in is something that will hopefully be unique to the person you're after, so '*"phil Bradley" librarian*' should cut out most of the false drops. Alternatively, add in a further qualifier such as '*home page*' or limit to a particular type of site, such as academic or government, if you know the area in which your target works.

Google has made some major changes in the way that they identify individuals, and this may make life a little bit easier when it comes to finding the particular person that you are looking for. The search engine has integrated its social network Google+ into search results. If a particular individual is active in the network they may appear in a Google+ box to the side of the search results, with a brief biography and a link through to their network biography. Secondly, Google is working to introduce a new 'author' tag, with a photograph of the author of a particular page, together with biographical details culled, once again from the Google+ network. This is not a surprising move, given the importance of social media and networks, and is clearly designed to try and keep people onside, rather than losing them to other networks.

Before we leave standard search engines behind it's just worth pointing out that the image search function might be useful as well. If you're not sure if the 'Phil Bradley' that you're after is male or female, run a swift search through an image engine just to check. This is also useful if you're dealing with a foreign name that you've perhaps not heard before, and who knows – you may get lucky and find a photograph of the actual person that you are looking for. You might also try the video search function as well – given that it is so easy to add video to the likes of YouTube, many people will have their own channels.

E-mail search engines

Some search engines are simply databases of names matched to e-mail addresses. The data is collected from a variety of sources such as newsgroups, social media sites, web pages, people who directly register and so on. Some of these are independent search engines, while others are associated with an existing engine. Yahoo!, for example, has a people search function and it can be found at http://people.yahoo.com. This is, however, of little value to my non-American (or non-American researching) readers, since the search facility is limited to people who are based in the USA, and unfortunately there isn't an option for other country versions of the database. However, if you are searching for a USA resident, it's a valuable service, listing locations of people, maps to their residences, telephone numbers (if listed) and links to run background checks on them for a fee. The USA is generally well served for search engines that will provide details of individuals, such as 411 locate, at www.411locate.com/people-search, Address Search, at www.addresssearch.com, and the Internet Address Finder, at http://email.iaf.net/email-search.html. The rest of the world is rather more limited, and so it may well be necessary to try different types of search engine to locate individuals. However, one last possibility might be to research the company or organization that you think they work for, see how e-mail addresses are used, and try sending an e-mail to the account that you hope is active, and cross your fingers!

People finders

A people finder attempts to do more than just provide an e-mail address. When possible they will give you a phone number, street address, and so on. Furthermore, once you have that type of information you could then begin to use one of the street mapping services to take a virtual drive along their road and take a look at their house. This does, however, get us dangerously close to the 'stalker' level of research, but I would seriously suggest that you do attempt to find yourself on the internet, just to see how much personal information is available, much of which you will not be aware of! If you do happen to find material that you're not happy about there isn't a great deal that you can do, as it depends on who owns the data.

> >

For example if a friend has mentioned you on Facebook, you could ask them to remove the reference, or if you appear on Google Streetview and they haven't already blurred your face, they will do so. However, goodwill is the key issue here, so a polite 'softly softly' approach is advisable.

192, at www.192.com, is a good example of the people finder type of service. If you have a vague idea of where a person lives, simply search on their name and 192 will return address details, a view of the road in which they live via Bing, their telephone number, electoral roll details, information on their house and so on. The majority of this data costs money, but it is available, perfectly legally. A similar American product is Anywho (www.anywho.com/whitepages) and in Canada you could try Canada 411 (www.canada411.ca), while the WikiWorldBook, at http://wikiworldbook.com/free-people-search, takes a more global perspective, and also links into social media networks as well. Pipl, at http://pipl.com, is also a global search engine, and this one pulls similar information together, and tries to create a variety of profiles of individuals for searchers, making it easier for them to identify the particular person that they are after. A search for my name, for example, found LinkedIn accounts, Amazon accounts, YouTube videos, Facebook accounts, and so on. The problem with Pipl was that it found too much information for me – I didn't realize that there were quite so many namesakes! However, if you want to look for person globally (while adding in a location, even one as broad as a country) it's worth trying out. Finally, the engine with the rather science fiction name of ZoomInfo (www.zoominfo.com) is also one that bears investigation. It includes a number of filters, such as job title, location, company and industry keywords, and it located 'me' very quickly and accurately.

Social media tools

The growth of social media, and the irrepressible rise of social networking, now provides the people searcher with a whole new raft of tools to use. Some of the early tools are still with us, such as **Friends Reunited,** at www.friendsreunited.com, for the UK and **MyLife,** at www.reunion.com, in the United States. There are other global services such as:

➡ **Alumni** at www.alumni.net (a global service)
➡ **Around** at www.around.co.uk (a global service)
➡ **Forces Reunited** at www.forcesreunited.org.uk (a UK service for members or ex-members of the services)

《 《

➡ **Netintouch** at www.netintouch.net (a global service)
➡ **Wink People Finder** at http://wink.com/find-classmates (a US and Canadian service).

Facebook and LinkedIn

There are some social media sites which have become so ingrained into the internet over the past few years there is a very high likelihood that the person that you want will have registered with one, other or both of them; I'm referring, of course, to Facebook and LinkedIn. Facebook has almost 1 billion members worldwide, which would make it the third largest country in the world if we were comparing population statistics. The search function at Facebook is fairly basic at the moment, but you can put in a name, and you are almost certain to get more results than you expect.

>> **Did you know?**
Facebook has over 1 billion users (www.youtube.com/watch?v=TXD-Uqx6_Wk).

Some people are quite happy to provide a lot of personal detail, so it may be very easy to identify the person that you are looking for, but other people have their accounts so tightly locked down that it's almost impossible – it really is a case of pot luck, I'm afraid. While there are a few search engines that attempt to search Facebook they are all very limited and the results that they return are not at all comprehensive, so a search for a person could return zero results, but I wouldn't be confident that they were not using the site.

LinkedIn, at https://www.linkedin.com, is often regarded as a 'professional' networking site, with an emphasis on making contacts in your professional sphere of activities, rather than sharing photographs of the family pets. Since the site is widely used by recruiters looking for new staff, search options are quite extensive. You can obviously search on name, keywords, location, country, postal code, title, or school that someone went to. Furthermore, there are a

>> **Did you know?**
Every second two new members join LinkedIn (www.youtube.com/watch?v=TXD-Uqx6_Wk).

large number of filters that can be incorporated into a search; industries, seniority level, function and so on. If you have some basic details of the person that you are looking for, LinkedIn is certainly an excellent place to start your search.

> >

Twitter

Twitter, at www.twitter.com, while not having quite the reach of giants such as Facebook, does have many millions of users. There are plenty of different ways to search the resource, the first of which is to actually use Google instead. A search for '*site:twitter.com*' and then the name of the person that you're looking for will return a list of results that contain not only the name of the person you're looking for in their Twitter 'handle' but also those who are using nicknames, but whose real name is a match. Finally, Google can return matches where individual tweets contain the name of your target.

If you prefer to go directly to Twitter it's worth making the point that you don't have to have an account in order to search it. Simply point your browser to https://twitter.com/#!/search-home and start looking. You can do a simple search on your target's name, although I would suggest putting it into double quotes to make sure Twitter realizes that you want to search on the whole name as one element, rather than on two unrelated names. There are also a number of advanced functions that searchers can use in order to find specific people. If you're fairly sure that you have got the right name for someone, try a search string such as '*from:philbradley*' to see all of the tweets that I have sent (this will work with me, but some people protect their accounts for various reasons, and so this sort of search will not always return any hits I'm afraid). Alternatively, try '*to:philbradley*', to see if anyone is talking to the person that you're seeking. You could also try a search '*@philbradley*' to see instances where I am referenced on Twitter. With these two options it won't matter that someone has their own tweets protected, you should still be able to locate them via a third party. One final method to try, if you're running out of options, is to try a geographic search. If you know where the person you're interested in lives (the more specific the better!) Twitter uses the search functions '*near:*' and '*within: mi*' and so a search would look something like '*near:bath*' or '*within:15 mi*'. You can also use '*near:<location>*' in conjunction with other search terms, such as '*near:bath "American Museum"*', if you think it's possible to find your contact that way – although to be honest, at that point, if you have that much information on them you should pretty much have found them using other methods!

> **>> Did you know?**
> The typical reader of the world's top blogs is 38 years old (http://royal.pingdom. com).

Finding people you don't know

At first glance this seems a bit weird, but it's something that we do all the time. I may need to find a trainer who can run a session on mobile technology, but I don't know anyone offhand who could do that for me. So it's really simply just a case of finding people with a certain amount of authority that you can then research in more detail.

Obviously, you can use a lot of the resources that have been previously mentioned in this chapter. A Google search will bring back suggestions of individuals who are active on Google+ in a particular subject area. Simply type in the subject that interests you – sometimes you will be fortunate enough to see some names and faces popping up in the right-hand side of the screen in the place of advertisements. You can then click on an individual and see information such as their date of birth, location, any Wikipedia entry they may have, their education and more recent posts on Google+. You will also be able to see similar individuals, as defined by Google.

Once again, Twitter can also be useful here. Run a search using appropriate keywords and see who is tweeting about that subject. Take a look at their biographies, look at their other tweets, see who they follow and who follows them and in a fairly short space of time you should have a small number of useful names. It may also be worth looking at some Twitter search resources that identify experts in particular areas. ExpertTweet (http://experttweet.com) is one such example, tweeting requests to experts, and helping you find them. WeFollow (http://wefollow.com) works in exactly the same way, but it also has a very interesting 'most influential' section, based on influence rather than a straight count of followers. A slight downside of engines like this is that they rely on people joining them, so they shouldn't be regarded as comprehensive, but again, they're a really good place to start searching.

Facebook isn't a great deal of help directly, but if you can find a Facebook group for your area of interest, it may be worth spending time 'hanging out' in the group to see who posts material, who responds, and so on. If all else fails you could always ask a question yourself to see if anyone can suggest recommendations.

Another approach that often pays off is to search one of the many sites that host presentations. Conference organizers will often put PowerPoint presentations online and so a Google search for an appropriate keyword and '*filetype:ppt*' will focus a search, and adding in a type of site such as '*site:.ac.uk*' will narrow the search even further. Alternatively, visit sites

〉 〉

such as Slideshare, at www.slideshare.net, or Authorstream, at www.
authorstream.com, to identify individuals who are sharing slides on a
subject that is of interest to you. Also consider using YouTube, at
www.youtube.com, to see if people have posted appropriate videos in
your area of interest. Another video search engine, eHow
(www.ehow.com) provides links to a lot of videos produced by experts.
Finally, since we're looking at presentations, take a look at Lanyrd
(www.lanyrd.com) which lists conferences that are taking place around the
world (see p.130). You can often see details on who is taking part, links to
their presentations, and so on.

There are some search engines that are worth considering if you're
looking for experts. The Expert Engine, at www.expertengine.com (which
is currently in private beta testing but hopefully should be open by the time
this title is published), is a place worth stopping by in your search. Profnet,
at www.prnewswire.com/profnet, is designed for journalists who are
looking to get quotes from experts and the site is designed to match both
together. Expertclick (www.expertclick.com) lists thousands of experts in a
wide variety of different categories, although of course the definition of
'expert' will differ, but it's a good starting point.

Allexperts (www.allexperts.com), created in early 1998, was the very first
large-scale question and answer service on the net! They have thousands of
volunteers, including top lawyers, doctors, engineers and scientists, waiting
to answer your questions. All answers are free and most come within a day,
and they are reasonably comprehensive. Once again of course, you should
check the answers (and experts themselves!) to ensure that you're satisfied
with their level of authority. A similar site, Quora (www.quora.com), hosts
questions and answers, which often turn into interesting discussions. It is
discussed in more detail on p.167.

The Journalists Toolbox (www.journaliststoolbox.org/archive/expert-
sources), which is produced by the Society of Professional Journalists, lists a
great many other resources, and while they are aimed towards their
profession, they nonetheless provide some inspiration and links for people
looking for experts.

A search engine vanishing act

I am often asked if it's possible to erase yourself entirely from the internet
and, quite frankly, these days I don't believe that it can be done. However,
there are a number of things that you can do at least to limit what people

can find about you. Now in some senses this has very little to do with internet search per se, so feel free to move straight onto the next chapter (I won't mind) but, equally, learning how to reduce your internet 'footprint' does provide useful knowledge about some aspects of search that don't get mentioned elsewhere.

If you have a Google account, log into your Google dashboard at www.google.com/dashboard and you will see that there is a record of every YouTube video that you have watched, the Google searches that you have performed, when you search, favourite websites and much more. The dashboard does allow you to adjust your privacy settings; this doesn't cover everything, but at least it's better than nothing. You should also check your web search history at the same time at www.history.google.com to delete either individual entries or the entire history. If you find yourself on pages that Google has cached, as mentioned previously, ask the person who has put the information online to delete it. If they comply, you can then check the Google cache to make sure that the old page is no longer available, and if it is, you can request that Google removes the cached version. Details on this are available at http://support.google.com/webmasters/bin/answer. py?hl=en&answer=1663691. Of course, this is entirely useless if the person who has referred to you chooses not to remove the content in the first place, as is their right of course (unless you have been libelled, which is going to be a painful and probably expensive thing to prove), so all that you could do in that case is try to push that particular page down the rankings, ironically by adding more information about yourself, written in such a way as to make Google believe that the new page(s) have more value than current ones and ranking them more highly; most people never check on the second page of Google results, don't forget!

If you are unhappy with your Facebook presence there are plenty of privacy settings that can be changed, but since Facebook is constantly tinkering with these I'll simply surrender at this point and say 'find the options yourself'! Two important points though – don't post material publicly where it can be picked up by search engines and, if everything else fails, you can always delete yourself entirely from Facebook.

If you have spent much time online you may well have created accounts on a variety of social media sites, and a quick way to find these is to use the NameChk site at http://namechk.com. This links to over 150 social media sites and you can simply type in your username. The search engine will then display a list of the sites on which that username is registered – it may not be registered to you, of course, but it's a useful starting point.

〉〉〉

Finally, there are a number of companies that will do the hard work for you, if you feel that you're unable to do it yourself, or you don't have the time. You will however need the money, as these services can cost hundreds or even thousands of pounds. A search for '*reputation management*' will find any number of them for you.

Summary

Looking for specific people on the internet is a hit-and-miss affair. People are understandably concerned about their privacy and many will go to extreme lengths to protect it, making them very difficult to find. Others will change e-mail addresses on a regular basis as they move from provider to provider, and may change their name or details on social media websites. Finally, even if you do have the right name, that's seldom going to be enough detail to track someone down, as there will be hundreds, if not thousands, of people who share the same name. The more information you have, the easier it will be to find someone, but there's little to beat an accurate and current telephone number!

CHAPTER 10

>> People-based resources

Introduction

We have already seen just how important social search engines are becoming when we are attempting to find information on the internet, but there is also another aspect of people-based searching that we should also bear in mind. There are a large number of searchable resources which have been created and written by individuals. Probably the most obvious of these is the Wikipedia, at www.wikipedia.org, but there are question-and-answer websites, search engines and wikis that can also prove to be a valuable resource. In this chapter I'll look at some of these and highlight their strengths and weaknesses.

Wikipedia

The Wikipedia, founded by Jimmy Wales, is badged as 'the free encyclopedia that anyone can edit'. Alternatively if you prefer, it's a 'multilingual, web-based, free-content encyclopedia based on an openly editable model' (http://en.wikipedia.org/wiki/Wikipedia:About). It's written collaboratively by unpaid volunteers who can write and make changes to most articles – with a few limited exceptions, often on moral, religious or political grounds.

It was started in 2001 and there are currently over 4,200,000 articles in the English-language version alone. If it was printed and bound in book form (with each book containing 1,600,000 words) it would take over 1770 volumes to contain it. In order to get up-to-date figures, the best resource is the Wikipedia page on the subject at http://en.wikipedia.org/wiki/Wikipedia:Size_of_Wikipedia. Anyone can edit the Wikipedia – casual users or readers right through to expert academics. Editors look over pages, and there are editing programs to ensure that bad edits are corrected. If there are disagreements on a subject editors will work together to ensure that current thinking is properly reflected in the article. The fact that anyone can edit an entry is often used as a criticism of the resource, and there is a certain amount of justification in that; however, in most instances edits are seen by a large number of people quite quickly and can be rectified and corrected. Of course, the more esoteric the article, the less likely other people will see it, and so something that is incorrect could well remain in the article for some time.

Wikipedia can be searched in a number of different ways. There is an overview of the resource, which is a basic outline of knowledge that has been divided into 12 subject branches, followed by outlines of subjects, breaking them further into branches and levels, and finally a list of academic disciplines. There are also lists of related articles, such as countries and territories and lists of people by nationality and occupation. Searchers can also gain access to alphabetical indexes, timelines and featured content. If that isn't enough for the keen searcher there are an increasing number of spoken articles, collections of articles that can be viewed as books, portals, categorical indexes and glossaries. Finally, there is of course the ubiquitous search box.

When searched, Wikipedia will prompt the user with suggestions (similar to the Google Instant Suggestions option), which may help more closely define their search. It's also possible to do a null search: users can simply click on the search icon (a magnifying glass), which will then bring up an option for advanced searching. It's then possible to limit a search to specific types of Wikipedia data, such as files, articles, user talks, the media wiki and so on.

> **›› Did you know?**
> 1.2 trillion searches were done on Google alone in 2012 (www.bestvpnservice.com/blog/internet-statistics-how-the-internet-performed-in-2012).

If there is an article that matches the search that's been run, the user will be directed to that specific article. If there are any issues with it, such as a requirement for citations, problems with citation style, or wording which promotes the subject in a subjective manner, these will be highlighted at the top of the page. Articles have a brief introduction, a contents section, an image (if appropriate), a brief factual summary, a discussion of the subject in appropriate detail, notes, references and further reading. Readers of the page can indicate their view as to its trustworthiness, objectivity, level of completion and how well it is written. Finally, to ensure transparency, readers can view the revision history for any particular page that interests them. If a searcher is looking for a subject which may have several potential meanings they will be able to view a disambiguation page, allowing them to decide which aspect of the subject is the one that they are interested in.

As Wikipedia allows anyone to edit articles there is always a question mark over its authority and reliability. Considerable research has been undertaken on this subject, and in general most people are now of the view that it can be considered a reliable source of information. Ironically, one of the best places to see both pro and anti views is the Wikipedia article on its own reliability, which can be found at http://en.wikipedia.org/wiki/ Reliability_of_Wikipedia. Anyone who uses the Wikipedia, or works with those who do, should of course take into account authority, potential bias, the speed of removal of outdated or incorrect material and so on. I am quoted in the article previously mentioned, as I said in 2004 that I did not know of any librarians who would use it, but given the way in which it has been developed, I'm happy to say that I would certainly use a Wikipedia entry as an initial jumping off point for research, but would also consult other sources as well – which any information professional would. I do find it particularly useful, however, if I need to locate the 'official' website for something, or if I just have a casual interest in a subject.

Question-and-answer sites
ChaCha

ChaCha provides free and real time answers to questions that have been posted online at www.chacha.com, by mobile app or by texting via mobile phone. It launched the first people-powered mobile answers service in January 2008 and to date over 2 billion questions have been answered. It has over 32 million users every month, who connect through a wide variety of devices, and there are over 50,000 guides around the world who are able to take a question, find an answer to that question, and then post a response; for this they receive a small amount of remuneration. As with any such service, it relies on people asking the right question in the right way (and if you're an information professional you'll know that's not always the case) and that someone else answers it correctly.

ChaCha has a number of search options: questions, categories, galleries, quizzes and a search box. The questions section simply provides users with a recent selection of questions and is arranged chronologically. It's therefore not of any use to a searcher per se, but is quite a good indication of the type of questions that the service receives, and the type of response the questioner receives. A few random examples that caught my eye and which give a fair summary of coverage are as follows:

Q: What is neoclassic? A: Characteristic of a revival of an earlier classical style

Q: How much does an aerospace engineer earn? A: The average salary starts at $55,000 for 1 year of experience to $106,000 for 20+ years of experience.

Q: How many valence electrons does Beryllium have? A: Beryllium has 2 valence electrons, 4 electrons, 4 protons and 5 neutrons.

Q: How many feathers are on a goose? A: I can find no exact count of how many feathers are on a goose listed online. It varies from goose to goose.

There are a few things that strike me immediately about the service – firstly, there's no citation evidence or links to the source of the answer, and no indication as to who provided the answer or what their experience in that particular subject area is. Consequently, while an answer may be vaguely interesting, searchers will really need to dig a lot further to get confirmation of the answer that the ChaCha guide has given them.

ChaCha questions and answers can also be viewed by the category approach. There are seven different categories, from entertainment to scitech, with subcategories underneath them. Each section is broken down into sections, such as 'last month's popular questions' and top trends. A gallery is essentially a page of content on a subject that provides answers to related questions, an overview of a subject, social media share icons and various 'quizzes'. Quizzes are simply that, and ChaCha has a great many of them, ranging from quizzes to see if you are addicted to particular things to personal traits and general knowledge. Once again, while these may be quite fun to do, there's no indication of who put the quiz together or the veracity of the answers.

The final search option in ChaCha is the ubiquitous search box. As the searcher types in his or her query ChaCha provides instant suggestions, similar to the approach taken by Google. ChaCha will attempt to provide the searcher with an appropriate answer, as well as a list of other questions and answers in the same subject area. Unfortunately, these are very often hit-and-miss. While ChaCha is very friendly and easy to use, I think that it suffers badly from a lack of authority, and many of the answers that I looked at were brief to the point of inaccuracy.

Mahalo

Mahalo, at www.mahalo.com, was launched in May 2007 as a human-powered search engine; over the last five years it has developed into a site where users can 'learn anything'. It provides a wide range of content, including text-based information and how-to videos. These videos often form part of their Courses application, which is a series of lessons on how to become expert at a variety of things, such as getting the most out of Photoshop, learning Beatles songs on guitar or learning pilates.

Users can search Mahalo in one of two ways – either by drilling down into the 24 main categories and browsing through the resources that are available, or by using the search box. The first option requires patience, serendipity and the hope that someone has prepared some content that matches your interests, while the second approach provides data that matches your query. However, this is something of a random approach, and it may well be necessary to rethink

> **>> Did you know?**
> It's estimated that Facebook could become the largest 'country' in the world at sometime between 2016 and 2018 (http://royal.pingdom.com).

your search terminology in order to get exactly what you want. For example, a search for '*Confederate*' or '*Confederacy*' only returns videos from YouTube or Bing, and images from Google, Bing and Flickr. The broader term '*American Civil War*' provides a brief overview of the conflict (with the emphasis on brief) and some 'Fast Facts'. While it is not clear who has provided this data there are options for adding in references and citations, which is an advantage over ChaCha. It's perhaps slightly unfair to expect Mahalo to have in-depth information on subjects like that since, despite the 'learn anything' tag line, its real emphasis is on learning how to do practical things.

Finally, Mahalo does have a Questions section, where people can post questions and hope to get answers from the site community. However, as with ChaCha, it's something of a pot luck affair.

Quora

If you are beginning to despair in the idea of human-powered search and Q&A sites I would suggest that you point your browser to Quora (https://www.quora.com). It says of itself that it 'aims to be the easiest place to write new content and share content from the web. We organize people and their interests so you can find, collect and share the information most valuable to you.' If you have a question on health, for example, community users such as doctors will be sent the question, and you'll be able to see the answers they give. So you can share your questions with people who have a particular interest and first-hand knowledge of a subject.

Asking questions is the easiest way of finding the answers, and each question page is intended to become the best and most complete resource for people with the same or a very similar question. Anyone can try to answer the question, and you can see exactly who those people are and what their qualifications are, and each answer can be voted up or down.

Quora also uses the concept of 'boards', allowing users to create their own collections on subjects that interest them, such as links, videos, photographs and text. A board creator can invite other people to contribute to a board, and Quora users can choose to follow these boards and focus on the creator's personal viewpoint on a subject, hobby or indeed their profession.

The range of questions is immense. For example, in the area of librarianship alone there are questions relating to public libraries, e-books, circulation policies and emerging technologies. At the other end of the spectrum there are animated discussions on various questions relating to Dr Who. I've asked a variety of questions myself, on subjects varying from 'which bands have done modern rock versions of classical music tracks?' to questions about Facebook and Google. I can see the number of

> **>> Did you know?**
> Barack Obama's tweet "Four more years" is the most retweeted tweet, at 819,000+ (http://royal.pingdom.com).

people who have viewed the question, the people who have answered it, and the number of people who are following the question and who will be informed when a new answer has been posted.

Quora users can choose to follow other people and be followed in turn, and they can also follow particular topics that are of interest to them. When you follow someone you can see their biographical information, their followers and people they follow, the questions that they have both asked and answered on Quora as well as the topics that they are following. This all provides users with more information on the individual who has responded to their question(s) and the level of expertise or authority that person has. In this respect the answers provided by the Quora community are going to be superior and more authoritative than those provided by other resources that don't provide searchers with the same level of data.

>>

Yahoo! Answers

Yahoo! Answers (http://answers.yahoo.com) is a similar resource to the others mentioned, in that it's a place where people can ask and answer questions on any topic that interests them. When asking questions the questioner categorizes it and it's then available for four days, a period that can be extended or shortened. Once answers have been supplied, the questioner can pick a best answer, or let the community vote on one. People who wish to answer questions can do so by viewing open questions that are related to a topic that they are familiar with. If the given answer is considered the best, extra points are awarded, on top of points for answering the question in the first place. The points concept is one of the ways in which Yahoo! Answers provides authority to the process.

As a searcher, you can browse the 26 categories, which have their own subcategories. 'Pets', for example, has eight subcategories available to narrow the query. The 'top answerers' are also displayed and their biography pages can be viewed, which also helps provide some context for the authority of their answers. Questions are arranged as 'open', 'in voting' and 'resolved', and can be sorted by currency, most popular or fewest answers. This is not a particularly helpful approach for the searcher, who is left with nothing to do but trawl through them, hoping to find what they need by luck.

A better approach is to use the search box. Answers are provided, pre-sorted by relevance, although there are two other filters, by currency and by most answers. Alternatively, the search can be refined by keyword matching in question or answer, by limiting to a particular main category or by location, question status, number of answers or date submitted.

Wordever

The Wordever resource, at www.wordever.com, is designed for users to create and share information on topics that are of interest to them. It could therefore be used by students who are collating material for their studies, scientists for research, librarians for subjects that they specialize in, teachers who are using it to provide access to more information on subjects that they teach, and so on.

The advantage of a system such as this is of course that someone else has done all the hard work of collecting the information and sharing it for you, allowing you to come along and simply make use of it. By the same token, the disadvantage is that you probably don't know the person who has created all that material, and so it's very difficult to assess the value of the content; it may be absolutely accurate, or there may be glaring holes in it, and if it's a subject area that you don't know well, it's going to be difficult to tell.

The method used on the website is to allow – by the use of a bookmarklet – members to clip items that are of interest to them into a collection. This then adds the article to your profile and you can also re-clip items from other members that complement your own. Wordever also allows its members to comment on clips, add links to other collections and so on.

Search is via the usual search box, and results are displayed on the screen with title, an image, date, summary, views and comments. There is also a link to the individual who created the clip(s) so that you can check with biographical information (although, of course, since it is provided by the individual themselves this is no guarantee of accuracy), a link to their other social media accounts, a display of their topics of interest and their collection of clips. Finally, the users' influence score, based on followers, likes, comments, views and re-clips, is shown. To an extent, this does get around the problem that was mentioned earlier, but until you start to use the service it's difficult to tell if a score of 1000, for example, is really good or rather bad.

Other resources

If you are still keen on human-powered answers, you may wish to explore other sites, such as AnooX, a social networking-based search engine at www.anoox.com, and Wikia [answers] at http://answers.wikia.com/wiki/ Wikianswers ,

Summary

The value of people-answering services such as the ones that I have mentioned in this chapter is sometimes questioned, and I can understand why. However, the concern is obviously not about 'people' per se, since all of the information that we come to use and rely on is created by people in one way or another: it's about the extent to which we can trust the information that they give us. We need to consider, weigh and evaluate this information just as much as any other that we get, and not take it at face value. Equally, we shouldn't dismiss this type of resource, as a lot of the data that we get will come from experts in their fields and we are in a very real sense going directly to the source of good-quality information. Finally, of course, we can always use tools such as these as our initial starting point for a search, and check the information that we get with other tools – if we're really stuck they can at least provide a jumping-off point!

CHAPTER 11

>> Academic and other specialized search engines

Introduction

The majority of the search engines that we've looked at so far are fairly general in their approach: they will give you whatever they can find related to the words or phrases that you have used in your search. While that may be acceptable for the majority of queries, there comes a time when it's necessary to go for a different type of data – that which is more academic, for example, or for specific types of users, or which deal with particular information, such as conferences. Now, it's true to say that much of this material can be obtained via a straightforward search using appropriate functionality, but it's a rather drawn-out process. There are, however, many search engines that limit the information they index, leading to more accurate results, which may also not be available by a 'normal' search, as the information is hidden or invisible. (The hidden web is discussed in more depth in Chapter 6.)

> **>> Did you know?**
> 88.1% of US internet users aged 14+ research products online (http://chowcommunications.ca/marketing-communications/part-4-the-correlation-between-internet-research-and-online-shopping-statistics).

The key thing to remember about search engines of this type is that they are almost always specialized in nature. While it's true to say that some general, multidisciplinary engines are available, most of them will focus on a specific subject – such as PubMed, which deals with biomedical information – or a very restricted, almost niche, market – such as GENESIS, which deals with women's history. As you would expect, there are literally hundreds of these engines available, and there is no complete listing of them. The Wikipedia has a good collection of them (http://en.wikipedia.org/wiki/List_of_academic_databases_and_search_engines) and

ᐸ ᐸ

CompletePlanet, the deep web directory, lists over 70,000 speciality search engines at http://aip.completeplanet.com. I am not going to attempt to cover even a small number of potential search engines in this chapter – I simply want to provide a brief overview or 'taster' for the kind of search engine that you can expect to find.

Academic search engines
Academia

Academia is part social network, part database, part search engine; you can find it at www.academia.edu. It defines itself as a 'platform for academics to share research papers. The company's mission is to accelerate the world's research.' Well over 2 million academics have joined the service, adding over 1.5 million papers and listing over 700,000 research interests. Academia offers a simple search box, with instant suggestions as you type. Results are broken down into a variety of areas; people, documents, journals and jobs, for example. Documents may range from papers that have been uploaded by individual researchers that can be downloaded and read in a .pdf format, through to links to web pages or to other social media sites such as Pinterest. If you need to find an expert in a particular area, this is a good place to start, as you can quickly see their interests, what they have published, who they are following and their recent activities on the site.

BASE

BASE, or the Bielefeld Academic Search Engine, at www.base-search.net, provides access to over 40 million documents pulled from over 2400 sources; the full texts of about 75% of the indexed documents are available. The sources included are selected and reviewed by BASE staff to ensure that, as they put it, 'data garbage and spam do not occur'. Searchers are presented with a search box from which they can choose to search an entire document, or title, author and subject fields.

Results are displayed in field order, including title, author, description and publisher, with links to the originating URL and content provider. Search results can be sorted by relevance, author, title or date. Furthermore, BASE offers options to refine results by various fields, such as author, subject, Dewey Decimal Classification number, content provider, and so on. Records can be checked in Google Scholar, e-mailed, exported or added to a list of favourites. Searchers can also get an RSS or ATOM feed for their search, they can save the search and add a search plug-in to their browser's search box, if it has one.

BASE also has an advanced search function, with six different field options that can be combined, as well as the ability to specify content sources (geographical), publication dates from and to, and document types, from books to sheet music.

INFOMINE

INFOMINE, at http://infomine.ucr.edu (not to be confused with the .com address, which is a site that is all about the mining industry), badges itself as a 'scholarly internet resource collection'. It's a virtual library of information which is of particular interest to students, academic staff and researchers at university level. INFOMINE has been created by librarians, particularly from several American universities, but other colleges and universities have also contributed to its growth. The database provides access to data in subject areas such as medical sciences, cultural diversity, maps, social science, the humanities and the visual and performing arts. It also provides links through to some basic search engines, as well as general reference information. INFOMINE has been in existence since 1994, which makes it one of the very oldest of the search resources that I've listed in this book.

As you might expect from a tool that has been created by librarians, the search functionality is extensive and powerful. Basic searches retrieve terms that are found in the title, author, keyword or description, while advanced and subject category searching also provides searchers with the ability to choose which fields are searched. All of the usual search functions are available – Boolean Operators, exact phrases, truncation, proximity searching and nested logic. The search fields in advanced search include all of the ones previously mentioned, but also record origins (created by a person or a computer crawler), resource types, free or fee-based material, or resources that have been added to the service in the last 20 days.

Search results are rather short, unfortunately, giving little more than a title and brief summary of the resource that's been returned. For example, a search on 'social media' that I ran returned a link to the site 'Pew Internet and American Life Project: Social Networking' with the summary 'Reports, presentations, commentary, and survey data on Americans' online social networking activities'. This really doesn't give the searcher much to work with, and as a result there is a considerable amount of clicking through to the listed resource to check it out in order to see if it is of value.

However, it would be churlish to be dismissive of the service. Searches can be narrowed down very quickly and easily, so if the initial 'social media' search didn't work well, it would have been simplicity itself to go into the social sciences and humanities section and then limit to free resources that are found in the news and newspapers, for example. Results could then be ranked by relevance or by title (though not unfortunately by date).

LexisWeb

LexisWeb (www.lexisweb.com) is the home of LexisNexis, which is a global provider to legal, risk management, corporate, government, law enforcement, accounting and academic markets. It provides customers with access to billions of documents from over 45,000 sources. Search results are – in common with other engines in this area – very comprehensive and they provide searchers with far more than a few words of summary. Searchers can obviously run straightforward searches, but can set their 'search scope' by limiting to over 60 practice areas. Results can then be narrowed by site type (news, government, commercial, law firms and so on), related topics, citations, legal terms, jurisdiction, source and file format, to name a few options.

LexisNexis is obviously a very well known company which has made a business out of providing researchers with the information that they need, so it will come as no surprise to learn that much of the material they make available is via a commercial arrangement. Searchers can either subscribe or they can buy individual articles, each individually priced. However, each record does provide a useful excerpt and bibliographic details, which means that it may be possible to track the article down via interlibrary loan. However, there are many records that use web pages as their source, which makes it far easier to get access to them!

LibGuides Community

LibGuides Community can be found at http://libguides.com. Over 55,000 librarians have produced over one third of a million guides (333,350 to be precise) to different subject areas. These can be searched for all institutions, academic, public, special libraries, school libraries, partner sites or guide authors. Results are displayed by title, summary, author, source, date and tags. The guides themselves are produced using the commercial product Libguides (produced by Springshare, http://springshare.com/libguides) and so there is an element of consistency in them, but since they are produced by different librarians, covering different subjects for different readers, do expect considerable variety.

OAIster

OAIster, at http://oaister.worldcat.org, is a union catalogue of over 25 million records, representing digital resources from more than 1000 contributors. It's a multidisciplinary search engine which searches the collections of many libraries worldwide using WorldCat, the world's largest network of library-based content and services. Search is based on the 'two-pane' system, with results in one window and a menu on the left, similar to that used by Scirus (see p.178), for example. Searchers are provided with a simple search box, but with instant suggestions as they type. Results include an image, title, author(s), language, publication data, editions and formats, libraries that own the item and in some instances the ability to view the item there and then. Searchers are able to narrow their results in a variety of ways, such as by downloadable archival material or articles, by image, e-book, map, audiobook or even musical score. Alternatively, this can be done by author, year of publication, language or topic.

Since OAIster works hand in glove with WorldCat, it's also possible to search for items in local libraries – if their collections have been included in the database, obviously.

Science.gov

Science.gov (www.science.gov) has as its strapline 'Your gateway to US Federal Science'. It searches over 50 databases and over 2100 websites from various US federal agencies, providing access to over 200 million pages of authoritative US government science information. Consequently, it's a rather nice example of a meta-search engine, searching across all resources to find appropriate results. The results summaries are very helpful – title, database, author(s), source and date. There is also an excellent summary section for each result that is far more than the few words that we're generally used to seeing – commonly in the range of 50 or more words.

Science.gov also provides searchers with a helpful filtering menu: by topic, authors and dates, for example. There is also an excellent clustering visualization tool for the results in the form of concentric circles, which breaks the subject of the search down into narrower elements, with narrower ones under those, and even narrower again. A search for 'dyslexia' can be broken down into learning disabilities, students, processing, developmental dyslexia and children with dyslexia. If I choose to narrow the last of these down I have a choice of five options, include 'words', and this itself can be broken down into narrower categories, such as phonological awareness. It's one of the very best visualization tools that I've seen, and it's both simple to use and visually appealing. Science.gov also allows searchers to limit by source, or to sort by rank, date, title or author, or to choose textual results or multimedia-based results. There is a link to the Wikipedia entry for a subject, alerts can be created for the search, and individual results can be marked for later printing or e-mailing.

Scirus

Scirus (www.scirus.com), 'for scientific information only', regards itself as the 'most comprehensive scientific research tool on the web'. It indexes over 545 million scientific items and the content covers journals, scientists' homepages, courseware, pre-print server material, patents and institutional repository and website content. It helps searchers to quickly locate scientific, scholarly, technical and medical data. It filters out non-scientific sites (the rock group REM is missing from results, but information on sleep is easily located), and it also searches digital archives, repositories and journal databases, finding information that other engines not only don't return, but can't find in the first place. Results are returned based first on location and frequency of search terms (what Scirus terms as a 'static ranking') and secondly on the number of links to a page ('dynamic ranking').

> **>> Did you know?**
> 75% of searchers do not look beyond the first page of results (http://searchenginejournal.com/24-eye-popping-seo-statistics/42665).

As you might expect from a search engine of this nature, it provides very comprehensive details on what it indexes, and this is available in detail at www.scirus.com/srsapp/aboutus, but to give you an indication, it provides access to 498,000 articles from the American Physical Society, 25.2 million patent records from LexisNexis, 21.8 million Medline citations and 11.1 million full-text articles from Science Direct.

The results screen is very sophisticated, based on a two-pane system – the right-hand (and major) pane has the results, in title, author(s), publisher, date and summary format, with links to the appropriate source such as website, or in the case of paid material, to the publisher's site. The left-hand pane provides a menu of options, allowing the searcher to filter by content source or file type and the opportunity of refining the search. Results can be arranged by relevance or by date, and they can be e-mailed, saved or exported.

Advanced search options include the ability to limit words in specific fields, publishing date, information type (abstracts, books, pre-prints, reviews and so on), file formats, content sources and subject areas. In summary, Scirus is an excellent example of a specialist database; very clear boundaries, excellent subject coverage and a good collection of search functions.

Summary of academic search engines

As I have previously mentioned, it's not possible to give a thorough and comprehensive overview of all of the academic search engines that are available; there are simply too many of them to include in an entire book on the subject, let alone a chapter! However, in giving an overview, I hope it should be clear that academic search engines are in an entirely different category when it comes to internet search. The data is more limited, and rigorously selected by experts in their field. Search functionality is usually of a much higher level, together with the opportunity to sort and rearrange results. Finally, these engines provide excellent methods of filtering results to get very precise information; if a general internet search engine is akin to a blunt axe, academic search engines are the equivalent of a surgeon's scalpel. Unfortunately, in common with other internet resources, academic search engines are subject to closure on a disappointingly regular basis, so if you're wondering why I haven't mentioned BUBL or INTUTE, for example, it's because they have ceased updating. The sites are still there, but of less value every day. Pinakes, at www.hw.ac.uk/libwww/irn/pinakes/pinakes.html, is not exactly a search engine itself, but is more of a subject gateway, providing access to over 30 different academic search engines, and has itself not been updated since September 2011. However, the engines that it references, which cover subjects such as archaeology, economics, law, maths, engineering, physics and the visual arts are still going strong, so if you are looking for a particular resource, it's worth paying the page a visit.

‹ ‹

Search engines for children

Having looked at one end of the academic spectrum, I wanted to also take a look at the other, and provide a listing of search engines that are suitable for children. I looked at about a dozen different engines but unfortunately, for a variety of reasons, I really couldn't find any that I could confidently recommend; they all had something that I thought made them unsuitable. Rather than simply limit my coverage to a single paragraph however, I will briefly cover some of the things that I looked for when assessing these engines, so that if you decide to take a look for yourself you'll have a template to work from.

First of all, what age is a child? A search engine for children below 10 should look very different to a search engine for young teenagers, but a lot of engines really didn't seem to take this on board at all. Obviously the younger the age group, the more basic the search, the simpler the results and there's probably going to be a design element of bright bold colours, pictures of animals and so on.

I did, obviously, search for specific words and terms, just to see if the search engines provided unsuitable results. To save you having to think of some yourself, I tried 'dogging', which is a British term for a certain type of sexual practice that generally takes place in car parks (but which is also the name of a children's book, so might be a searched-for term), blue tits – for obvious reasons – and schoolgirl – again, for obvious reasons. I could have chosen a lot of other terms, of course, but I think that these three were enough to point to the extent to which a child can surf safely.

Some engines were capable of filtering content, so that I could get material on birds, for example, without adult images, but many took the easy way out by blocking the term entirely. Some search engines merely returned no results, but others did flag up that an incorrect search had been run. These error screens were just poor, with no idea that the terminology they used would be either inappropriate for, or indeed incomprehensible to, children – or worse, that the children would quite likely feel that they had done something wrong and had looked for 'bad words' when they were innocently searching.

I was also disappointed that while some engines were able to work out the difference between blue tits as a description of a physical situation or as a type of bird, too many were not, and just didn't give any help at all. Very few provided alternatives, and as we can see with search engines that provide a clustering approach, this is not actually that difficult to do. It wouldn't be that hard for an engine to return a result that said something along the lines of 'We couldn't find anything on blue tits, so we did a search for birds instead'. If a child isn't helped at this crucial point, he or she is just going to be put off searching, rather than encouraged.

There was also the really big problem of Google adverts. While the domain owners seem to take care to try and limit inappropriate results, they don't seem to have given much thought to adverts, which can be as objectionable as the content they're trying to block, and which lead directly to inappropriate sites for children – completely unacceptable at all. Either block adult sites, or do as some of the others have done, which is not have advertising at all – or screen it correctly.

In summary, while lots of children's search engines are available, it's next to impossible to find one that correctly filters material, provides a range of materials, gives sensible help and advice screens and doesn't show inappropriate advertisements. Perhaps the best solution is for an adult to sit down with the child and search with them, teaching them good practice and reassuring them if and when they go wrong.

Other specialized search engines

We're really in miscellany heaven (or hell!) with this chapter, since this is really a catch-all area for search engines that I wanted to mention, but couldn't find a home for in any of the other chapters. Some readers may look through this section and shrug their shoulders and move on, while others will shout 'Eureka!' as they find exactly the tool that they've been looking for. I hope that you're in the latter category!

Alternative.to

Alternative.to, at www.alternative.to, searches for alternatives for different things. This is a useful search engine if you need to check out an alternative to a particular car, piece of software, beverage, food, camera and so on: simply type it into the search box and see the alternatives that are presented. Alternative.to also has a category approach, which I found generally quicker and easier to use. There is a social element to the search engine, as people can vote alternatives up or down, add their own articles and propose their own alternatives.

BananaSlug

BananaSlug, at www.bananaslug.com, takes a rather different approach to the concept of search. The searcher types in a search term and BananaSlug runs the search on Google and adds in a random word to provide an element of serendipity to the results. BananaSlug offers several categories of words to enable the searcher to focus the amount of serendipity used, and these categories vary from archetypes to jargon words and themes from Shakespeare, for example. I couldn't honestly recommend this for serious searching, but for a few moments of fun it's worthwhile.

Factbrowser

Factbrowser – 'the research discovery engine' – (www.factbrowser.com) is unsurprisingly a search engine that is designed to provide searchers with facts on the subject of interest. Users can either choose from one of six major categories, such as technologies, companies or regions, and then from a sub-category, or they can simply type their subject of interest in the search box. It's not really very much use for historical information, so don't expect to get anything if you search for 'American Civil War', for example, but if you focus more on current information and technologies you will get some useful content. The results page gives the fact at the top of the hit, followed by the title of the source, date that it was added, where it was added from, and any keywords.

Fanchants

Fanchants (http://fanchants.com) is a search engine that will provide users with access to recorded football (soccer) chants. It's probably news to you and me, but football chants are taken very seriously by some fans, and this database has a collection of thousands of them – over 13,000 in the UK alone. The search engine provides access by country and by team. However, it's also possible to search by a number of options, such as anthems, classics, funny, vintage and the delightful-sounding 'avin a go. The chants are available to listen to as MP3 files, lyrics are provided and brief background history given. Chants have been recorded directly from the terraces and so they give listeners a really atmospheric sound.

Findhow

FindHow, at www.findhow.com, rather gives the game away with its name – it is a search engine that helps you to find out how to do something – from changing a tyre to citing an article in a paper. It's obviously very practical in nature, but other than that the remit is wide, covering subjects as diverse at careers, money, writing, pets, hobbies, and the automotive industry.

Knowem

Knowem (www.knowem.com) is a useful engine if you are heavily into using social media. It allows you to check over 550 different social media websites, such as Twitter, Blogger, Typepad, Delicious and Pinterest, to see if a particular name has been taken. If you have been tasked with securing your brand name this tool will prove to be invaluable, or if you want to protect your own name and ensure that someone else with the same name doesn't get to register it first, Knowem will check the websites for the name that it's been asked to search on. The first search will highlight popular social media sites, greying and crossing out icons where the name has been taken, but providing a link to any resource that hasn't had the name taken, together with information about the site. It's then possible to narrow the search to look at aspects of social media such as blogging, bookmarking, design and entertainment. Furthermore, Knowem will also provide details of the availability of domain names and trademarks.

MillionShort

MillionShort is an engine that may well cause some consternation when first viewed, at http://gb.millionshort.com, because what it has done is remove the top 1 million most popular websites from its index. Alternatively, you can choose to remove the top 100, top 1000, top 10,000 or top 100,000 sites. We're all aware of the 'fact' that most searchers never look beyond the first page of results, and this engine is giving people an opportunity to really dig down much further to find the gems that might be hiding dozens of pages down in the results. It's not entirely clear to me how they are defining their figures, because I am sure that some of the sites that I saw are certainly within the million most popular sites on the web, but I still found lots of information that I wouldn't have done without using MillionShort, so, that small criticism aside, it was an interesting experience!

‹ ‹

Numberfetch

Numberfetch is a search engine that you'll only want to use rarely, but when you do, it can help save your sanity. It's at http://numberfetch.com and it is designed to let you search for UK landline and freephone numbers to call, instead of using the exorbitant premium-rate numbers. Simply enter the name of the company that you want to contact, and Numberfetch will provide a variety of options and information about the organization that you're interested in.

ProCog

ProCog, short for Proficient Cognition, called itself a 'transparent search engine', and what it meant by that is that its real strength was to provide you with information about a particular website. This can be especially useful if you want to get some more background information on a particular site or page. Unfortunately it no longer exists as a search engine in its own right, and its functionality has been pulled into Gigablast at www.gigablast.com. Under each

> ›› **Did you know?**
> 36% of search engine results clicks are for the first organic (i.e. non-advertising) link (http://searchenginejournal.com/24-eye-popping-seo-statistics/42665).

result users can see options to view: the cached site; backlinks to see who is linking to it; a scoring system; and an SEO option. This provides information on a SiteRank, matching queries, monthly traffic and so on. So although the site has very recently closed, the functionality is still available, and it is still useful for researchers who want to dig into the facts behind a site as much as what is on it.

Quixey

Rough numbers suggest that over 600,000 apps are available for iPhone or iPad, and around 400,000 for Android devices. The problem becomes quite acute when you're trying to find just exactly the right app to use. Quixey, at https://www.quixey.com, is a potential solution. It provides a list of apps for iPhone, iPad, Android, Mac, Windows and so on, and you can filter to just free resources. The results pane displays the app icon (which can sometimes be useful if, for instance, you are searching directly in the iTunes store and are given a large number of similar apps), the title, designer and the platform the app is designed for. There's also a fly-out option on the right-hand side of the screen which displays screenshots of the app in action.

Eat By Date

The shelf life and expiration date guide at www.eatbydate.com is a useful search engine that tells you how long you can safely eat food past its sell-by date. Simply type in the food item that you're interested in (yoghurt, bacon, etc.) and this site gives you an interesting new perspective. As well as providing information on the varieties of food (canned, fresh, opened) it tells you how to decide if something shouldn't be eaten, how to store it to extend its life and other useful information. This is an interesting search engine which does one simple job very well.

SymbolHound

SymbolHound, at http://symbolhound.com, is an engine that some people will just look at blankly, while others will jump up and down in excitement about. It's an engine that – as the name suggests – searches symbols for you. Google has started to expand into the area of symbol searches, but if you want something like ===javascript or ruby $$ this is going to make life much easier for you. It has an advanced search function with the usual suspects, such as all terms, any terms and exact phrase. Results are clear, with URL, summary and title. So, if you need to search for symbols like &, %, and π this is one engine that you really need to check out.

USZip

This will obviously have a limited value on the eastern side of the Atlantic, but for my US readers USZip (www.uszip.com) will prove to be a really useful tool. Simply type in a location to see all of the relevant zip codes, or type in a zip code to find the specific place that you're looking for. Once you've found the place that interests you the real value of the search engine comes into play. There is a wealth of knowledge about the location at your fingertips. Total population, housing units, land area, demographic information (gender, age, race), public school and library information, universities, colleges, hospitals, crime rates – all nicely presented with useful charts and graphs. This is a really nice tool and one worth keeping in mind.

Wolfram|Alpha

Wolfram|Alpha at www.wolframalpha.com is a rather different search engine. In fact it's not a search engine at all in most senses of the word; it calls itself a 'computational knowledge engine'. Many searchers, when exploring a new search engine, will often start by looking for themselves. We normally know where we're referenced, how many references there are and so on, so it's a useful starting point. However, if you do this over at Wolfram|Alpha you get information about the names 'phil' and 'bradley'. We learn that Phil and Bradley are male given names, latest information for US births (Wolfram|Alpha is currently using data produced in the year 2011 for this), history of US births from 1880 to date, estimates for current US population and estimated current age distribution. The source data for this comes from six different places, all of which are listed. It's a shame that we're only getting content from the USA – adding in UK or England just confuses the engine, and we get no results.

Trying a date also gives really different information (remember the computational element here!), because if I type in a date such as April 9 1865 I learn a lot about the date – that it fell on a Sunday, it was 144 years, 1 month and 10 days ago. (Lovely little cut and paste function there which I only discovered when trying it!). It's also the 99th day of the year, the date that the American Civil War ended, sunrise/sunset information and the phase of the moon. A search on the same date in Google emphasizes the historical information, rather than anything else.

Another example of the computational element: a search for '*population England China India France Germany*' provides a summary of the total population for those countries, highest and lowest, tabular data, population history, and a huge slew of data on the demographics. This content is taken from many different (listed) sources, and they're fairly current. While it did give the population for my local town, this was dated to 2004. On the other hand, the same search in Google gives me a more recent, but much less precise figure.

Wolfram|Alpha can also provide you with a great deal of information about you, based on your Facebook account. If you allow the engine access to your account it can do a huge amount of number crunching and will serve up a fascinating array of facts, such as exactly how old you are, average post length (words and characters), total likes, total comments, word frequencies, significant words (also available as a basic word cloud), most liked post, most liked photograph, most commented-on post, top commentators, check-ins, weekly app activity and interface activity by device. Not only that, but information on friends' genders, friends' relationship statuses, ages, oldest friend, youngest friend, friends' locations, spoken languages, religious and political beliefs, birthdays, common names of your friends, friends with most mutual friends, and friend networks!

I've produced a short video which shows some of the things that Wolfram|Alpha can do, and how powerful it can be when used in conjunction with other search engines: it can be found at http://youtu.be/3IL9Vo8h2Ic. Suffice it to say, if you are a reference librarian, and/or ever have a need for facts and figures about a subject (which is most of us at one time or another), this is one search engine that is really worth getting to know inside out.

2lingual Google Search

2lingual Google Search (www.2lingual.com) is a dual-language search engine that makes it easier to search across Google in two different languages. It currently supports 37 different language options, and when it is searched it will perform the 'normal' search and a cross-language search in the language of the searcher's choice. Results are presented side by side in two different panes. It obviously makes more sense if you can speak the language that you're searching in, but even if not, since 2Lingual does an initial translation for you, it's still possible to get some useful material. It's also helpful to see just how different the results are between two language sets.

Summary

To adapt Shakespeare, 'There are more search engines on the internet, Horatio, than are dreamt of in your philosophy.' It's simply not possible to be comprehensive when looking at search engines, as there are simply too many of them. The best advice that I can give is that whatever you are interested in, there's going to be at least one search engine that covers it, and if there's one, there are going to be several. It's just a question of finding them, evaluating them and then using them.

CHAPTER 12

>> **News-based search engines**

Introduction

Several questions arise when looking at the concept of news search. First, what exactly does 'news' mean now? Global and national 'news' is a fairly clear concept, and we can take that down to the next level of local news. However, is it 'news' that your next-door neighbour has painted his fence? To you it may well be very interesting and valuable to know what product he used and how effective it is, because you can then go and buy some paint yourself from the same manufacturer if you have been shamed into painting your fence too. However, your friend at the other end of the country may well not regard this as news at all (though if you paint your fence it may be) – so we could perhaps define 'news' as being fresh information that is of particular interest to us and our friends and colleagues. Given the ease of use of social media-based tools, where we can share updates so easily it is perhaps understandable that people will view the concept of 'news' in a very different way than they did before this ease of access. Indeed, with cameras – both still and video – in most people's pockets in the form of their smartphones, everyone can suddenly become a journalist, and it's quite usual these days to see video footage appear on news channels which started off in a smartphone, or images in newspapers that have been taken (sometimes with, sometimes without, permission) from Flickr and other photograph-sharing websites. On a professional level, speeches and workshop discussions can also easily be shared, so while it's of no international or even national interest, what a speaker thinks about a subject is still going to be important news to the people who are dedicated to that particular subject. So 'news' now has to be seen rather more in the context of what an individual defines as news.

Secondly, what sort of time period are we looking at here? Books can have a production cycle of several months, magazines and journals perhaps a month, newspapers will define as news anything that happened since they were last published, let's say that's roughly a day, and search engines can update their indexes as often as needed to reflect the changing content of news sites. We then have the news sites themselves, which try their best to keep up with the breaking stories of the day, and closely allied to that we have blogs; once again we're talking about hours or minutes. Finally we have the greatest news pipe of all – Twitter, which can present a news story that is seconds old.

Thirdly, we have to consider the idea of authority as well. In 'the old days' it was relatively easy to work this out – we could assume that an article had been peer reviewed prior to publication, a book had been edited, and newspapers had a particular bias that everyone was aware of. However, if I get a news item off a blog, or as a tweet, it doesn't necessarily have the same type of authority that it would have had otherwise. In the early days of Twitter, the only way that one could be certain that a 'celebrity' was actually the famous person you thought was tweeting was if Stephen Fry rang them up, asked them and confirmed it in a tweet. While it's slightly amusing that he was acting as a de facto validation source, the rather more important point is that we now need to consider the context of the news item – not just who said it, when and where they said it, but who their friends are, and the extent to which their extended network can validate them. Unfortunately, it's not really that easy; the need to get a story out as quickly as possible can sometimes take precedence, as a daily tabloid found out some time ago. It ran a story based on a tweet from Steve Jobs, which stated that he was going to have to withdraw the iPhone 4 due to technical problems. The journalist working for the newspaper had built up a story based on a single tweet and hadn't checked the actual biographical details of the account, which made it perfectly clear that it was a fake/parody account. At the other end of the spectrum, someone can tweet something which they don't even realize is news. Sohaib Athar started tweeting descriptions of events that happened close to his home in Pakistan, and it was only later that the world realized that he was live tweeting the attack on Bin Laden by American forces. So – can we, or should we, trust the established newspaper and professional journalist, or should we trust someone who is reporting exactly what they are seeing in front of them? Of course, it's not really that simple, but the concept of authority, validity and trustworthiness becomes more important every day. End-users probably will not realize this, and indeed they may unwittingly perpetrate a myth. In January 2012

〉 〉

there were reports that the Cuban leader Fidel Castro had died. This story was tweeted and retweeted hundreds of thousands of times, but of course it wasn't true. So, even though a large, indeed a huge, number of people say something, it may be really meaningless.

Finally, we have to consider how we can deal with news that we're not supposed to have. Wikileaks, for example, is a not-for-profit media organization which provides a way for sources that wish to remain anonymous to leak information to the Wikileaks journalists. This may sometimes be highly sensitive information that should not be in the public domain. There are times when in the UK super-injunctions have been used by celebrities to keep details of legal cases that they're involved with out of the press, but the details have appeared in social media resources such as Facebook or Twitter. What are our ethical and moral duties here? If we are faced with a request for information, and we're able to get the information because it has appeared in the public domain, should we use it, provide it with a caveat, regard it as entirely unreliable and ignore it, or something else?

The concept of 'news' is therefore fraught with many and varied questions, and there are very few answers, so perhaps all that we can do is to keep an open mind, educate our members and just do the best we can! Having raised several spectres I will now take a step back from them and turn my attention to the actual tools that you can use in order to find newsworthy information.

General search engines

Many of the major search engines such as Google, Bing, Yahoo!, DuckDuckGo and Blekko will provide access to news stories. Consequently it's very easy to use your preferred search engine as a one-stop shop when it comes to news information, but it does help to have an indication of the sources that the engine uses, how the stories are rated, if there are any inherent biases towards the material, and the extent to which you can get a rounded and comprehensive view of a particular story.

Google

In my opinion, Google provides the best news coverage from the general search engines, and you can find it at https://news.google.com. It provides some really good functionality and users of the service have a great deal that they can customize. As well as the 'look and feel' of the page, users can choose what resources they have displayed on the page by personalizing it with various sliders, so if world news is really important the slider can be shifted to the right, resulting in more stories and the entertainment slider moved to the left to decrease information on celebrities, for example. However, it's also possible to add in any news topic that is of interest, and Google also offers the option of adding in ready-made sections such as social networking, space, physics and so on. Therefore, users can create custom sections to locate news items that are local to them, they can add country editions and can even decide how the news is presented – sorted by most users (of a section), highest rated or newest, for example.

News stories are displayed clearly, with different news sections to the left of the main stories and recent items, local items and editor's picks to the right, forming an interesting and effective triptych. Each news item has its origins clearly marked and related stories can quickly and easily be pulled up, to add in-depth coverage to a subject. If available and appropriate Google will also display video news clips from major news sources such as the BBC news. Google News has an advanced search function, and search terms can be limited to particular elements of the news coverage, such as the title, the source or the country the article is published in. However, it's only available as an option when a search has been run, which is quite irritating if you know exactly what you want, but have to run a search in order to get to a position where you can do the exact search that interests you.

When searches have been run, searchers can create an e-mail alert for the subject that they have searched for. They can choose the terms of the query, the type of information that's returned to them, such as news, blogs, video or discussions, how often they get an e-mail (as it happens, once a day or once a week), how many results, and the e-mail address the alert should be sent to. There is no limit to the number of alerts that can be set up, and they can be as simple as an individual word, or a much more complex search query. Searchers can also save the search as a RSS feed, which can be incorporated into their newsreader. There are many newsreaders available since Google closed their RSS option, Google Reader, and I have listed many alternatives at http://philbradley.typepad.com/phil_bradleys_weblog/2013/03/20-alternatives-to-google-reader.html. However, the most popular appears to be Feedly at http://cloud.feedly.com#welcome, as over 3 million Google Reader users have switched to it.

> >

Bing

Bing's options, at www.bing.com/news, are a little less 'full on' than Google's, and the news page is far less busy, with a search box, some leading headlines and below that leading headlines in a variety of different subject areas such as world, UK, business, politics and so on. Those subject areas can be expanded if preferred, so that the engine just displays all the leading stories from a subject section. Finally, users can of course search for whatever interests them, with results displayed either as the best match or the most recent. However, it's not then possible to limit further without more work, since stories on the subject of 'community libraries', for example, will return all stories on the subject, regardless of country, which is an annoying limitation of the service. Searchers can subscribe to RSS feeds for stories that interest them, but there isn't an option for creating an alerting service.

Yahoo!

Yahoo! News, at http://uk.news.yahoo.com, is another busy screen of news. Under the search bar the engine presents a variety of news categories such as UK, world or technology, and then presents news stories, with an emphasis on image rather than text. Added to that is a series of advertisements which are not always clearly indicated as such, leading to some confusion. The rest of the news screen is a mixture of images and textual summaries for different categories, 'most popular' news items, latest videos, a poll on a current news story, editor's picks, slideshows, weather and so on. The Yahoo! news resource can obviously be searched, with results being displayed and filtered by either relevance or time. Searchers can then further filter by source and/or time. The search can also be saved as an RSS feed as well.

DuckDuckGo

DuckDuckGo does not have a dedicated news section, but rather uses the !n bang option (see p. 73), which pulls results directly from Google's news feed. However, because of the nature of the search functionality that DuckDuckGo offers there are a wide variety of other news-based search functions. Users can search via key broadcasters, such as !bbc, and they can search international resources, by magazine, newspapers, speciality sources and weather channels.

〈 〈

Blekko

In common with DuckDuckGo, Blekko uses a specific search operator, but instead of the 'bang' or exclamation mark, Blekko uses the 'slash the web' function, whereby users type in their search term and then follow that with /news; this brings up results that can be displayed by date or relevance. There are a total of 11 other news slashtags (which can be found at http://blekko.com/ws/+/view+/blekko/news) for various subject areas. Results are rather limited, however, giving searchers little more than the headline, a small summary, source and date, which is rather disappointing.

Specialized news search engines

There are a small number of search engines that simply report on the news – gathering data from news websites such as television stations and, newspaper sites. They have a single focus, which is to get news to you as quickly as possible. You may therefore find them to be a rather more appropriate choice if you just need global or national news that is regularly updated.

AllinOneNews

The AllinOneNews search engine, at www.allinonenews.com, claims to search 1800 news engines from 200 countries. It's a very basic engine, which starts by displaying top stories on the home page, with a left-hand menu of subjects. Each story has a headline, source, date and time of day, source URL and brief summary. However, the rather basic approach doesn't mean that it's of little value – quite the contrary in fact, as this engine pulled up a lot of recent material for me on the test searches that I ran, several only a few hours old. It's not a particularly exciting engine, but it does do a good job without any bells and whistles.

Infonary

Infonary (http://infonary.com) is described as a 'real time news digest'. It has a very basic home page, with a small number of headlines, and it also takes headlines from leading UK resources such as television news and newspaper sites. There are a variety of video news items from different video sites such as YouTube. As well as the normal search box there are several categories of news which are available, such as politics, sports or technology. It is also possible to view news via country or alphabetically by subject. Once users move away from the category approach and into personalized searching for key terms Infonary finds results from news sites, search engine news, YouTube, blogs and Twitter. Infonary is updated regularly and provides a good service, although it's rather let down by the very bare interface.

Newsmap

Newsmap (www.newsmap.jp) is at first glance a very confusing page, because it has a large amount of headline content contained in different sized squares across the page, all in different colours. However, given a few minutes' perusal it all becomes clear. First, users need to locate the tab across the very top of the screen which gives them a choice of country – about 16 options, heavily biased towards the West. The next thing to check is the bottom of the screen, which has a colour-coded index – headlines with red backgrounds are world news, purple backgrounds are health news, and so on. Finally, the lighter the colour, the more recent the news, and the larger the square, the more important the news. This sounds terribly convoluted and messy, but it's a very quick concept to pick up, and the system does provide a considerable amount of granularity, so that with a couple of mouse clicks a user can visually focus on technology stories from the USA, or health and sports stories from Argentina. The colour and size focus really does come into play when running a keyword search, however, as the main stories can leap out of the page at the searcher, helping one to quickly isolate lead stories.

News Now

News Now, at www.newsnow.co.uk/h, was launched in 1998, and is currently visited by over 3 million users a month. It's an aggregation service, and so it matches breaking news stories in real time to keyword-based topics. In common with other news services it provides small 'boxes' of information on particular topics, which can be clicked on as appropriate, with the original story opening in a new browser tab. News Now also offers a menu of subject areas such as hot topics, science, sports and arts and culture which break down into narrower subjects. It's therefore really easy to go from 'sport' to 'football' to 'the Premier League', to a club and then to transfer news and details on particular players. At every point in this focusing process the searcher is shown how many new stories are available, which is very effective. Searchers can simply type in their topic(s) of interest and the engine will provide information arranged by time: the last hour, two hours ago, back to the last seven days. If preferred other date ranges can be chosen. News stories are taken from over 40,000 sources and auto-refresh every five minutes.

Silobreaker

The Silobreaker search engine (www.silobreaker.com) was founded in 2005, and provides a commercial suite of products for enterprise search and media monitoring. However, its news search engine is a free product that helps to showcase what the company can do.

The home page has a rather 'newspaper' look to it, with small items in column-based format. It is supported by advertisements, but these are quite obvious, and kept to the right-hand column of the page. When the page loads it provides access to a wide variety of different news stories, from political items to crime, science stories, finance, technology and so on. The format for these stories is all the same – an indication of when the story was first reported, the last time it was updated, summary report and an indication of the total number of news stories available for the researcher to delve into. Finally, it has a number of what it calls 'entities' or keywords to further define the story.

Silobreaker has a number of special features, and these change content on the fly according to the search that is being run. Users can check out recent video-based news stories from YouTube or news agencies. There is an 'In Focus' section, listing people, countries, political parties, subjects and so on that are in the news. They provide a fast-track method of catching up on a particular story or subject area. Next is a 'Network' graph, which illustrates relationships and associations around the subject of the search. There is a 'Hot Spots' section, which is a global map and will show places in the world where information or events surrounding the search topic are particularly prevalent. The section on 'Trends' is in the form of a graph showing media attention trends for several subjects related to the search. There is a section listing Blog postings and audio/video content and another which lists press releases. These can all be sorted by date or relevance.

There are a number of tabs on the home page covering global issues, technology, science, business, energy and countries. Clicking on any of these leads to a selection of current news stories, with further tabs to

〉 〉

narrow the focus. Clicking on 'technology', for example, provides options on internet and IT, telecoms, gaming, AI and robotics. It's also worth noting that there's an RSS feed for each of these sections as well, so it's very easy to keep up to date with the general news in a specific area.

Silobreaker comes with the usual search box, and it defaults to a 360° search, which is a general, all-round coverage of the news resources they have available. When users begin searching, Silobreaker provides a variety of search suggestions, and also indicates to the user the type of suggestion it has provided – an entity (or person), organization, publication, company, and so on. This is really helpful when it comes to trying to clearly define a subject – users do not have to think of extra qualifying terms to distinguish apple the fruit from the music label or the computer company.

Searchers are then able to scroll through the set of results, choosing a particular entity, or simply browsing the news stories. Alternatively, they may also want to focus on any of the previously mentioned sections, or check out a selection of tweets that mention the search subject. Once the searcher finds a news story that he or she wishes to investigate in more detail the link will expand to a bigger summary and an option to read the full article. There is a link showing what others report on the same story, which is an elegant way of escaping the idea of a 'filter bubble' (see p.8), just showing users similar stories from the same perspective, and there is a link to other related stories.

Silobreaker has an advanced search option, which I'm sure you are able to imagine by now, as it is very similar to those that you have likely already experienced – all words, an '*OR*' and '*NOT*' option, the option to limit to documents from a particular publication or country, particular language, type of document and publication date range. There are other options, but these are limited to premium subscribers. Search functionality also allows searchers to use filters directly in the search box, so it's possible to search for '*Person:*' or '*Publication:*', for example. The use of proximity search is also available using ˜ and the number of allowed middle words, so '*"George Bush" ~2*' will provide results containing 'George Bush', 'George Walker Bush' or 'George Herbert Walker Bush'. Silobreaker also supports group search expressions between Boolean operators, an example being '*barack obama AND smoking AND NOT ("smoking gun")*'. Searches can be focused even further, as Silobreaker has a filter or 'drill-down' search within a search function. Searchers can filter the results by clicking on a drill-down icon.

There is much more to Silobreaker, however. As well as the 360° search, users can instead choose to visit the Network section. This takes the idea of

‹ ‹

the network option previously described into entirely new territory. Instead of just a few links between subjects the searcher is presented with dozens. Silobreaker provides a series of sliders for subjects such as company, organisation, person, keyphrase and so on which can be tweaked to bias the network information according to taste. Each item is clickable, allowing the searcher to find out exactly why a particular person or subject has been included in the network. The Hot Spots feature is designed to provide a geographical aspect to a search. By hovering over a particular hotspot on the world map, you can get Silobreaker to display a small dialogue box with an overview of the story that relates to that area. It is also possible to refilter the Hot Spot option to provide access to stories from the last week or the last month, or a specific time range. Finally, the Trends option does exactly as you might expect – it allows searchers to drill down into a subject by looking at trending information over a period of time, to see what relates to, and is popular about, the search subject. Users can compare people, companies or products to see who or what gets the most attention from the media, examine the reasons for it and configure the selection of topics for yourself.

In summary therefore, Silobreaker is a tremendously powerful news search engine, and it makes Google News, which had been widely regarded as the premier news search resource, look rather shallow. Silobreaker is a really useful tool for those professionals who have to keep up to date with the news, and who moreover need to be able to draw a variety of stories together in order to analyse them.

Ten by Ten

Ten by Ten, at http://tenbyten.org, has a refreshingly different take on the news. Rather than provide headlines and a search box, the user is given a 10 x 10 cube of images, with a listing of 100 words to the right of the box. Searchers simply cursor over the images and the appropriate keyword on the right-hand side is enlarged. Clicking on a link provides a list of headlines which can be clicked on and visited. Ten by Ten is an interesting cross between a visual search engine and a news search engine. It's effective if you enjoy searching via images, so would be quite attractive to many students that I know, although it is rather let down by the fact that the same image(s) can appear several times in a grid.

> >

Other specialized engines

There are of course plenty of other alternatives available if you're unhappy with any of the ones that I've discussed above. Try Rocket News, at www.rocketnews.com, World News, at http://wn.com, Daily Earth, at http://dailyearth.com, Headline Spot, at www.headlinespot.com, or News Lookup, at www.newslookup.com.

Newspapers and traditional media resources

An obvious place to look for news stories is where we've always looked for news in the past – newspaper and television websites. There are quite simply thousands of news sites which go from the tiny local newspaper site that's updated once a week to the huge news resources from organizations such as the BBC which are updated minute by minute. Obviously each of these resources has their own bias, but that is to be expected. Nowadays we can expect each resource to update continually throughout the course of the day with new information and breaking stories, and to include video reports, and even live reporting, as and when necessary. Having apparently dismissed these tools in a paragraph, however, there are some sites that I would like to particularly draw your attention to.

Newseum

The Newseum site, at www.newseum.org/todaysfrontpages, shows 879 front pages from 91 countries. It's enlightening and frustrating by turn, since the front page IS all that you get, but to be fair, there's a link to the website itself. Consequently it has limited value, but it's a good way to see how subjects are treated around the world.

Google

Google has a newspaper archive of hundreds of broadsheets, some going back into the early 1800s, and it is international in scope. It is arranged alphabetically, so you need to have a fairly good idea of exactly what you are looking for, but there is a search function that allows users to jump straight to a particular article in a journal. Google also provides a very handy 'related articles' link to similar stories. Perhaps the most interesting aspect of this collection is that the newspapers are provided visually, so that it's possible to move around a newspaper, looking at the advertisements for example.

Unfortunately Google has decided not to continue developing this resource, but they are leaving it online for researchers, so if you are looking for archival information, this could be a good starting point.

The Paperboy

If your needs are more current, The Paperboy (www.thepaperboy.com) has a searchable collection of over 6000 online newspapers and e-papers. Content is displayed in magazine format, but users can click on a world map, choose by country or simply enter a search term.

The British Library

If you are serious in a desire to read news, the British Library provides access to the British Newspaper Archive at www.britishnewspaperarchive. co.uk and thousands of new pages are scanned every day – the current figure is over 5,500,000 pages. However, this is a commercial product, and does not have a free option.

RefDesk and Internet Public Library

The RefDesk site, at www.refdesk.com/paper.html, also has a useful listing of US and national newspapers from around the world, neatly divided by US state or country. It provides excellent coverage and links to almost 50 UK newspapers, for example. They are, however, slightly outdone by the Internet Public Library site at www.ipl.org/div/news, which lists almost 120 UK resources, as well magazines.

The Library of Congress

The Library of Congress has a newspaper and current periodical reading room at www.loc.gov/rr/news/oltitles.html, which links to newspaper archives, indexes and morgue resources. As you might expect, there is a strong US bias to the content, but there are also plenty of international references and links as well.

'Good news' sites

Finally, on a lighter note, you may be interested to know that there are a

〉 〉

large number of news sites that are devoted to positive news stories. When talking and teaching about news search I often have discussions about how grim all of the news appears to be, so it's quite nice to be able to highlight a few sites that focus on good news. I certainly wouldn't consider replacing any of these with the tools that I have previously mentioned, but if for some reason you're feeling a little down, take a brief look.

Good News Network (www.goodnewsnetwork.org) has various news sections, just like regular news sites, with top stories, RSS, a subscription service, inspirational quotes and so on. HappyNews, found at www.happynews.com, describes itself as 'all the news that's fun to print'. Again, there are various sections, columnists, quotes, and links to 'unhappy' news sites. Good News Broadcast, at http://goodnewsplanet.com, is a very busy site, with an emphasis on YouTube videos and very feel-good, though in my opinion not quite so much a 'news' items site as the previous two. Gimundo, at http://gimundo.com, has the strapline 'good news served daily': good news hotspots via Google maps, videos, RSS, best of the web and so on. I really like their take on the news – 'higher gas prices mean less accidents' being one excellent example. The Great News Network, located at www.greatnewsnetwork.org/index.php, has news by category, region, submit news, and an RSS feed. In its 'About' section it really does define exactly what this type of news resource is all about: 'The Great News Network is meant to

> **>> Did you know?**
> Wikipedia is the sixth most visited website in the world (http://open-site.org).

supplement your daily news sources – not replace it. Its role is to show that there is hope, people are making a difference, and that a lot of things are getting better.' Up Beat, at http://upbeat.net, is promoting good, positive and upbeat stories. Positive News is a UK-based site at http://positivenews.org.uk . It's the web-based version of a paper-based quarterly; not so much current affairs, more the feel-good, sustainable-future type of information. Yes! Magazine, at www.yesmagazine.org, again looks like a website of a paper-based newsletter/magazine. There is more on political issues than current affairs from the look that I took. As a brief aside, when researching this section I looked at a lot of different sites, as you can imagine, and I followed up links to find resources that were quite often several years old. While several more 'traditional' news sources had closed, all of these 'positive' news sites were still in existence, so there's a message in there for us all somewhere!

‹ ‹

News curation tools

Of course, the definition of what is 'news' is going to be different for each and every one of us. Up to now I have looked at national and international news resources, but there are two other types that we should consider. The first is news relating to individual subject areas, which while not of national or international interest may still be very important for each of us in our jobs. The second type of news is going to be rather more personal; what our friends and colleagues are looking at, highlighting and sharing.

I don't expect to find a great deal on the BBC news about developments with search engines, new and interesting Web 2.0-based utilities or things that are happening within the library world. I could of course quite easily set up my own RSS feeds and news alerts to keep me informed, but because much of this information will not appear on the news, or via news sites, these tools can only provide me with a snapshot. It's at this point that my colleagues and their activities come into their own. I have already looked at the value of social media search engines in Chapter 7 and the role that colleagues can play in them, and this is the subject I'm returning to now. We are all familiar with the Facebook 'Like' button, the Google +1 button, blogging about resources, adding them to bookmarking services, and so on.

>> **Did you know?**
At 2012 Q2, 16% of adults in the UK had never used the internet. This is 10% lower than in 2011 (www.ons.gov.uk/ons/rel/rdit2/internet-access-quarterly-update/2012-q2/stb-internet-access-2012-q2.html).

Even if we don't always do this ourselves, friends and colleagues do. It can be very useful to see what others in your social circles are looking at, commenting on and sharing, because if they like something or find it interesting, there's a high chance that you will experience something similar yourself. However, it's simply not possible to spend all day checking out these resources, looking through friends' profiles and so on – there simply isn't enough time. This is where news curation services become useful. Simply put, you can provide a resource with access to your Twitter account, or perhaps your Facebook account, and let it gather data on the likes and references to resources that contacts find and make. These can then be presented to you in an easy-to-use format, allowing you to skim very quickly through that highly personalized news. While there are a few of these available for the browser, they have particularly come into their own in various apps for smartphones and tablets, though in some cases they are available for both.

It's worth pointing out that although a lot of these products ask for your

> >

Facebook or Twitter details and then access data produced by your contacts, they are really only acting as a mechanism for drawing together information that these contacts are already sharing with you.

Addict-o-matic

Addict-o-matic (http://addictomatic.com) has as its strapline 'Inhale the web; instantly create a custom page with the latest buzz on any topic'. Sharp-eyed readers will be aware that I've also mentioned this site as a social media search engine in Chapter 7, but I think it deserves another reference here as it does pull in results from a variety of news resources such as Bing News, Google Blog Search and Ask.com news. This is a slightly different product from the other engines in this category, in that it doesn't provide a home page of global or national news; it has a category approach, but the user is expected to know what they're after, and to create a search for themselves.

Curate Me

The Curate Me product, found at www.curate.me, searches the stories mentioned by friends and colleagues on Twitter and Facebook. It can then combine these and deliver them straight to your inbox. Key stories can be quickly scanned, shared and passed on in return, or read in depth directly on the web page.

Flipboard

Flipboard, at http://flipboard.com, is the one that you'll probably be aware of, if you are at all familiar with this type of resource. It's made up of small subject cubes: when you open the app you see a display of squares, which you can tap on to take you into more detail, with stories displayed in a similar cube or magazine format. When you swipe across the screen, you do get a quite pleasing flip effect

> **›› Did you know?**
> New Yorkers received tweets about an east coast earthquake 30 seconds before they felt it (www.youtube.com/watch?v=TXD-Uqx6_Wk).

as the page 'turns'. Clicking on a story opens up the original tweet or status, displays the story on the screen, and links to the full story on the website. An upward swipe loads it directly for you to read. New sections can be added easily, and they're just a tap or two away. It's a very well regarded resource, and it makes excellent use of the visual and touch-screen elements of tablet devices. You can link your Flipboard account to your Facebook and Twitter accounts, as well as link to news feeds and search results for tweets covering specific subject areas.

Flud

Flud, at www.flud.it, is a new entrant into the field. It styles itself thus: 'a modern, beautiful and personalized mobile news ecosystem with a vision to empower its users to interact with each other to access, engage and broadcast content that is relevant to them. You probably visit hundreds of sites a week to look at content you love, but, until now it's been a pain to do and far from classy.' In common with similar applications, it pulls data from a variety of different sites and resources defined by the user and displays them in a magazine format. Clicking on a story opens it on the right-hand side of the screen and you can view stories in web view or as straightforward text. You can also e-mail it to other people, add it to Facebook or tweet a story. It's easy enough to add new resources, based on RSS feeds. You can also pull resources in from Google Reader as well, which is useful, but not uncommon, as most of the other resources also offer the same functionality.

News.me

The Daily Briefing from News.me, at www.news.me, brings together a handy collection of stories shared by friends and colleagues across social media platforms. These can be viewed either by visiting the website, or by reviewing the daily e-mail which it sends to you. The resource provides a brief headline, source, summary and details of the colleagues who have shared the story.

Paper.li

The Paper.li service, at http://paper.li, is a content curation service. Users can publish and share their own newspapers based on the topics that interest them, which others can share. It can automatically find and curate stories of interest based on feedback from users, and from the stories shared by the people that an individual user follows.

〉 〉

Pulse News

This is another free app at www.pulse.me, and the blurb from the site says
'It incorporates colorful panning story bars and fills them with content from
your favorite sources. Pulse redefines news, giving you the opportunity to
experience the news you desire from traditional sources, your favorite blogs
and social networks – all in one beautiful interface.' You can choose up to
five pages of content, with 12 resources in each. This is one of the things
that does annoy me about this one – a limit of 60 news feeds really is a
limit, and not in a good way. It does look very neat, however. It works on
both tablet devices and directly on the web. Clicking on a story opens it on
the right-hand side of the screen, and you can simply scroll across. It's very
elegant and smooth. It's easy to edit resources and add more if necessary,
and of course it syncs seamlessly across devices.

Scoop It! and Scoopinion

A web-based tool, Scoop It!, at www.scoop.it, is designed to act as a
personal aggregation tool that lets users bookmark stories of interest to
them using the bookmarklet, and to share these stories with friends and
colleagues. It's simple to create a topic, and when a user finds a story that
would fit well into their magazine they can 'Scoop it' and add in any
commentary that they wish, or simply leave it as it stands. Another similar
tool is Scoopinion, at https://www.scoopinion.com.

Storify

If you wish to curate and share stories by bringing together content that is
scattered across various social media sites, then Storify (http://storify.com) is
a useful tool to consider. Users can build a consistent creative narrative,
pulling in content from sites as diverse as Twitter, Facebook, YouTube and
Flickr. Status updates can be dragged and dropped, reordered and edited as
necessary. The story can then be embedded anywhere on the web.

Zite

Probably my personal favourite of all of the news curation tools that I have
tried is Zite, which you can find at www.zite.com. It styles itself as 'your
personalized magazine', and is very attractively displayed on the screen.
Users can create a variety of sections: some of them are available as defaults,

others can be created by the users themselves. The product opens onto a Top Stories section, pulling key articles from each of the sections. These can be tapped on in turn, which then open out from the initial paragraph into the entire article. Various tickboxes allow users to inform Zite if they liked or disliked the article, and if they want more on that particular subject. Consequently, over the course of time Zite 'learns' about the user's interests and is able to tailor the magazine more closely to his or her particular interests. Each article can be tweeted, added to Facebook, bookmarked or e-mailed.

Other tools

As I am sure you expect by now, these are far from the only news curation tools that are available on the web. While they work in a variety of ways, they all exhibit characteristics similar to those previously mentioned. So if none of those attract you, it's worth exploring resources such as Amplify, at http://amplify.com, Bagtheweb, at http://bagtheweb.com, Feedly, at www. feedly.com, Summify, at http://cloud.feedly.com/#welcome, or Trap!t, at http://trap.it.

Summary

Searching for news is already becoming one of the most interesting and fast moving areas of internet search – mainly because no-one really knows what it means any more! Consequently we're seeing the development of news search engines, the collation of content, the delivery of content and even the definition of that content changing continually. People are becoming journalists, so as well as reading the news we're more capable than ever of recording and publishing it, which brings the associated difficulties of authority and validity. With the ever-increasing use of mobile phones we will see news being brought to us all of the time, and it's going to be tailored down to where we physically might be located, with a search engine working in tandem with the GPS option on the smartphone. News really is all around us now.

CHAPTER 13

>> Multimedia search engines

Introduction

In the earlier days of internet search video and multimedia were very much the poor relations. Most people used dial-up connections to access the internet and the equipment needed to create video or make voice recordings was either expensive to purchase or complicated to use – often both! By 2011 74% of UK households had a broadband connection (http://stakeholders.ofcom.org.uk/market-data-research/market-data/communications-market-reports/cmr11/uk/1.3) and the total number of global broadband subscribers grew to 643,770,042 by the end of 2012 (www.ispreview.co.uk/index.php/2013/04/world-broadband-users-reach-643-7-million-fuelled-by-fibre-optic-connectivity.html). Due in part to the cheap availability of webcams and, more importantly, the increased sophistication of smartphones, over 100 hours of video are uploaded to YouTube every minute, and 4 billion

> **>> Did you know?**
> YouTube uses as much bandwidth per day as the entire internet did in the whole of 2000 (www.stateofsearch.com/how-massive-is-google).

hours of video are watched every month by over 1 billion unique users. In 2011 YouTube had more than 1 trillion views, which equates to around 140 views for every person on Earth (www.youtube.com/yt/press/statistics.html). I think we can safely say that sharing and watching video on the internet has become a serious business. Of course, a large amount of the content shared and viewed is simply for entertainment (although how one defines that is open to question – what is entertainment for one person may well be serious research for another), but with news items being shared on video sites, 'how-to' videos, educational material, discussions from Google+ hangouts and so on, content found on video has to be taken into account when searching. In this chapter I'll look at some of the ways in which searchers can utilize the flood of content that's available and suggest some search engines to use in order to retrieve it.

Traditional search engines
Google

As we have seen in previous chapters, most search engines have a 'video' option. Google is perhaps a little bit greedy, with two choices – their own Videos resource, which can be found in the general menu or visited directly at www.google.com/videohp, and also a link to YouTube. Google Video is the poor relation of the two and it has a chequered history, in that it's been listed for closure, then saved. However, as Google has something of a reputation for killing products at reasonably short notice, especially those that are under-performing, it's not a tool that I would want to rely on. Since Google owns YouTube, that's where I'll focus, but as YouTube is a separate site in its own right I'll return to it later in the chapter.

Bing

Bing provides access to videos via the menu bar at the top of the search screen, but it also has a link at www.bing.com/videos/search. The video search option provides immediate links to top videos, viral videos, TV, news, celebrity and so on; much of the offering is primarily focused on the entertainment market. A search results in an infinite scrolling list of videos, each with a thumbnail, the length of the video, title, date and where it's located. Videos can be viewed directly on the search engine website, but links are available that take the viewer directly to the originating site. Bing provides links to related searches, and there are filters for length, resolution and source. One quick word of warning, which not only relates to Bing's offering, but to many others: you may well be advised to have some filtering or SafeSearch option in place, as even an entirely innocent search may return pornography.

Others

DuckDuckGo utilizes the 'bang' search option and simply links searchers to other video sites, so a search for '*dog !video*' runs a search at Google video, and '*dog !vimeo*' takes the searcher directly to results at Vimeo. Blekko has a

'/video' option, but it also has a variety of other media related slashtags such as '/news', and '/tv'. Exalead has a video search option available at www.exalead.com/search/video or above the search box. Results can be sorted by relevance, newest, oldest, rating, length or view count. Searchers can filter results by source or category.

Video-specific search engines

Most search engines will have a video search option as we've seen from the previous examples, but in most cases they are simply indexing other resources such as YouTube, so it makes sense to go directly to the specialist search engines themselves. There are a great many engines of this type, some of which attempt to provide access to any and all videos, while others tend to specialize in a particular type of video, such as educational or historical. Let's take a look at a few of them. I should warn you in advance that you may find this section to be a huge time sink, as you explore one collection, think 'I'll just watch one more' and you find that several hours have passed!

blinkx

blinkx has a video search site at www.blinkx.com. It provides a search home page with the usual search box and also 15 categories from news and politics to health, sports, celebrity and travel. Content in each category is arranged chronologically, with links to featured contributors such as the Huffington Post, ITN and Reuters. When I started typing in my '*library*' search blinkx gave me various suggestions such as 'library, public library, national library' and also some matching channels. The results that I obtained were all news-related, the most recent being 18 hours old. Each result took up most of the screen as a large thumbnail featuring details of the time it was uploaded, the source, the title, an option to add as a favourite and a link to sharing the video. Underneath the thumbnail was a brief summary. Unfortunately there was no indication as to how many videos were available, and since the results were on an infinite scroll I couldn't even count page numbers. blinkx provided some basic Boolean functionality such as '*NOT*' and '*OR*' as well as the option for phrase searching via double quotes, but there wasn't an advanced search option.

The channels option was not well documented, but since blinkx offered me ones from the Library of Virginia and the LibraryChannel I am assuming that they are user-generated resources – they certainly contained appropriate content, and anyone familiar with YouTube will have no difficulty in navigating their way around.

Dailymotion

Dailymotion, at www.dailymotion.com, attracts over 112 million unique monthly visitors who view over 2.5 billion videos per month. It has 34 localized versions in 16 different languages, and is based in France. The content is varied, with an emphasis on entertainment, but there are lots of useful news clips from global news corporations such as CNN International. Videos can be browsed via categories such as news, sports, arts, music and so on, or searched via the search box. My search for '*library*' returned over 5500 videos and they were a mixture of news-based, anime (Japanese movie and television animation) and humour. Options were rather disappointing, however, since they were limited to searching for playlists, groups or users, sorting by relevance (most viewed, most recent or best rated) and filtered by HD content, 3D content or official or by language. Videos were displayed by thumbnail, with an indication of duration, title and source. By placing a mouse cursor over the thumbnail further information such as keyword and the number of views was also available.

Internet Movie Database

The Internet Movie Database or IMDb for short, at www.imdb.com, isn't strictly speaking a video search engine of the type that I'm referring to in this chapter, but since its focus is on films, television and news items, this is a sensible place to discuss it. It describes itself thus:

> the world's most popular and authoritative source for movie, TV and celebrity content. The IMDb consumer site is the #1 movie website in the world with a combined web and mobile audience of more than 160 million unique monthly visitors. IMDb offers a searchable database of more than 130 million data items including more than 2 million movies, TV and entertainment programs and more than 4 million cast and crew members.
>
> www.imdb.com/pressroom/about

This makes the search engine a prime tool when searching for video-based information. There is of course the ubiquitous search box, but it comes with a pull-down menu to limit search to titles, TV episodes, keywords, characters, quotes and plots. There is also an advanced search function, and this expands out into options to limit search by release date, genre, 'title groups' (such as Oscar-winning), companies, locations and so on. The '*library*' search resulted in film titles, characters, keywords and companies. Narrowing my search down to the keyword option I was presented with over 880 titles, with thumbnails, summary, date of production, rating and votes from IMDb users. The IMDb also provides current affairs information about the film and television industry, listing new movies, coming soon, top news, television news, celebrity news and even movie showtimes. Although it's not possible to view videos at IMDb, it does link to trailers, and since it is owned by Amazon, options to purchase the films themselves, or to rent them by post.

Trooker

Trooker, at www.trooker.com, is an unusual video search engine, since it's a multi-search engine – it searches for content on YouTube, Live Video, Myspace, Dailymotion, CBCNews, Brightcove and Crackle (some of which I discuss in this chapter) from a single search box. Results are arranged chronologically by search engine, and they can be viewed directly on the Trooker site if so desired. Trooker has a nice feature in that it's possible to create an account, keep favourite videos in 'sets' or playlists and share these with other people. Consequently, it's quite valuable for information professionals who have to collate and present material for a library member, since all videos can be linked in a single URL.

YouTube

I have already mentioned some of the frankly mind-boggling statistics surrounding YouTube, so I shan't repeat myself. Suffice to say, if you need to find a video, YouTube is probably the best place to start. A search will return a listing of videos in the main section of the screen with a thumbnail shot of a frame, an indication as to the length of the video, the title, authorship, upload date, number of views and a brief summary. Videos can be filtered by upload date, result type (which is to say by video, channel, playlist, film or show), duration, features (high definition, closed caption, creative commons, 3D or live) and they can be sorted by relevance, upload date, view count or rating.

‹ ‹

Videos can be viewed in full screen or embedded on the YouTube page, and the viewer can obtain more information on the video if it's available, read or contribute to comments, like or dislike a video, obtain a transcript, view statistics and flag videos. Finally, if you have registered with YouTube you can subscribe to a particular channel to keep up to date with any new videos that are uploaded. The ability to search by channel is very helpful – once you know that one exists of course. It may be necessary to do a straightforward search to begin with, such as '*CILIP*', but this will then return videos that have been uploaded by the user 'CILIPMarketing' and a second search will return all of their video uploads. Alternatively, it's worth just searching for an organization or a person – a search for '*phil bradley*' will highlight my own channel as well as videos of the country and western singer for example.

Searching for educational videos on YouTube is covered separately in this chapter, on p.215.

Vimeo

Vimeo (http://vimeo.com) has as its focus the individual user who wishes to upload video to share with friends – it's a little bit like Flickr in this respect. Consequently a lot of the videos will have limited or no professional interest to searchers in most instances. Having said that, there are a large number of videos available – my basic search for '*library*' returned almost 50,000 results. The engine does have some advanced search options, so I could narrow this number down by searching for all videos, just ones that I had uploaded or videos from my contacts (thus emphasizing the social networking nature of the site). I could also limit by matching my keyword to title, description or tags, and date of upload. Options were also available to limit results by the number of plays that a video had already had, the number of likes or comments, the duration, quality and a Creative Commons licence.

Educational video search engines
BBC Video Nation

BBC Video Nation (www.bbc.co.uk/videonation/archive) is subtitled 'your views and experiences on camera and online'. Content is divided into over 40 categories, such as age, anger, disability, memories, school and work. There are also feature sections such as Africa, D-Day, Mother's Day and

Teachers, with local sites around the UK by county. Searching the site also linked into the BBC news generally, so my '*library*' search resulted in over 15,000 hits, from news (the largest category with over 10,000 results) down to health and parenting (with two results).

CriticalPast

The videos found by CriticalPast (www.criticalpast.com) tend to be focused on the 1940s, with over 57,000 videos in total and over 7 million images. The search options are not perhaps as flexible as one might like, but you can filter by colour, sound, language, date or location. My browsing seemed to suggest a fairly heavy US bias as well. There was a nice option to show clips from specific dates in history (which they link to suggesting that searchers put their own birthdate in, but of course it could be any day), and I tried this myself. I had one video clip from 1918, nine from 1930-39, eighteen for 1940-49, seventeen for 1950-59 and eight from 1960-69. Fifty were monochrome and three in colour, and 35 were silent. You can see therefore that the emphasis really is on the past, rather than current content. Once a clip has been chosen to view it's also possible to pull out still images from it. While both films and photographs can be viewed for free, they carry a heavy watermark and the price to purchase the film or still can be quite high. However, for viewing on the screen with a group of people, this site is quite useful. It's an interesting collection, and if you're into US history from the 40s, it's made for you. Other people may have rather slimmer pickings though.

eHow

The eHow site, at www.ehow.com, has the subtitle 'discover the expert in you'. It has over 30 categories, such as food, tech, money and health, and has over 2 million articles and videos on how to do things. It has a very practical focus, rather than entertainment. The section on 'Toys and Games', for example, has videos on how to play different card games, information on how to create a safe outdoor playground for children and how to fix a scratched Xbox 360 game. Rather than choose to browse the available categories searchers can simply use the search box. A search for '*library*' returned informative videos on teaching library skills, using your local library for reading activities, and the placement of a home library.

ScienceHack

ScienceHack (http://sciencehack.com) is a vertical search engine for science videos, each of which has been screened and approved based on accuracy and quality. It does not host videos itself, but indexes them from other sites such as YouTube. Disappointingly my *'library'* search did not return any results, but the videos suggested to watch instead will give an indication of the subject coverage: 'bionic hand', 'invasive fire ants lose heads to flies' and 'venus flytrap in action'. Videos load directly onto the search page, but they can be viewed full screen as well.

TeacherTube

TeacherTube, at http://teachertube.com, is designed to support the educational community with instructional videos. It's a safe venue for teachers, schools and home learners to share knowledge and information. Members of the site upload educational material, but they are also able to make constructive comments, rate videos and flag videos if they feel that they are inappropriate. The search engine provides access primarily to videos, but searchers can limit to audio, photographs or documents, too. The site is entirely free and no registration is required to use it, but it does contain a considerable amount of advertising.

TED Talks

TED Talks, at www.ted.com/talks, is another superb resource which provides access to over 1400 talks ranging from 2–3 to 20 minutes in duration. Search options include talks subtitled in different languages, events, date filmed, most viewed and rather quaintly, options to limit searches to talks that are e.g. 'courageous', 'funny', 'informative' or 'fascinating'. It's an extremely useful site to find short videos for use in training sessions, motivational work or education, or to keep up to date with developments in different subject areas.

Videojug

Videojug at www.videojug.com is another 'how-to' video site. It provides expert advice, with over 60,000 free professionally produced guides. Users can search via categories such as 'health and wellbeing', 'family and education' or 'technology and cars', or they can use the usual search box.

The majority of videos will assist in practical tasks such as how to wire a plug, facepaint children or create meals using particular ingredients.

YouTube

YouTube has an education channel at https://www.youtube.com/education which provides access to a wide variety of educational videos ranging from academic lectures to inspirational speeches and everything in between. There are over 700,000 videos available in over 800 channels. Videos are uploaded by YouTube educational partners, so the quality is high and appropriate for students. There are three categories of video; primary and secondary education, university and lifelong learning. Each category has subsections, so it's easy to quickly locate videos for primary and secondary students in the area of history and social science which are about geography for example. YouTube also has a section of the site which is designed for schools to use, and in order to use this it's necessary to have a school account with Google, not a personal account. The page at https://www.youtube.com/schools goes into more details on this aspect of YouTube, but briefly it's designed to ensure that students get access to appropriate material which has been customized for their school, since teachers and administrators can create playlists of videos that are only viewable within the school network. Finally there is another element of YouTube which has been designed for teachers at https://www.youtube.com/teachers and can be used to help them leverage video to educate, engage and inspire students.

> **>> Did you know?**
> 100 videos are added to YouTube every minute.

Other video search options
Break

Break, at www.break.com, is an entertainment site and search engine – trending on the site when I looked were dogs, cute cats, funny babies and news bloopers. I tried a search for '*library*', more in hope than expectation, and the majority of videos returned were either humorous in intent or mildly pornographic. (It's worth noting that in most instances the 'family filter' seemed to be of very limited use on this engine.) Having been mildly critical of the site I should also point out that it did have a fair selection of filtering methods – by video, picture, games or users, an option to sort by

‹ ‹

newest, views, rating or comments, the ability to search in specific channels and related genres.

Clipblast

Clipblast, at www.clipblast.com, appeared to be mainly a collection of Hollywood trailers, snippets from television shows and so on. If you needed to find information about films, music video, or celebrities, this resource would be quite helpful, although my '*library*' search did not return any results at all. There was heavy emphasis on 'adult content', so this is one that you may wish to leave until you can't think of anywhere else to search!

Crackle

Crackle, at www.crackle.com, specializes in movies and television programmes, using the slightly unfortunate phrase 'in guys' favourite genres – like action, sci-fi, horror, crime and comedy'. Surprisingly I found 49 links to videos with my '*library*' search, but the majority were cartoon or anime. However, since the site really is designed for entertainment purposes, it would be unfair to be critical of it on that point.

FindAnyFilm

FindAnyFilm (www.findanyfilm.com/search) is a database of films that are available in the UK. It's supported and funded by the UK Film Council and is very impressive. They claim that they have every film available in the UK. Nice simple interface – just type in the film that you're interested in, or browse by genre, A–Z or advanced search. Once a film has been located you get to see the trailer (if one is available), a full summary and film viewing options. The resource will find places where a particular film is showing, at the cinema, on TV, or on DVD or Blu-ray, if it's available for download, watching online or in other formats. There is also an 'alert me' function for each of those options as well.

> **›› Did you know?**
> It took the radio 38 years, the television 13 years, and the world wide web 4 years to reach 50 million users (www.statisticbrain.com/internet-statistics).

FindAnyFilm also links to related titles, 'have you considered' options, most popular, new, and so on. Advanced search allows searchers to limit to title, actor, director, keyword, genre (20+), language, release date and certificate. It will also find cinemas that are close to you, show you what's on, provide a map and website link and give you filtering options. When it was launched they claimed to be working with exhibitors, distributors and retailers to give viewers the best possible movie experience.

Metacafe

Metacafe, at www.metacafe.com, is almost wholly entertainment-based. The emphasis is on various channels covering gaming, humour, television shows and other similar subjects. Much of the content is American, so may have limited interest to searchers in other regions.

Tellyads

Tellyads, at www.tellyads.com, is a fun site, listing an amazing 5666 adverts to date. It has a very simple interface – a search box and an A–Z listing, so you really do need to know exactly what you're looking for, and it's probably rarely that you'll need a site quite like this, but it's worth knowing that it's there.

Other sites

12vid (www.12vid.com) has 12 top videos every day. It's a nice simple way to keep up to speed with some of the viral videos that are coming out of YouTube. There's also a search facility. This may well become one of those places that you just stop by every now and then to catch up. If you still have a thirst for more video, you may wish to try Blip tv, at http://blip.tv/, Ebaumsworld, at www.ebaumsworld.com, Mefeedia, at www.mefeedia. com, or Metacafe, at www.metacafe.com.

Audio search engines

As we've now looked at text, graphics and video in this book, it's logical to also cover audio search. If we exclude music search options, audio is something of a poor relation; while there are some search engines available they are quite few in number. Any attempt to properly cover music search engines would require at least a single chapter by itself, if not more. While

‹ ‹

there are obviously times when music searches are required, a lot of engines
are general in nature, and it would be repetitious to cover them in detail.
Moreover, many of these resources focus on playing music for
entertainment purpose (which is very logical of course) and they do tend to
get shut down due to copyright violations, so I hope that you will forgive
me if I leave you to find these for yourself.

Findsounds

FindSounds, at www.findsounds.com, has a 13-year history, which is
probably something of a record when it comes to internet search engines!
It's a sound effects search engine and it provides access to animal sounds,
birds, household noises, musical instruments, the noises that people make,
television and movie sounds and vehicles. Search options include file
formats and the number of channels – mono or stereo. Perhaps
unsurprisingly no sounds had been labelled 'library', so I used a fallback
search '*dog*'. This provided a total of 200 results, with a link to the original
source, a visual interpretation of the sound wave of the file and an
opportunity to listen to the sound itself.

The Macaulay Library

The Macaulay Library resource at http://macaulaylibrary.org is the world's
largest and oldest scientific archive of biodiversity audio and video. It
focuses on ornithology, and has as its mission 'to collect and preserve
recordings of each species' behavior and natural history, to facilitate the
ability of others to collect and preserve such recordings, and to actively
promote the use of these recordings for diverse purposes spanning scientific
research, education, conservation, and the arts'. Users can search recordings
by species, and results indicate the waveform, species, sound type (such as
call or song), location, date and length. There is also an option to view
video results as well. This is obviously a very specialized search engine, but
cannot be bettered in its area.

Playaudiovideo

Playaudiovideo, at www.playaudiovideo.com/pav_start.htm, provides access
to content as audio, video or image, and results are returned in that order.
Audio results display information on the filetype, the date the sound was

〉 〉

uploaded, the originating site, a link to its homepage and a cached version of the home page. Summary content is very limited to title and a short (almost meaningless in some cases) summary. Given that Playaudiovideo also gives access to other types of media this may well be a useful 'catch-all' site. Interestingly it did provide a dozen results for my '*library*' search, and I was also amused to see that one key search filter was for pornography, with a default set at 'Maybe'.

PublicRadioFan

The PublicRadioFan site, at www.publicradiofan.com, features listings for thousands of public radio stations and over 1750 podcasts. The majority of these are entertainment stations playing various types of music, but there are also links to news resources as well. Searchers can filter and limit to programs by category, source, name, by station, or excluding music.

Soungle

Soungle, at http://soungle.com, returns sound effects and musical instrument samples. Keyword searches retrieve effects with minimal information other than bitrate, waveform, time and brief descriptions. While it's quite basic in search terms, it does have a wide variety of files available, so if you were ever asked to find the sound of a creaky door, this would be a useful site to visit.

Soundjax

Soundjax (http://soundjax.com) indexes and renders waveforms and catalogues audio from the internet. Results are displayed with their waveform and an option to listen to it on the page, as well as download it. Each waveform also has mono/stereo data, filetype, playtime, bitrate and size associated with it as well. Search options appear to be quite limited – when typing in a search Soundjax will provide suggestions; typing in '*dog*' gave options such as 'dog growling' and prairie dog, for example.

Soundcli.ps

Soundcli.ps (http://soundcli.ps) contains links to over 10,000 sounds. Search results are very bare, with a link to listen to the sound file, a brief title and indication of the length of the clip. However, a mouseover onto the result provides other options – a download link and information on total downloads and links to similar and related sounds.

Summary

The amount of multimedia-based information will only increase – particularly as people add their own user-generated content via smartphones. It's interesting to see that in 'the old days' people tended to record multimedia to keep as a historical record, such as a child's first steps, but increasingly content is uploaded for people to share with each other via social media. Unfortunately it's quite difficult to actually index this kind of content, although YouTube has automated a captioning option, which works reasonably well. I predict that we'll see a lot more work in this area in the future, and that will make multimedia search even more useful.

CHAPTER 14

>> Hints and tips on better searching with sample search examples

Introduction

Of course, it's all well and good looking at search from a theoretical viewpoint, but none of us sits down looking at a blank search box thinking 'Now, what shall I look for today?' Everyone of us has our own specialisms and interests. I've tried to include very basic searches as examples in the book, but I thought that it might be of interest if I took a look at a few real searches, and provided a 'walk through' of how they can be solved. This is something that I sometimes do on my courses and it's quite popular. Some of these examples are my own, and others I've found already in existence on the internet; I've made it clear which are which.

Hints and tips on better searching
Domain names, URLs and web pages

Become familiar with the major domain identifiers, such as .com, .co.uk, .org and country codes. Organizations usually try and register memorable combinations of names and identifiers, but these days if they are registering a domain for the first time they may have to take whatever they can get, so if you're not finding the site that you expect at a .com address, try the .org or even the .org.uk version, for example.

It's worthwhile checking to see who a domain is registered to, if you have any doubts about the validity or authority of a particular site. In the UK the organization responsible for domain name registrations is Nominet and they have a very useful 'Whois' tool at www.nominet.org.uk/uk-domain-names/about-domain-names/domain-lookup-whois/whois-tool, which you can use to check a domain – as long as it has .uk in the address. You can see who a domain is registered to, either a person or an organization, their address, when the domain was registered to them and when it is going to expire. It's not a foolproof method, because a registrant can pay extra to have their details redacted and it won't find addresses that end in .com either – even if they are based in the UK. If you have no luck with Nominet, do a simple '*whois*' search within your favourite search engine and it will return a variety of different tools that you can use to explore domain ownership.

While on the subject of domains, please do check very carefully, and make sure the domain that you're looking at is the one that you think you're looking at. For example www.twitter.com is not the same address as www.tvviter.com (two v's do not a w make!) and the University of Southampton website can be found at www.southampton.ac.uk and not www.southamptonuniversity.co.uk. You may also find that if you receive an e-mail with a link in it, the link that is displayed on the screen is not necessarily the link that your browser will click on. It's therefore worth warning members of your library not to simply click on a link in an e-mail, but to type the URL directly into the browser themselves. Tricks like this are known as 'phishing' and are designed to get people to pass on details of their accounts, passwords and so on to a third party who can then use those details for nefarious purposes.

If you click on a link and get taken to what is known as a '404 error page', which is the way that the remote server tells your browser that it can't find the right page, it's always worth checking the URL and chopping a little bit off the end, up to the last forward slash. Keep doing that until you get to a page that does work, and see if you can trace the right page that way – or just go straight to the home page of the site and see if they have a search function. Alternatively, using the '*site:*' functionality that some engines offer is always a good way to find a page that might have been moved on a site. If that fails, try to identify the page via the '*cache:*' option on a search engine or use the Internet Archive at www.archive.org to find the information that you need.

Home pages and bookmarks

When your browser opens, the page that appears on the screen is what is known as the home, or start, page. This may be a page that takes you to your organization's home page, it may take you directly to a search engine, the home page of the computer manufacturer or some other page, which may or may not be helpful. However, there's no technical reason why you have to put up with this, and you should give some thought to producing your own home page. There are a great many tools available that will assist you in this, and a good example is Netvibes at www.netvibes.com. It's a free resource and is designed around the concept of modules or widgets that you can create, with bookmarks, search engine search boxes, RSS feeds, news items from newspapers or the media and so on. All of your information is therefore kept in one place for you, and because your page is hosted on their server (rather than stored locally on your specific machine) you can get access to it from any computer anywhere in the world. It's a very fast and effective way to keep on top of subjects that are of interest to you and provides helpful shortcuts to your favourite search engines.

> **>> Did you know?**
> 80% of all e-mails sent are spam (www.statisticbrain.com/internet-statistics).

If you frequently use different computers – perhaps a machine at work, one at home and a laptop for travelling – it makes sense to ensure that anything you bookmark or make a favourite can be copied into the browsers of those machines, or even from one browser to another on the same machine. There are a variety of bookmarking tools available, with one example being Xmarks, at www.xmarks.com, which will back up and synchronize your bookmarks across Chrome, Internet Explorer, Firefox and Safari.

Another option related to bookmarks is to use one of the many bookmarking services that are available. Examples are Delicious, at www.delicious.com, and Diigo, at www.diigo.com, which allow you to store your bookmarks on their servers and add in your own preferred keywords and summary of the page. It's then simply a matter of returning to the site when you want to find a web page that you need to view again, and find it using their search option. These tools are excellent when it comes to research as it's an easy job to visit a lot of pages, store them and use them for future reference. If you have pages that you visit regularly, however, you may wish to add them to your start page, or set your browser up so that it opens a specific set of tabs every time it starts.

If you have a number of searches that you run on a regular basis, there's no point in continually typing in the search term over and over again. Simply type it in once, get the results and bookmark the page. It's the search that is saved, not the set of results, and you can simply add in a time option to pull back the most recent searches, or indeed add in the option for displaying just the most recent hour's or day's worth of results to further narrow the search and simplify your life.

When you click on a result and visit a web page you often have no real idea of where you'll locate the term(s) that you're looking for. A very simple approach here is to use the Control key in conjunction with the F key. This will bring up a dialogue box at the bottom of the browser window and you can type in anything you wish at this point, and the browser will highlight the combination of characters that you've typed in. You can simply jump from one to the next until you find exactly what you're looking for.

When you are printing off a web page it can be very irritating to waste ink and paper with content (particularly adverts) that you don't want. There are plenty of tools that can be used to make it easier to read a page, or to print the page off. A couple of examples are Readability (http://readability. com) and Print What You Like (www.printwhatyoulike.com). You can simply add a bookmarklet to your browser bar, and when you need to print off a page it will create a printer-friendly version of the web page.

Get the most out of your browser

The browser is a very powerful piece of software, but one that is very often overlooked. Considerable development goes into making the browsers better, faster and more efficient than previous versions and, indeed, superior to the competition.

It's worth having several browsers on your computer. You can then set each browser up exactly how you wish, perhaps to open an entirely different set of pages for you, to load different variants of your user name, and so on. If you want to compare the personalization of results, for example, have one browser that logs you into your Google account, and another browser that doesn't. Run the same search in both browsers and see what different results are returned to you. Ideally, if you can have two actual monitors this makes life even easier – while it sounds like an unnecessary luxury, a two-monitor setup will save you large amounts of time. I'm using such a system myself, so that I can have one screen open to a page of search engine results in the left-hand monitor, with my word processor open in the right-hand one, and I can easily just look back and forth while I'm typing. The alternative is to constantly switch from one resource to another, which is a slow and tiresome approach.

Check to see what shortcuts your browser will offer you. For example, in Firefox, pressing Control and N will open up another version of the browser, Control and I bring up a search box for your bookmarks, Control

> >

and H displays your history and Alt and D puts your cursor into the address bar. Pressing the Home and End keys takes you to the beginning of a page or the end of it respectively.

Check to see what extensions can be added to the browser. There are literally thousands of these available, and they do all manner of things to make your searching and browsing life easier. Simply run a search for '*<browser name> extensions*' in order to see what's available to you, but keep an eye on the time, because searching for extensions can become quite addictive.

Searching

Hopefully you've got a very good handle on the whole search experience now, but it's always worth reiterating a few things. Although it's tempting to just use the same search engine all of the time, you'll be aware now that there are plenty of them out there. Try using one of the 'blind search' tools such as BlindSearch, at http://blindsearch.fejus.com, to compare results and then see which engine you actually do like the most. Alternatively, try the Blekko '*/monte*'

>> **Did you know?**
The total number of e-mails sent daily is 210 billion (www. statisticbrain.com/internet-statistics).

option to choose the best results from Blekko, Bing or Google. This particular function will run a search on Blekko for you, and will provide three columns of results. You can choose the one which you feel most satisfies the query that has been run, and can click on it. Blekko then displays the source of the search – Google, Bing or its own database.

Keep up with the changes to search engines: there really isn't a day that goes by without a new search engine starting up, one closing down or another changing what it does. I try to keep on top of this myself in my own blog at www.philbradley.typepad.com but there are also other sites that you should consider looking at, such as State of Search at www. stateofsearch.com and Search Engine Land at www.stateofsearch.com. If you really get bitten by the search bug, there are lots of communities that you can join on LinkedIn, Facebook and Google+.

There may be times when you really want to stay anonymous when browsing, for a whole host of reasons. Most browsers nowadays have a privacy option available, and there are plenty of extensions that can be added to the package to ensure that no one knows who you are or what you're searching for. However, there are also a fair number of tools available on the web which help in this process as well. Hide My Ass, at www.hidemyass.com, has what is called a free 'proxy' service which hides your IP address and protects your online identity. Anonymouse, at http://anonymouse.org, does the same job, as do many others – just search for '*anonymous browsing*' to get a list of some.

Don't forget to look beyond the first page! It's really easy to forget that the first 10 results are just that – the first 10, and there are plenty more after that. A cartoon that I saw recently made a very good point; 'Q: Where's the best place to hide a body? A: On the second page of Google'. It's worth checking with the options in your favourite search engine and changing the default number of results from 10 to 20 or even 50 if you can.

Don't forget to try nesting your searches. Rather than running a straightforward Boolean search, try adding in brackets (or parentheses) to focus your search more clearly. For example, try '*impeachment AND (Clinton OR Nixon)*'. Not all search engines will support this type of search functionality, but it's worth exploring the help screens just to make sure.

Always put your most important keywords first in the search string. Many search engines will just search for all of the words however you have typed them in, but others will actually provide different results once it realizes what you're really interested in.

Your answer may not lie in text, but may be found in a video, podcast or some other multimedia resource. Remember to query YouTube and other video search engines or do a Podcast search perhaps. It's amazing to see just what information is hidden away in different formats.

Please don't forget to be distrustful. It's a horrible thing to have to say, but when you are searching for news events some people will create web pages that are seeded with malware, and even the mere act of clicking on a page may cause you problems. So even though you desperately need news of a specific event quickly, don't just mindlessly click on the first result that comes up – search engines do try and ensure that dangerous links are removed, but there's always a risk that one might get through. If you need information on breaking stories, use a news search engine or go directly to one of the national or international news sites and search there.

>> **Did you know?**
If Twitter was a country it would be the 12th largest in the world (http://go-globe. com).

If you are out and about, don't forget that you can still search for whatever you need to find by using any of the many hundreds of apps that are available to you on your smartphone or tablet device. If you have a favourite search engine, do check to see if it has an app available; many of them do these days, and I can't see them becoming unpopular in the future – quite the opposite.

Set a time limit for a search, and stick to it. It's all too easy to keep searching for something long after you should have stopped. Have an internal clock ticking, and after 5 or 10 minutes, if you've not got what you were looking for, change your tactics.

Don't forget to leverage your contacts. If I'm having real difficulties finding something I'll often go straight to Twitter and ask my question there. Since I follow and am followed by lots of librarians someone can usually come up with a great tactic or strategy for me to use – or even the answer that I need, if I'm lucky!

Finally, don't forget that old and trusted method – printed resources! Despite all of the wonders of the internet age, with information at your fingertips, remember that books, journals and newspapers – or even microfilm or microfiche – may well hold the answer to your question.

Finding confidential information

Surprisingly, this is extremely easy to do, since people forget that Google will index a high proportion of material that goes online, and if they have not been careful about where material has been stored on a server, search engine spiders may well find it. Obviously, I'm not expecting people to go off and start hunting down what should be private and confidential information, but it's worth knowing how to do it, so that you can check your own site or that of the organization you work for, just to ensure that everything is as it should be.

There are a variety of search terms that may be helpful to use here. *'"This document is confidential"'*, *'"Not for distribution"'*, *'restricted'*, *'private'*, *'personal'* and *'classified'* are a few terms to consider, but I'm sure that you can think up many more. The *'filetype:'* option is a good approach to start looking for information of this type, since phrases will be embedded within documents, and may be overlooked. So a generic filetype search in Google as a starting point would look like this: *'filetype:rtf OR filetype:ppt OR filetype:pptx OR filetype:csv OR filetype:xls OR filetype:xlsx OR filetype:docx OR filetype:doc OR filetype:pdf.'*

This gets us a collection of filetypes; there are plenty more of course, but these are the most likely to yield useful results. Then it's a question of simply adding in appropriate terminology. The addition of *'"this document is*

ꞌꞌꞋꞋ

confidential'" returns about 9000 hits of a very wide variety. Some of the hits contain information that really should be confidential, while others refer to documents which are confidential ones – a false hit, in other words. The addition of further qualifiers, such as '*site:.gov.uk*' still returns over 2000 hits, though (which some may view with concern). The *filetype:* operator can also be used in conjunction with the '*inurl:*' search option, so we can run a search for '*filetype:xls inurl:"email.xls'"*, which returns a listing of documents in a spreadsheet format with e-mail details.

The use of the '*intitle:*' operator can sometimes identify material that should not be available for all and sundry to see, especially if used in the format of '*intitle:login inurl:passwd site@.co.uk*', as you can imagine. More generally, '*intitle:index of*' will sometimes return results that display a listing of files, which can then be viewed, and checked to make sure that there is no embarrassing data available. Many people have webcams connected to their systems, and these can be identified by searching for strings such as '*intitle:"active webcam page'"*, while searching for something such as '*intitle:login password*', '*intitle:"Index of" passwd*' or '*inurl:password*' may pull up documents where passwords are stored in plain text. If you ever need to check to see if music files were being stored on a system, a search for '*intitle:index.of mp3 beatles*' would display websites that had that music stored in such a way that it could be downloaded. You could always replace the '*mp3*' with some other file format, of course. Alternatively, a search for '*intitle:"Index of" config.php*' will return sites that have config.php files available, and if we skip over the technical details this file may contain username and passwords for specific types of database.

Searches can get much more complex and sophisticated, however, as we can see with a search for: '*-inurl:(htm|html|php) intitle:"index of" "last modified" "parent directory" (jpg|gif)*'.

To break this search down a little bit – we've told Google not to search in the URL field for various common file types, but we do want the phrase '*index of*' in the title field, plus the terms '*last modified*' and '*parent directory*' and images that are either .jpg or .gif. This search will then return matches that present the user with lots of directories that they can look through which contain images that they could, in theory simply download. Of course, by adding a '*site:*' function into the search you can just limit it to checking out your own site.

There are obviously many more searches that could be run, but since this isn't a book about hacking into websites, I think it best to stop at this point. I should also like to make the point that searching for other people's information is morally and ethically unsound, if not illegal in some situations. You may also discover to your cost that if you start to download any of the material that you find by searching in this way you have little or no guarantee that it does not contain a virus, and so I would again caution you against exercising too much curiosity. Limit your excursions to your own sites to ensure that they are not compromised!

Sample searches

Question: What colour is my car and do I park it on the road, facing the road, or away from the road?

Answer: In order to get the answer to this question you need to work out several things, not least of which is where I live. If you run a search for '*"Phil Bradley"*' you'll find that there are rather a lot of people with that name, and so if you add in the keywords '*librarian*' and '*address*' you start to get web-based material that is about me. One of the first results that comes up is my website, www.philb.com, and there is an option to contact me. Although I haven't provided my address, my landline telephone number is available and you could work out which part of the country I live in by searching on the STD code. You can then run a swift search on the BT website for the residential name and that immediately provides you with my address. However, if there were rather a lot of people with the same surname and initial, that still might be something of a problem. Consequently, you could decide to try and locate me by seeing if you could get my address from the details held on me by Nominet, the website registrar in the UK. That certainly gives you details on the domain, and an address for me, but these details are not always current. If all else fails, though, this is an approach that you can take, though some people have paid an extra fee to keep the registrant details private. Other approaches that might be worth considering are to use some of the people search engines mentioned in Chapter 9 or to delve into social media sites.

By now, if you are a diligent searcher you will have discovered at least three potential addresses for me, perhaps even more. The next thing to attempt is to work out the colour of my car. If I like my car (and clearly I do, since I'm talking about it) it's fairly logical to expect that I will probably have taken photographs of it. A usual first step would be to use the image function on one of the major search engines, but if you try this approach you will not find much of any value as there are far too many 'false drops'. However, searching for my name and the term photographs links to my

Flickr account. It's a fairly simple matter then to search my collection of images for cars, find any recent pictures, check to see if I say that you're looking at a photograph of my car, and then you're done. Everything is now in place for the final part of the puzzle. Using one of the map services such as Google Maps, it's a straightforward matter to type in the addresses one by one, and then view the road in a Streetview option. That should fairly quickly disclose an address with a car that should be recognisable by colour and make, thus answering the question.

That's a fairly easy example of course, particularly given that I knew you'd be able to work it out, but if I'd been away the day the streetview was taken it would have been a more difficult question to answer – but not by much, as there are enough photographs of my car outside my house in my Flickr collection that you could still have worked out the answer easily enough. However, if I had moved in the last couple of years it would have been rather more problematical, as these maps are not updated very often.

Question: Who created the sculpture that I have photographed at http://bit.ly/XhkuSe? It's an unusual piece of work, in that it looks slightly like a cross between a hare and a young boy. The only information that you have to work with is that I saw it while travelling to a conference in August 2012.
Answer: There are a number of ways that you could go about answering this query. Since there is a reference to a conference a good starting point would be Lanyrd, at http://lanyrd.com, but a search for August 2012 returns a lot of potential conferences, and even by limiting it to information-based conferences there is still an element of doubt as to which one I was at. However, Lanyrd has a search option that allows name search, so it's a fairly simple matter to track me down and see that I attended IFLA 2012, the World Library and Information Conference, which was held in Helsinki, Finland. A second quick search using a general search engine will confirm that I did indeed attend the conference. Alternatively, a blog search would have pulled up similar confirmation, since it's the type of event that attendees blog about. Then it's a simple enough search to look for 'sculpture Helsinki airport', and by choosing '*images*' rather than a web search you can find out that the sculpture was created by Kim Simonsson, and a quick crosscheck on her name confirms that she did indeed create the piece.

Alternatively, simply copy the photograph that I'd put online (which is fine, since I have chosen to make the image Creative Commons, with an attribution, non-commercial and share alike licence, upload it to Google's image search and it would then have produced similar images, linking back to the artist.

I'd next like to use a search example that I first discovered on Ted Talks, at www.ted.com/talks/markham_nolan_how_to_separate_fact_and_fiction_online.html which is a talk given by Markham Nolan. He is the managing editor of Storyful.com and he wanted to check to see if a particular video that he found on YouTube could be used as an example of very bad weather in the Florida area. All that he had to work with was the name of the person who uploaded the video, which was showing a downpour onto a swimming pool, when there was a lightening strike on a nearby tree – it's quite an impressive video to watch. The first thing he did was to search on a people search engine, Spokeo at www.spokeo.com, which located four people in the country with the same name. The first he was able to discount because the person concerned was in her 90s and lived in a desert area, but the other three lived on the east coast. Looking at the type of foliage in the garden where the swimming pool and luckless tree were, the best option to explore next was the individual living in Florida, and Spokeo also provided her address. However, in order to confirm his suspicions a quick check at Wolfram|Alpha for the weather on the date in question in the area that the woman lived showed that conditions for the day included rain and thunderstorms. It was then a simple matter to go to Google maps, type in the address and turn on the satellite view, and zoom in on the property concerned, and the swimming pool, with its very distinctive shape (including li-lo in the pool), was clear. Mr Nolan was then able to contact the woman to include her and her video in the story that he was writing at the time.

Here's a search that we can all appreciate. You can recall a particular book about the American Civil War, but you can't quite remember the exact title, or even who the author was. However, you can remember that the colour of the book was a mauve/purple colour with a photograph of a cannon on the front of it.
Answer: Simply go to a search engine with an image search function and run a search for '*American Civil War*' and then limit the results to photographs and choose the closest colour, and lo and behold, some books that will hopefully jog your memory. It's always worth remembering that you can now search for things by colour and type of image – perfect for hunting down that elusive book!

Searching for unquantifiable information: tastes and interests

All of the previous examples have been to find 'obvious things' such as places, images, people, folders and web pages. However, that's not the limit of what you can do when you put your mind to searching, as it's also possible to search for various other things, such as people's likes and dislikes. Take the film *The Good, the Bad and the Ugly*, for example. A quick Google search brings up some useful web pages, but it also provides me with a Knowledge Graph set of data, telling me when the film was made, when it was released, who was in it, and so on. However, underneath all of that, there is another section, 'People also search for', which shows me both the other two films in the canon, but also another spaghetti western that may appeal to me. This also works with other things as well – I can type in book titles and Google will tell me what else people look for, and a search for 'Hever Castle' shows Chartwell, Penshurst Place and Knole House, all historic properties which may well also appeal to the searcher.

However, Google is not the only tool that can be used in this way. Tastekid, at www.tastekid.com, encourages users first to tell it what they already like – bands, movies, shows, books, authors and games, for example. Tastekid will then provide suggestions for other bands, authors, films and so on. The more information that you're able to provide the engine with, the more accurate the results. I tried it with three examples of bands that I like, and was presented with lists of authors, books, games, television programmes and movies. While it didn't correctly identify my tastes every single time, it had a success rate of about 70% overall.

Other resources to test your searching skills

If you're a very sad person (like me) you may find that you really do actually enjoy trying to answer difficult search queries just for the fun of it. Luckily, there are one or two places that you can visit which will help you scratch that itch. As you might expect, Google has produced a series of lesson plans, with various categories such as culture and science. Most of the questions are fairly straightforward and designed for children, so are ideal to incorporate into lesson plans, but some are really fun in their own right and may well test your skills. You can find the Google lesson plans at www.google.com/insidesearch/searcheducation/lessons.html. There is also the 'A Google a Day' challenge, with trivia questions, a timer and points to be won; again it can be quite addictive and you think 'I'll just try one more'. You can find this at www.agoogleaday.com. Google also offers downloadable lesson plans and live search trainings, all of which can be found at www.google.com/insidesearch/searcheducation/index.html. Finally, Google runs an 'Advanced Power Searching with Google' course at various times through the year. Not only is it a useful course that is done (for free) online to give delegates a better understanding of Google, but it's a valuable way of keeping on top of changes to search and getting people to think more widely about the subject area. Details are available at their website at www.powersearchingwithgoogle.com. These are all a great ways of testing your own search abilities, and making sure that you're still on top of your 'Google Fu', as it's colloquially referred to.

Another useful site to hone your skills is the SearchReSearch site at http://searchresearch1.blogspot.co.uk; it's run by Daniel Russell, who is a Google employee, but this is his own personal blog. Daniel usually asks one question per week and encourages people to provide the answer, methodology and the time it took in comments on the blog. His questions usually relate in some way to what he is doing, or where he has been, and I certainly took inspiration from him for the earlier questions that I asked! The questions are generally reasonably hard to do and you really have to think laterally in order to get the answer, but they're always a real challenge of your ability to search Google.

Finally, you may well find that some academic institutions have sections of their sites that are designed to help students learn to search, so a good search to try out would be '*test search skills (site:.edu OR site:.ac.uk)*', so that you can get variations on the terms 'test' and 'search', limited to educational establishments.

Summary

Searching for information is neither as easy as the search engines would have you believe, nor as difficult as it might seem when you can't quite get the information that you're looking for. In the words of Corporal Jones from *Dad's Army* (a popular British sitcom), 'Don't panic!' if you can't get what you want immediately. Try another approach, think laterally and try a different resource. It's almost a certainty that the information you require is available somewhere; it's just a case of tracking it down.

CHAPTER 15

›› **Search utilities and resources to make life easier**

Introduction

I think that it's fair to say that the more that you search, and the wider variety of search engines that you are familiar with and use on a regular basis, the easier and more effective search becomes. However, there are plenty of tools that can be used to help make search even easier, and if they're available, it makes perfect sense to make use of them. Some of these are browser-based tools, so you might find that you have to contemplate using a different browser in order to get the most out of the system, while others work across all browsers. Others are smartphone- or tablet-based. One general point that I would make is that you shouldn't come to rely on any of these tools or utilities; the creator of the tool may lose interest, it may break if there is an upgrade to a particular browser, or it may be bought by a company that wishes to fold it into its general products, or is buying it to close it down. However, if there is a good tool, it's likely that someone else will come along and re-invent it, so don't let yourself be put off; if a tool is available, then use it.

Browser-based tools
Boounce

Boounce, at www.boounce.com, describes itself as giving you 'the power to leap from one search engine to another with a simple click' but in all honesty I think that's doing the service something of an injustice. It does only work with Firefox and Chrome at the moment, which is the major downside of the tool. Boounce installs a tiny add-on option to the browser which includes a search box, and the ability to search literally hundreds of search engines. The search bar looks like the one in Figure 15.1.

‹ ‹

Figure 15.1 The Boounce toolbar (reproduced with permission)

In order to use it, the searcher simply types in the word or phrase that they want to search for, or they can simply highlight what they want to search on any existing page that they happen to be on – it's not necessary to cut and paste into the search box – and then click on the search engine icon of choice. Boounce will then open up another tab in the browser and will run the search. You can click on each of the search engines individually, or you can do what they call a 'double boounce', which is a double click, loading tabs from all search engines, and you can visit the faster search engines first, and slowly make your way to those which take longer – a neat way of saving time. You can also then close the extra tabs that you don't need. At the bottom of the page of results, Boounce inserts a line of search engine icons that allow the searcher to re-run the search immediately on an alternative engine without any fuss or bother. Not only does this save the user time, but it keeps a variety of engines right in front of them; all they have to do is to remember which icon refers to which search engine!

You'll notice that to the right of the box marked 'Search' and to the left of the Google and Blekko icons there's a pull-down menu. This will open up over 20 different search categories, such as images, video, maps, health, food and genealogy. Within each of these categories there are subcategories, so for example under image search there are options for image search engines, live photo sharing, clip art, stock images, vector graphics and icons. Each of those can be loaded to provide access to yet more search engines; hundreds are immediately available – for the image search option alone there are almost 40 different search engine options.

This, however, is only the start of the tools that are available to Boounce users. Never likely to use the sports option? It can be deleted. And since categories can be deleted, they can be added as well. If you spend a lot of time searching through newspaper websites it would make sense to create a 'Newspaper' category. Simply click on the 'Create New Group' icon, and choose a name for the group that you want to create. It can then be clicked and dragged to the location in the pull down menu that makes most sense to you. Of course, at this point the group is unpopulated with any search options, and so this needs to be put to rights. Simply visit a web page that has a search engine on it – obvious examples such as the *Guardian* or the *New York Times* would be suitable candidates for our newspaper category. Place the cursor into their search box, right mouse click and then choose the option 'Add to Boounce'. The search option will then be automatically added to the category. Consequently, even if Boounce doesn't have access to the search engine that you feel is an absolute must for you, it can easily be added. Furthermore, Boounce offers users the opportunity of sharing their new search category with the Boounce community.

There is more to say about this tool, however, because it's possible to combine the use of it with Google Custom Search Engines. It's not quite as straightforward as I'd hoped, since the base URL for Google and Google custom search engines is the same, and Boounce doesn't see a difference. Consequently, what you have to do is to create your Google custom search engine, save it, and then import the HTML script onto a web page that you have access to. Then you simply create your new group (or add the custom search engine to an existing one) and add the engine in the manner previously described.

Boounce isn't a perfect tool by any means; the default set of search engines changes depending on the site that you're on (if I go to the CILIP site for example, the default suddenly becomes my Librarians group) and I can see exactly why that happens and why it's useful. However, it's irritating for a beginner, and especially when you want to add a search engine to different groups it makes life a little tricky. This is just a minor point, though, and as long as you're using a browser that is supported by Boounce it makes sense to use it to its fullest capabilities.

CloudMagic

CloudMagic (https://cloudmagic.com) describes itself as a 'search engine for all your personal data. It lets you search across Gmail, Facebook, Twitter, Dropbox, Evernote, etc. through one simple search box.' It can also be used on various flavours of smartphone as well. Simply sign up to the site and add in the accounts that you want to be able to search in and start to search. There's also an extension for use in specific browsers as well. CloudMagic currently searches across 22 different applications, such as Google Drive, various e-mail packages, Dropbox, Twitter, Facebook and so on. To that extent it's rather more of a personal search engine than a more general engine, but because it will search some social media-based content I've included it in this chapter. If you are looking for a unified search experience, pulling in material from a wide variety of resources that you use, CloudMagic is an option which is worth exploring.

‹ ‹

Greasemonkey

This is a tool that a lot of librarians use – it works within the Firefox browser, with some limited functionality within Opera and Chrome, and it's a powerful tool. It's available at https://addons.mozilla.org/en-US/firefox/addon/greasemonkey and it allows users to install various scripts which make on-the-fly changes to web page content. For example, new functionality can be added to embed price comparisons in shopping sites, combining content from different pages, and so on. A comprehensive listing of the scripts you can use is available at http://userscripts.org and if the word 'scripts' is putting you off, it shouldn't – if you're reading this book, you're quite capable of installing both Greasemonkey and different scripts, trust me!

Antivirus software

Probably not something that you would necessarily expect to find in a book on internet search, but several of the antivirus packages do provide add-on functionality that works with search engines to help indicate the trustworthiness of a site. The Norton Safe Web site at https://safeweb.norton.com is a good example of this. It has a simple search box with the question 'Is this site safe?' next to it. All the searcher needs to do is to input the site address that they're interested in and Safe Web will provide a free assessment of the potential danger level of the site, from 'safe' to 'caution' to 'warning'. Norton has also extended the use of their tool onto the browser bar as well, with the Norton Safe Web Lite search bar, which warns users of dangerous websites right in the search results. It's worthwhile saying that this can be used even if you're not a Norton user, or you prefer other virus-checking software; it's a freebie that doesn't interfere with other packages. McAfee Site Advisor at http://home.mcafee.com/advicecenter works in a similar fashion – it can be installed along with the virus software and used either in conjunction with Google (at which point it will highlight any dangerous sites) or as a downloadable search bar that can be installed into the browser.

It's worth making the point that it's always necessary to be on your guard when searching; not all search terms are created equal. If there is a big news event, such as the death of a well known person, an earthquake or a major sports competition, unscrupulous people will attempt to create websites and pages that are simply crawling with viruses and malware. As these pages and sites are new it's quite possible for a search engine to initially rank them quite highly, and although search engines do their very best to ensure that malicious content and sites don't make it onto the results page no system is 100% perfect. McAfee has produced a report on 'The Web's most dangerous search terms' which is available at http://promos.mcafee.com/en-US/PDF/most_dangerous_searchterm_us.pdf and it's worth reading in some detail. In brief, some of their findings show that sites which contain lyrics of pop songs are quite risky, as are sites that emphasis the word 'free'. Consequently, 'free music download' websites will often be dangerous places to visit – people have previously purchased their music on vinyl or CD and are looking to be able to download their music again for free, so they already have a mindset of being prepared to download something onto their computer, which is how malware, Trojans and other nasty files can get into a system. Celebrities can also be quite dangerous in their own right; McAfee also checks sites that supposedly provide information on stars of screen and television. Currently Heidi Klum holds the title of 'Most dangerous celebrity in cyberspace' as a search for her will result in an almost 10% chance of landing on a malicious website. Clicking on photographs, videos, screensavers and the like opens up the careless searcher to all manner of nasty material arriving onto their desktop or laptop. Other celebrities who may be considered dangerous are Cameron Diaz, Piers Morgan, Jessica Biel and Katherine Heigl.

Your choice of search engine may well also affect the danger that you find yourself in when searching. In April 2013 German independent testing lab AV-Test revealed that Bing serves back five times as many results that link to websites containing malware. Admittedly, this doesn't amount to a great deal – 5000 pieces of malware out of 40 million sites – but it's still something to take into account. The entire article is at www.av-test.org/fileadmin/pdf/avtest_2013-03_search_engines_malware_english.pdf.

While it's never fun to have to consider the dangers in searching it is something that does need to be taken into account; the internet is still not well policed and searchers need to be on their guard at all times.

Guiding tools

As we move ever closer to an internet world in which we act as creators and not just consumers, as a profession we're going to be able to advise our colleagues much more easily when it comes to pointing out good-quality material for them. Of course, we do this already and we're keen on producing lists of good websites to send to people, but we're now in a position to do this to an ever greater extent.

What would be better than having your own search engine, which just searched the sites that you wanted, and which returned the information that you knew could be trusted? Moreover, you'd be able to share such a search engine with friends and colleagues who could also benefit from good-quality content and a smaller set of results. I'm pleased to be able to tell you that such a resource does actually exist, and it's called a Google custom search engine. A visit to www.google.com/cse will – if you are logged into your Google account – provide you with the option of creating your own search engine. The idea is quite simple – provide Google with a list of sites that you want to be included in your own 'search universe', give the search engine a name and description and Google will do the rest. It will create the engine and provide you with a hosted page that you can direct friends and colleagues to, or you can use the HTML code provided to put on your own site or blog. When a search is run Google will limit the search to just those websites (or indeed web pages) that have been previously specified.

> **>> Did you know?**
> The most watched video on YouTube is currently 'Gangnam Style' by South Korean pop star Psy, which has had over 532 million views (http://go-globe.com).

There are hundreds of thousands of these engines already in common use, and you may well have even used one yourself without realizing it. It is however easy to tell – if you see the phrase 'Google Custom Search' in grey in the search box on a page this indicates that it's a custom engine that is searching a limited number of sites or pages that Google has already indexed. There is no limit on the number of custom search engines that Google allows people to create, so you could have one for your own website, another which searched a list of websites that you had created on another page on your site and yet another which searched your half-dozen favourite sites in a particular subject area.

If you'd prefer not to go to quite those extremes, Blekko has used its 'slash the web' concept to allow registered users to create their own slash tags, which will limit the engine to a specified collection of websites, in a very similar fashion to that offered by Google, although you can't embed the search box onto a page. However, you can share the slashtag, so if you visit the search engine, run a search and add '/philb' at the end of it, your results will come in the first instance from my website and weblog.

There are many other resources that can be used to create guiding tools, and even if you have no interest in them as a creator, it's worth looking at them from the viewpoint of the consumer-cum-researcher.

Pearltrees, at www.pearltrees.com, MuseumBox, at http://museumbox. e2bn.org, and Jog The Web, at www.jogtheweb.com, all offer users the ability to create lists and links of sites which can then be viewed in a variety of different ways, including sequentially, serendipitously or even via category in some cases.

Although rather a different tool, Netvibes, which can be found at www.netvibes.com, is a home or start page tool that could also be used in a similar way. It's a very easy service to use, since it is based on the concept of widgets or modules that can be edited and adapted for specific use, then displayed on a page. Therefore, it would be possible to create a series of bookmarks or favourites, modules that display in real time the result of canned searches, links to bookmarking services that update in real time when specific tags are used to describe certain pages, or modules that display news reports or updates on websites, for example. Dublin City Public Libraries, at www.netvibes.com/dublincitypubliclibraries#Home, have created an excellent set of pages, covering search tools, access to catalogues, links and information on news, entertainment, European press, traffic and travel, and so on. Not only can Netvibes users create an unlimited number of pages linked together via tabs, but the service updates instantly and is entirely free of charge.

RSS

RSS stands for 'Rich Site Summary' or 'Really Simple Syndication', depending on which person you talk to. An easy way out of the definition problem however is to simply refer to and think of them as newsfeeds. Websites which provide up-to-date news information, such as blogs, television, newspaper or media sites, all use RSS as a way to keep people up to date. In order to make the most of RSS it's necessary to use a resource referred to as a 'newsreader'. These are plentiful, and I have listed over 50 examples in my blog at http://philbradley.typepad.com/phil_bradleys_ weblog/2013/03/20-alternatives-to-google-reader.html and http:// philbradley.typepad.com/phil_bradleys_weblog/2013/03/even-more-33-google-reader-alternatives.html. (Google used to have a newsreader, but they closed it in spring 2013, which resulted in many other companies establishing or improving their own newsreader option.)

Once you have a newsreader you can subscribe to RSS feeds wherever you find them. These are generally indicated by the use of a small icon with the letters RSS on, or alternatively as a small orange icon with 3 quarter circles radiating outwards from the bottom left corner. Clicking on either of them will open up a dialogue box that will offer a variety of newsreaders (hopefully including your own!) which can be chosen. The newsreader will then visit the page on a regular basis, such as hourly, and if it finds any new information or stories it will bring the content back and will store it until you are ready to view it. When you open the newsreader it will display a series of headlines that can be quickly scanned through and if one appears particularly appealing it can be clicked open and read.

Using RSS in combination with a newsreader is a fast and effective way to keep up to date with the information that really matters to you, and which is particularly fast moving. Some search engines such as Icerocket (www.icerocket.com) will also provide an option to run searches for you in an RSS format. Basically what this then allows you to do is to run a search, subscribe to the RSS feed provided by the search engine and then use your newsreader to look at the most recent material as it becomes available.

Although RSS may sound rather complicated it's actually very simple and easy to use; the key is in finding a newsreader which you feel comfortable with. A more in-depth explanation of RSS is available on Wikipedia at http://en.wikipedia.org/wiki/RSS and a plain guide video from Common Craft can be viewed at https://www.youtube.com/watch?v= 0klgLsSxGsU.

Home or start pages

A home or start page is the page that opens when you start your browser – it might be your organization's home page, Google, or some other. There are plenty of these sites available, such as Netvibes at www.netvibes.com for example, which is widely used throughout the industry, but they do have a very particular use for searchers, since these tools usually have some sort of 'widgets' or modules available which help with search. For example Netvibes has widgets which constantly monitor search engines, running and re-running searches on average once an hour for you automatically, and returning new information as it occurs. Consequently it's not even necessary to search – simply look at the new material that's available in the module. Other modules can be used to monitor bookmarking services to see any new material that has been added for particular keywords. Alternatively, since home and start pages will often support an RSS module it's quite possible to run a search in a search engine, and take an RSS feed if one is offered, and add it to the start page. For example, I often find that new search engines will say that they are 'better than Google' and so it was the matter of a few moments 'work to create a search for that phrase (ironically in Google News itself) and then store this on my Netvibes page, so that it's very easy to keep up to date on such bold claims. You can see the results of this search in Figure 15.2 and this also gives you a feel for what other Netvibes widgets look like.

> **(14) "better than Google" - Google**   ↱ ✹ ✕

- **Apple Files For Advanced Street View Patent Which Is A Bit Better Than Google's - All about the iPhone**
  3 hours ago
- **Better than Google Glass? Baidu Confirms 'Baidu Eye' AR Glasses Exist, Hints at ... - Tech in Asia** 15 hours ago
- **What is Gmail Blue? It's Way Better Than Google Glass - PolicyMic** 3 days ago
- **It's Time To Stop Dumping On Apple's Software And Raving About Google's -- I ... - Business Insider**
  1 week ago
- **Medical search engine said to find 'zebras' better than Google - Network World (blog)** 2 weeks ago
- **Cry the beloved Google Reader - Fortune** 2 weeks ago
- **"Better Than Google" Claims: Why Doesn't Anyone Believe Them? - Search Engine Land** 3 weeks ago

  older ▶

Figure 15.2 A Netvibes search 'widget' from the author's own dashboard, www.netvibes.com/philbradley (reproduced with permission)

Netvibes in particular is a useful tool for the advanced searcher to get to grips with, since it provides modules for searching without leaving the Netvibes page. Simply type in the search that you need to run, click on the module option for a search engine and see the results coming up there and then on the screen in front of you. It's a quick and simple way of searching very quickly, without having to go to different engines one after another, wasting time. Netvibes also has a superb tool called a 'Dashboard'. Simply choose your subject of interest and Netvibes will create a dashboard for you.

‹ ‹

The dashboard is composed of several tabbed pages which are populated with modules that immediately pull back information from blogs, news sites, search engines, videos, social media conversations and so on. Creating a dashboard takes less time than it does to explain what one is, and it provides a rich variety of types of data; what's more, the modules continually update themselves without further input from the user, so fresh data is constantly being retrieved and displayed. Finally, Netvibes allows its users to have public-facing pages. The importance of this is that a searcher can create an in-depth sophisticated set of tabbed pages, pulling in content from a variety of sources that can then be made instantly available to the rest of the world. One good example of this is the Netvibes pages produced by Dublin City Public Libraries already referred to above.

If you find that Netvibes is not to your taste, don't despair! There are plenty of other options based around the same theme of pulling data together and displaying it for you on one or more pages, automatically loaded by your browser. Symbaloo, at www.symbaloo.com, badges itself as 'Your personal internet desktop' and it can be used to create a series of buttons or icons leading to different websites. It also offers more content via a tabbed system, so it's easy to create a start page which loads a variety of different subject-based tabs, which link to different search engines, RSS feeds and so on. It's also possible to create your own tiles with your own artwork to really personalize a system. Sitehoover (www.sitehoover.com/en) is a simple-to-use home page resource that works using thumbnails for sites that you input yourself. If you register (which you'll need to in order to keep the page you create) you can theme it, import bookmarks from Firefox, use RSS feeds and create public 'hoovers' as well. Nextaris (www.nextaris.com) is an all-in-one toolkit for searching the web, tracking news, capturing web content, sharing files, publishing blogs and private messaging. That's just three examples, but I have a more extensive list on my weblog at http://philbradley.typepad.com/i_want_to/create_a_personalised_start_page.

Other browser-based search options

All browsers give users an easy method of searching, but it's one that is often overlooked. With Internet Explorer 9 it's possible to search the internet directly from the address bar, and to choose which search engine to use. You can also let the engine suggest terms or results as you are typing your search. Simply start typing the search into the address bar and IE will

〉〉〉

produce a drop down menu with a list of search engines available at the bottom – simply click on the one that you wish to run the search with. If it's not available there's a link to search engine providers and others can be added from the list that's provided; there are over 60 different engines listed, from traditional engines to games search engines, newspapers and so on. Once a new engine (or engines) have been added they can be made the default search provider.

Firefox works in a similar fashion – it includes a search engine search box in the browser, and there is an option to add more search engines as necessary in a variety of different categories such as sports, news, video and music. A comprehensive listing of Firefox search tools is available at https:// addons.mozilla.org/en-US/firefox/search-

> **〉〉 Did you know?**
> The Google +1 button is used 5 billion times a day (http://go-globe.com).

tools and I would thoroughly recommend spending some time exploring them; there are over 1000 in multiple search alone, and over 330 news and blog add-on search tools.

Chrome also provides its users with a variety of different search tools. As you would expect, these include options to search various different engines such as DuckDuckGo, YouTube and Wikipedia search, plenty of search functionality for Google (Chrome is a Google product), and indeed it does seem that Google is using Chrome to pick up the slack when they stop providing their own search engine functionality. In early 2013 Google stopped providing a 'block this website' facility, but then immediately added a tool to allow exactly that in the Chrome browser.

One useful little trick that can be used with almost any browser is to find search terms (or indeed any words) on a web page. Simply press the Control Key (Ctrl) and the F key at the same time. This will pop up a 'Find' box at the bottom of the screen. Simply type in what you are looking for and as you type you'll be taken to the first instance of the set of characters on the screen. Once the entire word has been typed in, there are options for Next, Previous and Highlight all. Finally there's an option to match the case of the word(s) being searched for. It hasn't really got very much to do with search engines at all, but it's a very useful little trick, and surprisingly little known.

There are of course plenty of other browsers – Opera, Safari and Rockmelt all being obvious examples – but they tend to be used by a small number of dedicated followers, and I think that it's fair to say that users of such browsers tend to be power users who have all worked out how to get the most out of them, in far more detail than I'm able to go into here.

‹ ‹

Web page watchers

Having found a site or individual page that is of interest to you, you may well want to keep tabs on it, to see if and when the content on the page changes. Of course it's possible to simply save or print the details, revisit and compare, but that's a very laborious thing to do, especially when there are tools available that will do that for you!

Probably the best known of the tools that are available is the WebSite-Watcher at http://aignes.com, which will detect website changes for you, highlighting them on screen. It can monitor pages, forums, RSS feeds and newsgroups and provides a useful filtering system to ignore unwanted content. Unfortunately, the downside is that this is a paid-for product, costing in the region of €29. If you're looking for a rather cheaper option, Change Detection, at www.changedetection.com, is a free service, running since 1999, which will send e-mails to an account when the monitored page changes content.

> **›› Did you know?**
> There are currently approximately 3,881,516 articles in the English version of Wikipedia, which is enough to fill 952 volumes of the *Encyclopedia Britannica* (http://open-site.org).

Change Detect, at www.changedetect.com, also provides a free service. FollowThatPage (www.followthatpage.com) notifies you via e-mail when pages change and it can do 20 daily checks and one-hourly checks. A twist on the theme is Page2RSS (http://page2rss.com), which delivers updates to your favourite RSS reader or your Twitter account if you have one. As you would expect by now, having got this far through the book, there are always more options available, and a good summary is provided by Karen Blakeman at www.rba.co.uk/sources/monitor.htm.

The rise of apps

I discuss the future of search in the next chapter, but when looking at different ways of searching instead of using traditional search methods, it's also necessary to briefly look at the changes that are already taking place. In September 2012 people searched less than the previous month, and that's never happened before. Ben Schachter of Macquarie Securities noted this in a research note:

> Total core organic searches declined 4 percent y/y, representing the first decline in total search volume since we began tracking the data in 2006. While this month marks the first y/y decline in total search volume, growth rates have been

decelerating since February's recent peak at 14 percent y/y growth (for the prior two years, growth rates were largely stable in the high single-digit to low double-digit range).

www.businessinsider.com/peak-search-
google-search-query-decline-2012-10#ixzz2PZl3Y2Po

This isn't that surprising, and the reason for this is probably sitting in your pocket or bag right now – your mobile or smartphone. People are increasingly using apps to find the information that they need, without going down the traditional search route. If I want to find the most recent football results 'there's an app for that' which instantly shows me the latest scores and in-depth details of what is happening in particular games; I don't need to use a browser or search engine to find that information for me. If I want to locate the nearest bookshop to me in an unfamiliar city I'll open a map app and search for what I need. If you have a smartphone you will probably have already spent a lot of time looking at and downloading different apps for your phone. Findings from a survey in 2012 show that the average number of apps owned by a smartphone user is 41, which is an increase of 28% over 2011, and they're used on average for 39 minutes per day (http://offers2.compuware.com/APM_13_WP_Mobile_App_Survey_Report_Registration.html). The apps that we use will obviously differ from person to person based upon their own information needs, but a good place to search for apps is on The Next Web site at http://thenextweb.com/apps; I've also listed some useful search engines for apps in the next chapter.

This is obviously putting pressure on Google, which recognizes that even though it owns some of the most popular apps it needs to do more in the mobile market. It's fighting back with Google Now and Google+, but in April 2013 Facebook introduced Facebook Home, which is a new app that takes over the user experience on phones that run the Google Android operating system, which immediately alerts users to what their friends are doing on Facebook, with links to take people further into Facebook, such as the mobile app and Facebook Messenger. What's missing from this line-up, however, is a search option. Facebook is trying very hard to move people away from search and into the Facebook walled garden, where search will take place on their terms, retrieving information from their pages, not the internet as a whole.

There is no doubt that apps will continue to become more important, and in the next chapter I point you towards some tools and engines that you can use to find apps that are appropriate for search, based on your device and operating system. There is no doubt, however, that searchers now have the ability to entirely bypass traditional search and go to the best provider of the information that they're looking for. Consequently, in the next few years we may well see a swing away from single engine search to multi-app search.

Resources for further study

As you would expect, the internet is full of places that you can visit in order to find out more about internet search and to keep on top of this fast-moving subject area. In this section I'll do my best to point you towards some of the sites that I find are particularly useful, and that I suspect you will too. Hopefully you'll forgive me for starting off by pointing you towards some of my own material. My website at www.philb.com is the place where I put all of my longer articles that discuss internet search and social media. I also have listings on the site of useful search engines to use and when to use them, and a straightforward listing of search engines. There's also a section of over 4000 search engines divided by country and region. If you're interested in day-to-day changes in the internet search area I would suggest reading my blog on search at www.philbradley.typepad. com; I try to update this on a very regular basis with reviews of new search engines, changes to existing ones and anything else that I think is useful for searchers, as well as some stuff that isn't. I also have a second blog at http://philbradley.typepad.com/i_want_to, which has more of a social/real-time media focus, but hopefully you'll find some useful material there. I primarily use Diigo for bookmarking purposes these days and you can see what I bookmark at https://www.diigo.com/user/philbradley. I also automatically update my Delicious account at https://www.diigo.com/user/ philbradley with links that I post on Twitter, and you'll find me at https://twitter.com/philbradley – do feel free to follow me, and if your biography includes the fact that you're a librarian I'll almost certainly follow you back. If you're interested in keeping in contact I'm on Facebook at https://www.facebook.com/philipbradley and over on Google+ I'm at https://profiles.google.com/philipbradley. My public presentations are on Slideshare at www.slideshare.net/philbradley and I have a Scoop.it page on internet search at www.scoop.it/t/internet-search.

If you're interested in the subject of business, you may well find it's worthwhile taking a look at my colleague and friend Karen Blakeman's website at www.rba.co.uk. She has an absolute wealth of information on

〉〉〉

business resources and search strategies, covering industry sectors, news, statistics, stock markets, share prices and so on. If you need to know about companies, hers is the site to visit. A more general site on search, but which has a slant towards search engine optimization is the SearchEngineLand site at http://searchengineland.com, which is led by Danny Sullivan, who probably knows more about internet search than anyone else. It's a very informative site and updated several times a day. For something a little more 'newsy' you may want to take a look at Mashable, at http://mashable.com, or TechCrunch, at http://techcrunch.com. Both sites cover social media, Google, Bing and search in general, although they do have a much wider focus than simply those subjects, so you may need to hunt a little bit to find the information that you need.

Google+ has a number of communities which relate to search that may appeal to those with more than a passing interest in the subject. Take a look at:

➡ Internet Search, at https://plus.google.com/u/0/communities/ 104496223599483313097
➡ Advanced Power Searching with Google, at https://plus.google.com/u/0/communities/100573050943855316210
➡ Library Technology, at https://plus.google.com/u/0/communities/ 104744457137982942219
➡ TWiG, at https://plus.google.com/u/0/communities/ 105436080425968483787,
➡ Creating Professional Development about Search, at https://plus.google.com/u/0/communities/108291092137674093544.

Of course, it's always worth checking yourself to see if there are any new communities, and there probably will be, since this is a growing and dynamic aspect of Google+.

If you seriously want to get involved with keeping up to date with search engine news it's also worth subscribing to the various blogs that the engines make available. When they do anything new that's often one of the very first places that you'll hear about it. I've listed a few of them below, but bear in mind some may also be providing information about the company as well as the search engine:

➡ Ask Blog http://blog.ask.com
➡ Bing Search Blog www.bing.com/blogs/members/bing-search-blog/default.aspx

➡ Bing Webmaster Blog
www.bing.com/blogs/site_blogs/b/webmaster/default.aspx
➡ Blekko Blog http://blog.blekko.com
➡ DuckDuckGo Founder's Blog www.gabrielweinberg.com/blog
➡ Google Official Blog http://googleblog.blogspot.co.uk
➡ Google Webmaster Central Blog
http://googlewebmastercentral.blogspot.co.uk
➡ Yahoo! Search Blog http://yahoosearch.tumblr.com.

Finally, there are a variety of other quite outstanding individuals who blog about search, or various aspects thereof, and if you're looking for literate, thought-provoking and fascinating posts about the subject you should visit a few of these folk. John Battelle, at http://battellemedia.com, blogs on 'thoughts on the intersection of search, media, technology and more'. Gary Price runs an extremely informative and astonishingly current blog called Infodocket at www.infodocket.com and Tara Calishain has a blog called ResearchBuzz, at http://researchbuzz.me, and she has been covering search engines, databases and similar subjects since 1996. There are, of course, far too many people to mention them all, but I hope that having got this far through the book you're more than capable of finding them by yourself!

CHAPTER 16

>> **The future of search**

Introduction

During the development of internet search over the last 17 years or so, it always seems that people think that we've reached the pinnacle of search, only to discover that we're really just at a bend in the road, because there's always something new to consider. We had the macho wars of the early 2000s with search engines vying with each other to say that they were bigger, better and faster because they indexed more web pages. Then the search engines attempted to lock horns over which one indexed the most formats – web, news, video, blogs and so on, as well as which file formats they were able to view and to index. We're now into the realm of personalization – which search engine can give us the best and most relevant searches for our interests, or the opposing view, which engine can provide us with the most objective views, irrespective of who we are, where we're based and what we've searched for previously. Every time search engines overcome one challenge, there's another one waiting for them. Search is continually evolving, with new engines being launched, older engines silently disappearing and the major engines continuing to strive against each other. Then we have to consider other web-based resources that are also having an effect on how search develops, such as Twitter and Facebook. While they're not search engines themselves they amass huge amounts of data, which needs to be taken into account when we are trying to find the best and most recent information on a subject.

> **>> Did you know?**
> The future of internet search, and indeed the web itself, will be as a 'wordstream', which will kill the operating system, browser and search as we know it, according to David Gelernter of Wired Magazine (www.wired.com/opinion/2013/02/the-end-of-the-web-computers-and-search-as-we-know-it).

The rise and rise of user-generated content

Perhaps the largest single challenge to traditional search engines is the rise in user-generated content. We are very quickly moving away from the hegemony of the website to the importance of the material that individuals such as you and I create. Let's take a brief moment to consider just how much information we produce between us in a single minute on the internet, but before we do, please bear in mind that I'm writing this towards the end of 2012 – by the time you read this the figures will have escalated again!

➡ YouTube users will upload 48 hours' worth of new video.
➡ Facebook users will share 684,478 pieces of content and there are 6 million Facebook views.
➡ Twitter users will send over 100,000 tweets and 320 new accounts are created.
➡ Instagram users will share 3600 photographs.
➡ Flickr users will add 3125 new photographs and has 20,000,000 photo views.
➡ Wordpress users will publish 347 new blog posts.
➡ Six new Wikipedia articles will be published.

If we then extend that to what happens on the internet in a single day, enough information is consumed to fill 168 million DVDs, 2 million blog posts are written, 532 million Facebook statuses are updated and so many photographs are uploaded to Facebook that, if they were printed out and stacked up, the stacks would be as tall as 80 Eiffel Towers. These figures are taken from Domo.com (www.domo.com/blog/2012/06/how-much-data-is-created-every-minute), Intel (www.intel.com/content/www/us/en/communications/internet-minute-infographic.html) and Mashable (http://mashable.com/2012/03/06/one-day-internet-data-traffic).

Given the amount of data, it's simply not possible for search engines to keep up with the flood of information. Not only is it arriving faster than many of them are able to index, there are a great many more sites that demand our attention. For example, in the past I would have put up a PowerPoint deck just onto my website in order to share it with other people. Now however I can put the same deck up onto Slideshare, Authorstream, Slideshark, Google Documents, Lanyrd, Slideboom, ZohoShow, Sliderocket, Slideserve, and Scribd. That's without even researching sites; those are just some of the ones that came directly to

> >

mind. I don't need to use a traditional website to share my data, and therefore it's much harder for traditional search engines to index, rank and display content.

Currency and news

A second reason why search engines are going to find it hard to keep up is the speed of publication. When someone tweets content, that tweet is available to their followers (and to the Twitter search engine) within a couple of seconds. Consequently, we need to now rethink exactly what we mean about 'currency'. In the pre-internet days the publishing cycle of the book might well mean that 'current' related to content that was accurate nine months previously. With magazines we might be talking about a three-month turnaround. With a newspaper, we're down to about 24 hours, 12 or less if we're lucky. Google may be able to index a website the same day, or within a few hours of it being updated, and with blog postings, we're down to about 20 minutes. Twitter gives us the opportunity to report virtually instantaneously on what someone is saying at a conference, while smartphones allow us to take a photograph of an event, upload it, tweet it and project it onto a world stage in less time than it's taken to type this sentence.

As a result, what does 'news' mean now? In all honesty, I think it means whatever you want it to mean, but increasingly we have to define what we mean by that. In 'the old days' if a client asked us for 'the latest information on xyz' it was possible to take a bit of a stab in the dark and assume that they wanted material published in the last month or so. Nowadays however, that may well mean information published today. Before anyone points out that a good researcher or reference librarian should always ask what 'the latest' means, I'd agree, but would also make the point that publishing cycles would help define what that meant – now, we don't have publishing cycles any longer. I gave up buying newspapers when all the news that they could offer me was content that I'd looked at the previous evening, explored and discussed with my friends.

We also have to define what 'news' means, as well. A well known quote from Mark Zuckerberg (co-founder of Facebook) is 'A squirrel dying in front of your house may be more relevant to your interests right now than people dying in Africa.' (www.brainyquote.com/quotes/authors/m/mark_zuckerberg.html). While that might sound rather callous I think the point of it is that you're more likely to discuss the former event on Facebook or with your friends in other forums than you are to generally discuss the issue of poverty and starvation in Africa. There is of course 'news' and 'news'. We have local, national, regional and global news items; the elections, the wars, the earthquakes and sometimes very occasionally happy events as well. But to that list we should now add professional and personal news. News reporting services may well sometimes broadcast news that interests us on a professional level (although it depends on our profession of course) but I wouldn't expect to find a great deal on the national news of an evening that related to librarianship. However, that's not to say it doesn't exist – very far from it. In 'the old days' (sometime before 2005) I would expect to have to really hunt for the information that I needed, and would be relying on websites found as a result of a search engine query.

Accessing professional news now is something entirely different; while I still do have various Google e-mail alert services set up to inform me about new and interesting things, I find that I get a far better view of what is happening in the industry by following individuals. As previously discussed in Chapter 7 when I was looking at social media search engines, I can still search for the information that I need, but I'm doing that less and less. I now rely much more on news curation tools. Resources such as Zite (www.zite.com) and Pulse (www.pulse.me) have joined the ranks of the better known Flipboard (http://flipboard.com) but there is also ShowYou (http://showyou.com), which does the same for videos. These all work well on tablet devices, but if you don't have one available you could also check similar tools such as Scoop It (www.scoop.it), Headslinger (www.headslinger.com) or Learnist (http://learni.st) online. Of course, how well these work depends on the number of people or friends that you have in particular networks who disseminate information that you can then pick up. In our profession, therefore, it's going to become increasingly important to spend time creating information as well as consuming it, even if that creation is limited to linking to appropriate or interesting resources elsewhere. The more that we are able to engage online, the more value we can bring to our members, clients, customers or users. In this way we're able to leave the books, bricks and mortar behind and reach out to people virtually.

Where should we go?

It's always tempting to try to give a list of resources that you should spend time using but, in all honesty, that is doomed to failure. What I find useful is not the same as the tools that you may find useful, and we may both find that the tools we use will change over time, and may well disappear altogether. What's really important is not the tool, but the activity. You should talk to your library members to find out what they like using, and consider the value of those tools, exploring them and evaluating them. By all means pick up new tools and social networks and try them for size. Do a search for keywords to see how many other people in your sector are using the same tools, and while you're at it, have a search for librarians and libraries as well. For example, I have over 1000 UK librarians that I follow in my Twitter stream, and am connected to over 1200 on Google+.

Don't just look at a tool and then, having decided that it doesn't fit your requirements, move on, never to return. It's always worth keeping an open mind with these social media tools and go back to them on a regular basis, just to see if they have changed or improved for the better. Google+ is a good personal example of this. I would go to the social networking site on a regular basis, perhaps once a day, but seldom found very much that interested me or that was useful. Over the course of time my visits dropped to about once a week. However, when Google introduced the concept of 'communities' (rather like Facebook groups) and made it very easy to not only join, but to create communities, I found my use of the system increased quite dramatically, and I began to share material more frequently with communities, but also to engage with other members. It's now somewhere that I visit on a regular daily basis once again but, more importantly, I'm sharing material there to a far greater extent than I've ever done before. If I had just taken an initial look and decided that it wasn't for me, I would have done myself a disservice.

Taking search with you

With the rise of the smartphone, an increasing number of people have virtually instant access to search wherever they are and whatever they're doing. There are an increasing number of search applications that can be used with smartphones, irrespective of your device or operating system of choice. A report by Nielsen, *State of the Media. The social media report 2012* (www.nielsen. com/us/en/reports/2012/state-of-the-media-the-social-media-report-2012.html), makes interesting reading, for although it's primarily about

> **>> Did you know?**
> More consumers will access the internet by mobile devices than by desktop or laptop by 2014 (http://cliqology.com/2011/06/15-keys-facts-and-conclusions-to-know-the-future-of-the-internet-in-2015).

‹ ‹

social media resources it does, I feel, demonstrate that people are accessing web-based material while being mobile in ever greater numbers. Time spent on using mobile applications and the mobile web accounted for 63% of the year-on-year growth in overall time spent on social media, with 16% of their respondents saying that they connect to social media via a tablet device. The overall unique US audience using the mobile web increased 82% between July 2011 and 2012, with those using mobile apps increasing by 85%.

As you would expect, traditional search engines such as Google have their own apps. One example of the type of search app that is popular is 'Google Goggles', which works on both Android- and iOS-based devices. Prior to the app, the only way that you could search was by typing in your request, or speaking it to your device, but it's now possible to take a photograph of something, and Google will then provide you with more information. If you need data on a book, for example, open the app and take a picture of the cover. Google will then run a product and book search for you, without any further input on your behalf. I recently used the app myself while I was in an art gallery. I wanted more information on a particular painting that I was looking at, so I framed the image within the app, and within a matter of a second or two Google had identified the painting and provided me with access to in-depth information regarding it. The same thing can be done with landmarks, logos, contact information and wine labels and it can even translate text for you, so if you're faced with a menu that is in a foreign language you won't order the wrong thing. It's far from perfect, as it doesn't work well on things like plants, cars or animals, but Google engineers suggest that in the future we will be able to use the app to suggest a move in a game of chess (it can already do that with Sudoku puzzles), or identify a tree by taking a photograph of one of its leaves. Even if I don't want to use Google Goggles, the straightforward Google search app can work in conjunction with my smartphone, working out exactly where I am and using that knowledge to influence the results that I am getting. So rather than a generic search for 'pizza' I will automatically be provided with information on the nearest restaurants to my physical location. Alternatively, I could use the Google Maps application; just call it up, wait the few seconds that it takes to work out where I am, and then run a search for my favourite shop, landmark or other location: in essence a local search engine.

However, Google is not the only search engine that has recognized the power and importance of being able to take search with you on your smartphone; various other search engines have also created their own apps.

Yahoo! Search displays results and offers maps with a link to directions if appropriate, but it's otherwise a fairly basic application. Bing Mobile has voice-activated search: you can see what your friends like if you have connected it to your Facebook account (although this is not yet globally available), it provides travel information, local data, and also offers 'Bing Vision', which is similar to Google Goggles in that you can scan barcodes or QR codes and it will return product information for you. It too can recognize cover artwork from books, CDs, DVDs and video games. Ask has also produced an app that supports oral searches, and in common with the web-based version of the search engine it is strong on providing answers to reference-type questions.

If you're not keen on the major engines, and want to try something a little different, the previously mentioned search engine DuckDuckGo offering may appeal to you. In common with its web browser-based search engine, it doesn't track your searches and uses over 50 different sources, such as Wikipedia and Wolfram|Alpha, to give you relevant information. Speaking of Wolfram|Alpha, they also have a search engine designed for smartphones, and it's possible that you're already using it in part, since it's used in the Apple Siri Assistant. However, this dedicated app gives access to the full range of the engine's database, but at a price of £2.49; the other apps mentioned are all free. Blekko has a US-based app which is not currently available in the UK, but the Dogpile app at https://itunes.apple.com/us/app/dogpile-search/id526817899?mt=8 is available globally. This multi-search engine works with Google, Yahoo! and Bing, includes image search and a camera scan option for barcodes and QR codes. Now, having said that Blekko has an app, they've also just released a new product called izik (pronounced Issac) at http://izik.com, which is a search engine that has been designed to work specifically with tablet devices. It uses the concept that we're all familiar with, of swiping across a screen to move content. Rather than scroll down as per 'normal' search engines, izik provides content that is best viewed by horizontal scrolling. It works for the iPad and Android tablets, and you can view it on their mobile web version too (the same link as previously given). Simply search for what you need, and izik will display various categories of information – quick answer, images, top results and so on – tailored to your search. A search for '*dog*' returned categories such as pets and veterinary, while a search for '*library*' gave me history and genealogy. I think the results from izik are clearer to view and they are more user-friendly. Although there's less on a page, the side swipe will continually reveal more information.

izik didn't outperform Google everywhere, however; a search on Google for '3D printing' returned more recent material, and in greater amounts than izik found, and in my Everton test search, recent results were more easily found using Google. However, playing with izik on my iPad was an absolute delight. Side-swipe scrolling worked really well and was immediately comfortable. (If you don't have a tablet, try the web-based version mentioned above, and give it a whirl.) If you prefer to look down the screen, however, you can expand a category of results, and izik will display them down the screen. izik is a really nice idea – it's got a great design and it's very easy and intuitive to use. I have no doubt that, on a tablet at least, it's going to swiftly become my favourite search engine.

Of course, there are plenty of other apps that provide access to search – Amazon, eBay, BBC News and so on. If you are a keen mobile searcher you will probably have found many other apps that appeal to you as well, but it's always worth keeping an eye out for new apps, since they are being added all the time. You will note that in this section I have not added in any links to resources – this is mainly because the apps come in different flavours for the different devices that are available, but I am hoping that if you have managed to read this far you'll be able to find them for yourself!

However, if you are after shortcuts (and I wouldn't blame you if you are) there are several search engines that you can use in order to find mobile apps:

➡ The **AppExplorer**, at www.appexplorer.com, also provides ratings information alongside an in-depth summary for each app, version information and pricing details. Helpfully it's also possible to filter by category, price, average rating and device. AppExplorer also offers an e-mail alerting service for apps that haven't been created yet – simply provide them with keywords and when an app has been added which has a title or description that include them they will let you know.

➡ **Mimvi**, at www.mimvi.com, is a comprehensive engine which filters results based on device (iPhone, Windows, Android, iPad or Blackberry), provides a brief summary and gives a useful ratings listing for each app as well.

➡ **Quixey**, at https://www.quixey.com, styles itself as 'the search engine for apps'. Consequently, it provides access to not only mobile apps, but also desktop, browser and web-based apps. In the mobile arena this includes Android, Blackberry, iPad, iPhone and Windows phone. Search results are based on a summary of the app, but the result can be clicked on for a quick in-depth view on the results screen. Results can be filtered by device, free or paid apps. However, in common with uQuery, searchers are provided with infinite scroll results, so it's not easy to tell how many results have been returned.

➡ **uQuery**, at www.uquery.com, is an engine that focuses on the iPhone and iPad. Searchers can filter results, based on 23 categories, ratings, price, and it has a sort function based on relevancy, popularity, most rated and highest ratings. Display of results includes a screenshot, which does give it a visual appeal, but rather irritatingly it does not tell the searcher how many results have been returned and, since it provides infinite scrolling of those results, it's not possible to tell.

➡ **Yahoo!** has an app search which allows people to consume news on the go. The iphone app is 'all about delivering the best of the web – right on your phone.': http://yodel.yahoo.com/blogs/product-news/summarize-yahoo-app-delivers-better-mobile-content-discovery-070046174.html. It uses the natural language abilities of Summly, a company Yahoo! recently purchased to provide quick story summaries. The company has also improved the search experience with better video and image search functionality. Unfortunately at the time of writing it is only available in the USA, but it should be rolled out to the rest of the world in the near future.

If none of these engines appeal to you, do not despair! You can always try Appcurl (www.appcurl.com), Appolicious (www.appolicious.com), Appgravity (http://appgravity.com), Appsfire (http://new.appsfire.com), Appshopper (http://appshopper.com), Crosswa.lk (https://api.crosswa.lk), Kinetik (http://kinetik.com), Xyo (http://xyo.net) or any number of other options. Finally, if all else fails, you could always try the app store that the device provider has made available via the phone itself.

There's little doubt that – in the UK at least – mobile searching is on the increase. A recent report by the Direct Marketing Association (*Mobile Search 2012*, www.dma.org.uk/toolkit/infographic-mobile-search-2012) showed that seven out of every ten UK smartphone owners preferred using search engine apps for research rather than brand-based applications such as eBay or Amazon. Popular information searches included news (54%), high street retailers (30%), movie information (28%), local travel updates (24%) and finance and insurance information (15%). The reasons given for using mobile web search were for offers and deals, directions, brand information and somewhere to eat. However, while app-based internet search is popular, that doesn't make it a pleasant experience, since most people (60%) said that they found it was easier to search for information via a desktop or

‹ ‹

laptop computer than through a smartphone; one often quoted reason being that the load time was quicker.

Through the eyes of search

Almost as a postscript to this chapter, I'd briefly like to mention Google Glass, also known as Project Glass, which is not to be confused with the previously mentioned Google Goggles. This is a research project that Google is developing to produce an augmented reality head-mounted display, or HMD. The idea behind it is that the HMD would be attached to glasses and would project information in a smartphone-like format – hands-free and via natural language voice commands. Future developments may include integration directly into a pair of glasses. There is currently no date by which this item will be made available to the public for purchase, but it has been suggested that this might be as soon as 2014 (www.bloomberg.com/news/2012-06-28/google-s-brin-to-offer-eyeglass-computers-to-consumers-by-2014.html).

Although it's tempting to consider this simply as science fiction, Google is investing a lot of time and energy into the project. Where this will take search is really anyone's guess, but if it is possible to have a device that can be worn constantly to provide users with information on what they are seeing without further interaction on the part of the user, search really will be everywhere. Furthermore, if it's possible to see information through the HMD, it's equally possible to start recording what the wearer is seeing. In fact, at the Spring 2012 fashion display at New York Fashion Week models wore Google Glasses down the catwalk, and were filming the audience (www.msfabulous.com/2012/09/ny-fashion-week-diane-von-furstenburg. html). This then leads to a situation where people are able to record everything that they do and see, tag it in real time and store it in the cloud for later recall as necessary. A total of 13.3 years' worth of HD quality video can be contained within 1 petabyte of storage space, and while that is still far out of the reach of most private individuals' pockets the cost of storage space is continually decreasing. Consequently, we can almost see on the horizon the day when people will be able to store and then search for everything they have experienced, let alone everything that they want to know about. Once we're at that point,

>> **Did you know?**
According to an analysis by the US company Cisco, over 50 billion devices will be connected to the internet by 2020 (www.siemens.com/innovation/apps/pof_microsite/_pof-fall-2012/_html_en/facts-and-forecasts-growth-market-of-the-future.html).

we'll be able to share our experiences and build up really accurate pictures of the world around us, jointly tagging and combining what we are doing. Perhaps the concept of a Star Trek Borg-like 'collective' is not too far away after all.

Summary

It's difficult to talk about the future of search, because we're already living it, with developments occurring so quickly it's almost impossible to keep up with them. However, some things are perfectly clear – an increase in the content that we produce, greater importance of the role of the individual in search as social media takes over from websites and mobile search becoming increasingly important. We're very close to the point when our smartphones will know where we are, what we're doing, and what we're likely to search for. All of the information that we need, when we need it, without even thinking about it. Just imagine – you get up in the morning and leave the house; your smartphone applications know your route and they can check to see if it's blocked, and if a quicker way is available they can tell you. They can find you interesting local places to eat at and can recommend what you'll enjoy based on the recommendations of other visitors. You can be kept up to date with things that matter to you – stock prices, news items, how your sports team is doing – all in real time. You'll be able to find if your friends are in town, and your apps can talk to their apps to suggest an evening out, perhaps at a bar you both like, or at a sports or musical event. If you're still thinking that's science fiction, then it's worth taking a look at the Google Now product (www.google.com/landing/now), which can do just about all of that for you already. So, as I said, we're already living in the future of search. Technology doesn't have to try and keep up with what we want to do any longer – rather, it's our job to try and keep up with the technology!

Index

⟨ ⟨